BROADSIDE

BROADSIDE

HOW WE REGAINED THE ASHES

STUART BROAD

**SIMON &
SCHUSTER**

London · New York · Sydney · Toronto · New Delhi

A CBS COMPANY

First published in Great Britain
by Simon & Schuster UK Ltd, 2015
A CBS Company

Copyright © 2015 by Stuart Broad

1 3 5 7 9 10 8 6 4 2

Simon & Schuster UK Ltd
1st Floor
222 Gray's Inn Road
London WC1X 8HB

www.simonandschuster.co.uk

Simon & Schuster Australia, Sydney

Simon & Schuster India, New Delhi

A CIP catalogue record for this book is
available from the British Library.

Hardback ISBN: 978-1-4711-0159-5
Ebook ISBN: 978-1-4711-0161-8

Statistics and scorecards compiled
by Ian Marshall
Typeset and designed in the UK
by Craig Stevens and Julian Flanders
Printed in the UK by CPI Group (UK) Ltd,
Croydon, CR0 4YY

CONTENTS

1

AM I DREAMING?

Have you ever been somewhere perfect, but wanted to be anywhere else?

I'm lying on my bed in Sydney's Intercontinental Hotel, in a room with one of the most spectacular views on earth, in one of the most stunning cities I've ever been to. The air is clear and there is a beautiful piercing blue sky above as yachts jostle for position on the shimmering turquoise blue water. The workhorse ferries service Circular Quay while massive ocean liners deliver excited tourists into the bustling port. The magnificent Sydney Harbour Bridge dominates the skyline while the Opera House completes my picture postcard view. In so many ways, it's a scene of perfection.

But it's lost on me. I want to go home. My curtains are drawn, the lights are out and my phone is off. I don't want to see anyone, be seen by anyone, and least of all speak to anyone. The walls are closing in. Leave me alone.

The remnants of my room service lunch lie barely touched on a tray on the floor. This can't be happening. Not again. I want to go home.

'I'm not leaving the room,' I think to myself. 'I'm too embarrassed. Were we really that bad?'

Three days earlier, we'd played Bangladesh in Adelaide in the penultimate group game of our Cricket World Cup. In every sense, it was a must-win game. But we lost. Badly. With one match still to play against lowly Afghanistan, we are out of a tournament we'd had hopes of winning. We have no excuses. We've been outplayed and out-thought. And we are getting hammered for it. I feel alone.

None of us who'd boarded the plane from Heathrow so full of optimism just ten weeks earlier could in our worst nightmares have envisaged we'd under-perform so spectacularly. We are ashamed. We've let our country down.

'Cheerio Chaps: Poms are Bangered and Mashed,' crowed the front page of the *Sydney Telegraph*.

'Cheerio Chaps: Poms are Bangered and Mashed,' crowed the front page of the *Sydney Telegraph* the morning after our tournament-ending 15-run loss to Bangladesh.

All the other papers are revelling in our misery too, while the abuse on social media gets so bad I delete the Twitter app on my phone.

We'd lost, and in spectacular fashion, managing one solitary win over Scotland while being thrashed out of sight in every other game.

At times, I'd felt completely helpless to stem the tide. I was fit and bowling pain free for the first time in a year, following major surgery on my knee. But I didn't hit my straps. I had tried my best, but I'd come up way short. We all had. At times, teams found it easy against us. As a proud Englishman, in a country that loves to hate us, that is what hurt the most.

Barely 12 months earlier, I'd flown home from Australia believing we'd hit rock bottom after being whitewashed 5-0 in an Ashes series that had ended the careers of some of England's greatest-ever players and accelerated the end for others. If anyone had told me then that a year later I'd be back here again, feeling just as low, suffering the same abuse, I'd have thought it was a sick joke.

But I'm not laughing. The lights are out. Leave me alone. I want to go home.

I'm not the only one in a dark place. Just across the corridor, my close friend and team-mate for almost a decade, Jimmy Anderson, has the 'do not disturb' sign hanging off his door handle.

Occasionally a team-mate pops his head around the corner of the door. But no one wants to talk. We've been abject and we want to go home.

And it's not just the players. Earlier that morning our assistant coach Paul Farbrace – one of the nicest blokes you could ever meet – had gone out for a brief stroll around Circular Quay on the steps of our hotel.

He made the mistake of wearing an official England tracksuit. Within minutes of leaving the hotel foyer, he was copping abuse from Aussie fans revelling in yet more misery for the England cricket team.

'Losers!' one ungracious local screamed in his face. Farbs about-turned and headed straight back to the hotel. His stroll lasted five minutes. He wanted to go home.

Somehow, we must pick ourselves up and play one more, now meaningless, game against Afghanistan. If losing to Bangladesh had been bad, losing to Afghanistan would be catastrophic.

We drag ourselves to training, but we're flat. Even our coach Peter Moores, normally so full of energy and enthusiasm, looks drained and withdrawn. Our captain Eoin Morgan, appointed in place of Alastair Cook just two weeks before we'd flown out, appears distant and shell-shocked. He talks manfully about pride in the shirt and leaving with our heads held high. But you can tell he's hurting. We're all in shock.

But we're also professional cricketers representing our country and we still have a game to play. Kids dream of doing this. We're privileged to do this, but it feels like a nightmare. It's Friday the 13th, but for once, our luck is in and we produce a decent enough performance to beat Afghanistan by nine wickets.

But there are no celebrations. We fly home the next day. We've got more flak to face. Brace yourselves, boys. It's an Ashes summer.

I'm in my usual spot in the Trent Bridge dressing room. Ian Bell's sitting next to me, where he always does. I'm staring at the red Dukes ball in my hand.

Outside I can hear the crowd chanting my name. I've taken eight for 15 and we've bowled Australia out for 60 before lunch. In the process I claimed my 300th Test wicket for England. Eight for 15? All out for 60? Three hundred wickets? Did that really just happen? This is surreal. Am I dreaming?

Jimmy Anderson's there, too. He's not playing in this Test after injuring his side in the last game at Edgbaston. But he's done his job. His haul of six for 47 at Edgbaston had helped us win the Test match.

This match is not won yet, but Jimmy and I share a look. We know the little urn is coming home.

'Well done, mate,' Jimmy says. 'I'm proud of you.'

It's a special moment. But I still can't believe it. The surroundings are familiar but the emotions are not. I've never felt like this before. In fact, I've never felt better.

Eight for 15? Sixty all out? Three hundred Test wickets? Is this real?

This match is not won yet, but Jimmy and I share a look. We know the little urn is coming home.

I'd woken at 6am that morning at my home in West Bridgford. Once I'm awake on Test-match day, I stay awake. I was extremely nervous. With Jimmy not playing, I was feeling the heavy burden of responsibility that comes with leading England's attack in an Ashes Test match.

I was the local boy, playing at my home ground. The pressure was on. And I'd delivered. But eight for 15? Sixty all out? Three hundred Test wickets? Really?

That evening as I walk across a ground I've walked across so many times at the close of play for both England and my county, Nottinghamshire, I glance up at the scoreboard.

England 274 for four, lead Australia by 214 runs.

I've spoken to the media – Sky, *Test Match Special*, Channel Five, daily newspaper reporters, the ECB website – and said the right things, of course: 'This Test match is not won yet. The Australians will come back hard at us in the morning. We've got a long way to go in this Test match. The Ashes are not won yet.'

But inside I know. There is no coming back for Australia. They are dead and buried. We have our feet firmly on their throat. We are 2-1 up already and this fourth Test, and the Ashes, are as good as in the bag.

I float over the ground towards the Radcliffe Road car park where my car is parked. My phone goes. It's my friend Nottinghamshire batsman Michael Lumb.

'All right Lumby?' I ask matter-of-factly, as if it's a normal day.

'All right? What the hell just happened? That was incredible! You just took eight for fifteen in an Ashes Test match. You must be absolutely buzzing!'

We chat briefly and I promise to catch up with Lumby properly after the match has finished. I hang up and continue across the outfield in the warm evening sunshine. The stewards usher me through a crowd of several hundred fans. Normally, at the close of a day's play, there are barely 30 diehards. But this is different. There are hundreds of fans all clamouring for my attention.

'Broady, can you sign my shirt?' One little boy asks, wide-eyed and grinning. 'And can you write eight for fifteen please?'

'Sure,' I say. I was him once.

'Broady, can you sign my programme?' One lady asks. 'Can you write eight for fifteen on it?'

'No problem.'

'Broady, can you sign my ticket?' A young girl asks. 'Can you write eight for fifteen on it?'

'Of course.'

The Intercontinental Hotel feels a very long way away.

I edge towards my car, but I'm here for an hour. More autographs. More pictures. More selfies.

Finally, I reach my car and gingerly climb in. I start the ignition, and breathe. The journey home takes a little over five minutes.

As I pull in to the driveway, almost three hours after the close of play, my girlfriend Bealey is there to greet me along with our dogs Jackson and Blue.

'Oh my God!' she cries. 'What have you done? That was incredible.'

We go inside and she's cooked chicken fajitas for me. They're my favourite. Normally I can eat five after a day's play. Tonight, I can barely manage one. I'm not hungry. I feel on edge. My head's spinning. I can't believe what's just happened.

The doorbell rings. It's nine o'clock.

'What do the neighbours want at this time of night?' I ask.

But it's Dad, with a bottle of red.

'Well done, son,' he says. 'I'm proud of you.'

We sit down in the living room and Dad pours me a glass. I take a sip. It's decent stuff.

'Eight for fifteen in an Ashes Test match?' he says. 'Wow! Who'd have thought that my premature little baby boy who weighed the same as a bag of sugar when he was born would take eight for fifteen in an Ashes Test match and bowl the Australia out before lunch? Unbloodybelievable.'

I smile.

Dad doesn't stay long. He knows I'm tired. He played Test cricket himself and knows I must rest. Sleep is everything to a professional sportsman. Every day you need to get up and go again. No rest, no recovery. No recovery, no performance. No performance, no win. No win, no point.

I go upstairs and climb into bed. I can't sleep. My mind is racing. Bealey is there. This is so surreal.

I once took seven for 12 against Kimbolton School Under-15s and remember thinking how ridiculous those figures were. That could only happen in a schoolboy game, couldn't it?

I begin to drift off.

Eight for 15? Sixty all out? Three hundred Test wickets? Is this really happening?

I am dreaming.

2

A MEMORABLE
YEAR TO FORGET

Of all the 28 years I'd been alive, 2014 had proved to be by far the most difficult I'd faced so far.

It started off abysmally with a crushing Ashes whitewash Down Under, briefly improved with a backs-to-the-wall Test series win against India, before ending in pretty ordinary fashion when a former team-mate published a book seemingly intent on tarnishing the most successful period in English cricket history.

Add to that being hit full in the face so hard by a cricket ball travelling at 88mph I needed corrective surgery to fix a double fracture of my nose, seeing my friend and captain Alastair Cook almost resign the Test captaincy, before undergoing major surgery on my knee after nearly a year of agonising pain caused by repeatedly crunching my front foot into rock-hard pitches while delivering the ball.

Then, just as things started to settle down, Cooky was sacked as one-day captain in December only a fortnight before we were due to leave for a lengthy build-up to the World Cup in Australia.

It's a sporting cliché to describe a year as a roller coaster, but I genuinely cannot recall a year where my emotions on and off the field had been pulled in so many different directions. From desperation Down Under, hope at home against India, agony at Old Trafford, exasperation at Kevin Pietersen, to sorrow for Cooky, the year had it all.

At least I was settled at home. My girlfriend Bealey moved in to the house I'd bought just up the road from Trent Bridge in the leafy Nottingham suburb of West Bridgford, and my off-field affairs were being well managed by my agent, Neil Fairbrother at ISM, after a turbulent time with a previous management company.

Perhaps most importantly, I was fit. My knee had been causing me problems for more than a year and I'd been diagnosed with patella tendonitis – or 'jumper's knee' – in early 2014 but, as is the case with so many professionals, I'd put off having surgery until there was a gap in the busy fixture schedule which would allow me to recover without feeling I needed to rush back to play.

Very few people knew the extent of the discomfort I'd been experiencing. As a professional sportsman in the public eye, you will naturally be asked questions about your form and fitness, but you often have to play a bit of a game with the media in order to hide any sign of weakness or vulnerability from opponents.

The last thing I wanted was to hand an opposition batsman a needless competitive advantage by letting him know that pretty much all I was thinking about at the top of my run was how much pain I was going to be in when I delivered the ball at him.

I didn't want opponents knowing I had to get up sometimes in the middle of the night during Test matches to sit in a near boiling hot bath just to try to numb the pain enough to get up the next morning and bowl again.

I didn't want them knowing I was only able to drive my car for about ten minutes before the pain got so bad I had to pull over and stretch my leg out.

So I hid it. The media knew I had a problem, but very few knew just how bad it was. Ultimately, if you declare yourself fit to play in a Test match, or any match for that matter, you are judged on your output. Cricket is unique in that the results of your day's work are published for the whole world to see at the close of play. No matter how much pain you might be in, the only thing that counts is your figures.

Mine were decent in 2014 – 30 wickets in eight Tests at 26.70, including six for 25 as we took control of the series against India at Old Trafford – but I knew I could bowl even better if freed from the shooting pain which caused my knee to swell up grotesquely by the end of each day's play.

On top of that, I had to contend with the fallout of top-edging a bouncer from Indian fast bowler Varun Aaron which had left me with a double fracture of my nose, two of the worst black eyes I had ever seen, and a strange clicking at the back of my jaw which I still experience to this day.

Fortunately, the long-overdue knee surgery, carried out in early September a few days after the final Test at The Oval by Hakan Alfredson, the world-leading specialist from Sweden who had previously operated on football star Zlatan Ibrahimovic and others, was a resounding success.

During the surgery, which involved them opening the knee up and taking blood vessels out of the tendon which had been causing the pain, they also noticed I had a sharp piece of bone which was partially rupturing the tendon. Over time that was going to cause damage, so they had to slice that piece of bone off. I was in immense pain afterwards – so much so that I'd bitten into the inside of my mouth. The surgery caused extensive swelling immediately afterwards, but it didn't take long for me to feel the benefits of going under the knife.

As a professional sportsman, you are required to put your body through an extraordinary level of exertion on an almost daily basis.

As a professional sportsman, you are required to put your body through an extraordinary level of exertion on an almost daily basis, with packed international fixture schedules making it incredibly hard to find enough time to recover properly during a calendar year.

But the flip side of that, playing for England at least, is that the medical care you're afforded is absolutely world-class. It's in the ECB's interests to look after their players and there were a couple of occasions in 2014 – with the other being when I was struck in the face – when I had cause to be thankful for the highly skilled medical care I received.

After several weeks of extensive physiotherapy and rehabilitation with the England medical team in the UK, I joined up with the England Performance Programme in Potchefstroom, South Africa, in December for a couple of weeks of sunshine training that did me the world of good. I travelled with Jimmy – who was also recovering from a knee injury which meant he missed the seven-match ODI series in Sri Lanka that would ultimately lead to Cooky being sacked – and I was able to start bowling properly under the watchful eye of my former England coach Andy Flower, who was now in charge of the Performance Programme.

Andy, without doubt the finest coach I'd ever worked with and the most successful in English cricket history, had stepped down from the top job following the Ashes whitewash in January before being on the receiving end of some appallingly uninformed and personal abuse from people outside cricket who didn't even know him.

I always found Andy to be tough but fair and a man of the utmost integrity. He was never afraid to tell you exactly what he thought of your performance – good and bad – but that meant you always knew where you stood with him. He was a hard task-master, but I never doubted his motives for one second. He wanted England to win, and to achieve that he needed tough cricketers to survive in a hostile environment. Towards the end of his time in charge, perhaps he did get a little too prescriptive, too bogged down in the fine detail. But what coach wouldn't when his players were letting him down as badly as we did in Australia? Some of the things that have been said of him since he stood down have been beneath contempt, and I'm certainly not about to re-open old wounds by dignifying them with airtime here.

I hold Andy Flower in the very highest regard as a coach and as a man. He'd stood up to Robert Mugabe's dictatorship with his black-armband protest alongside Henry Olonga in 2003 and shown loyalty, leadership and vision during his five-year tenure as England coach. Those who'd spent much of the previous 12 months abusing him weren't fit to lace his boots in my view, and it was good to catch up with him in Potchefstroom away from the glare of the media and other prying eyes.

The facilities in Potchefstroom were excellent and the boys in the Performance Programme were a really good bunch of lads. We trained hard and it was interesting to see a few of them batting and bowling close up. When you're on a central contract with England, you don't get to see or play a great deal of county cricket, but I'd heard some good things about a young Durham fast bowler called Mark Wood and it was good to see him bowl in the nets and out in the middle.

He was definitely sharp, with a slightly unusual run-up which culminated in an explosive delivery stride and skiddy pace off the pitch that gave several batsmen the hurry-up.

I liked him off the field as well, where it became evident pretty quickly he was as mad as a March hare. One afternoon I was resting in my room after training and I heard this banging on my door. It was absolutely hammering it down with rain outside – one of those thunderstorms you seem to get only in South Africa – and I opened the door to see Woody stood outside with this great big wheelie bin next to him.

'Will you push me?' he asked.

'You what, mate?' I replied, before he climbed inside and directed me around the corner. We were staying on the university campus and the rooms were arranged along corridors close to the playing fields and world-class training facilities. There were a number of different athletes and sportsmen staying on the campus, training for a variety of sports and disciplines.

One of the athletes was the former Olympic, World and Commonwealth 400-metre champion Christine Ohuruogu, who also happened to be fast asleep in her room when Woody ordered me to stop pushing him when we ended up outside her door.

Woody didn't know her from Adam, but that didn't stop him shooing me away before knocking loudly on her door and flipping the lid of the wheelie bin back down with him still inside. After what seemed like an age, a clearly sleepy Ohuruogu opened her door, only to be greeted with the unexpected sight of a large green wheelie bin sitting immediately in front of her. With heavy rain and thunder hammering on the roof above, she clearly didn't know what on earth was going on.

Then, without warning, Woody burst out of the bin and started wailing like a banshee in Ohuruogu's face. She physically leapt in the air. To say she was shocked would be something of an understatement. I thought she was going to have a heart attack as this crazed Geordie cricketer who she'd never met before screamed in her face from out of a soaking-wet wheelie bin. She spent several moments trying to work out if she was still dreaming, before bursting into fits of giggles.

I couldn't believe Woody's front. Luckily for us Ohuruogu, once she'd gathered her senses, saw the funny side as she realised she'd been the victim of a practical joke. But it was a first taste for me of Woody's infectious sense of humour and willingness to act the fool. It was refreshing and I loved it.

On a personal level, the camp proved incredibly helpful as I started bowling at close to full tilt for the first time since surgery. It was so nice to be able to bowl without the pain I'd been in before and to get back to concentrating on how to get individual batsmen out rather than worrying about how much each delivery would hurt.

Crucially, I was able to get miles in my legs after a lengthy lay-off which had seen me lose a lot of what little muscle I previously had on my right leg. Getting some definition back was important and I was able to report back to coach Peter Moores after the trip declaring myself fully on track to be fit for the upcoming World Cup.

I'd obviously kept an eye on events in Sri Lanka while I was working on my rehabilitation. The seven-match series had been designed, along with the 6 January departure for Australia, to give us the best possible preparation for a tournament for which, historically, England had been accused of not being properly prepared. The aim was to provide a no-excuse environment which would see us leave no stone unturned in our bid to go one better than Graham Gooch's team had done in 1992, when they lost in the World Cup final to Pakistan.

Unfortunately, things didn't go to plan in Sri Lanka, which is one of the toughest places in the world to try to win cricket matches. The 5-2 series defeat wasn't a disgrace, but Cooky's captaincy and batting, which had come under intense scrutiny the previous summer, were once again under the microscope for all the wrong reasons.

I genuinely believed his one-day and Test captaincy had come on leaps and bounds the previous summer against India, when he'd shown a willingness to take a few risks and come up with some clever and imaginative field placings. He'd also batted his way out of a slump and back to form with a superb 95 in the third Test at the Rose Bowl, where he received the most incredible ovation I'd ever heard just for passing 50. I could feel the hairs on the back of my neck stand up at the same time the crowd did, as they gave the clearest indication possible of their support for a man who had been through the emotional and psychological mincer following the Ashes whitewash and our embarrassing second Test capitulation to India at Lord's.

I was worried he was going to give up the captaincy after that defeat when some spineless second-innings batting saw us bowled out for 223 as Ishant Sharma bounced us out to finish with seven for 74. Cooky was taking a kicking left, right and centre and there was no doubt he was very close to resigning the captaincy. He was struggling badly with the bat and his captaincy was coming in for sustained criticism. It was totally out of order, and it was wearing a good man down.

Allied to the personal abuse, Cooky was struggling badly with the bat, and with our ever-present wicket-keeper Matt Prior requiring surgery on his Achilles, which would eventually force him to retire from cricket altogether, he faced the prospect of losing another close friend and star performer from his squad. The year before in Sydney, after we'd lost the Ashes 5-0, I'd spoken at length with him and persuaded him not to resign. I told him the team believed in him and that his form would turn around. I felt the same now. He was a world-class cricketer, arguably England's greatest-ever batsman, who was going through a dip in form that any player who is in the team long enough will inevitably go through. He'd been in a similar slump against Pakistan in 2010 and batted his way out of it with a hard-fought hundred at The Oval. A player of his calibre would inevitably come good and, as soon as we started winning again, the barrage of criticism he was currently facing would disappear into background noise. The team needed him to carry on. England needed him to carry on.

In the end, to the relief of everybody in the dressing room, Cooky agreed to stay on and fight another day. But it was touch and go.

After our abject showing at Lord's, we turned the series, and the summer, around in spectacular fashion to run out comprehensive 3-1 winners courtesy of some of the most aggressive, attacking cricket we'd played for several years. Cooky finished the series with almost 300 runs at 49.66, while newcomers Gary Ballance, Moeen Ali, Jos Buttler and Chris Jordan all made important contributions. Joe Root also batted superbly following a difficult winter Down Under which had seen him dropped for the fifth Test, while Jimmy Anderson was at his imperious best, taking 25 wickets in the series. Personally, I was pretty happy with a haul of 19 wickets at 23 considering I was being severely restricted by the pain in my dodgy right knee every time I bowled.

All of a sudden, things were looking much brighter for the team and for Cooky, who no longer carried the weight of the world on his shoulders and began to look forward to leading England into his first World Cup as captain.

But it wasn't to be. Despite him regaining form in the Test arena, one-day runs continued to elude him. Sri Lanka in December proved the final straw for England's selectors, who took the drastic decision to leave him out of the World Cup squad after more than two years in charge of that team. Eoin Morgan – consistently our best one-day batsman over the past few years – was appointed less than three weeks before our departure for Australia, and Cooky had to accept he would not be part of the one-day side.

It was incredibly tough on him being sacked so soon before a World Cup. As a friend, I felt for him. He was absolutely gutted when he heard the announcement of the 15-man squad.

But, as harsh as it was, he knew as well as anyone that professional sport can be ruthless. The only thing that really matters is scoring runs, taking wickets and winning. He'd managed just 119 runs in six knocks in Sri Lanka at an average of less than 20. The thing that probably counted against him most, though, was a strike-rate of just 67.23, which was at least 20 below what most one-day openers would require for their team to stand a chance of winning the World Cup. One half-century in his last 22 innings left him without much room for manoeuvre, or runs to change the selectors' minds.

... professional sport can be ruthless. The only thing that really matters is scoring runs, taking wickets and winning.

It was a sad end to what had already been incredibly tough year for him, but he took it on the chin like the great man that he is, wished us luck, and stepped aside for Morgs to take over.

I hadn't felt any adverse reaction to the surgery on my knee while in Potchefstroom and, although well short of being fully match fit, I felt the lengthy warm-up spell in the build-up to the World Cup would give me ample time to get up to speed. The plan had always been for me to have the surgery, take my time with the rehab, and get myself ready in time for the World Cup. Mooresy had stressed to me from a very early stage that he had no intention of rushing me back and he didn't want me to feel under any pressure to do so. I appreciated that. Not all coaches would have been so sympathetic.

On 6 January, we flew out from Heathrow for the beginning of what would be, if all went to plan, a 12-week trip that would see us play 12 warm-up games, including a tri-series tournament involving India and Australia, immediately before the World Cup began in earnest on 14 February, when we would take on hosts Australia in front of 84,000 at the Melbourne Cricket Ground.

From a planning point of view, it was clearly not ideal changing captain less than three weeks before we left for Australia, but when we met up at Heathrow we felt confident, energised and there was a real sense we could prove our many doubters wrong.

Predictably, and perhaps understandably, we'd been widely written off before our departure by the media. Our one-day results had been far from impressive over the previous 12 months, with only 15 wins from our last 37 matches. But despite that, I sat on the plane, looked around the squad and saw players such as Alex Hales, Jos Buttler, Joe Root, Mo Ali, Belly and Morgs himself who were all more than capable of clearing the ropes with the kind of power hitting needed in one-day cricket these days. On the bowling front, I felt excited about the prospect of being able to run in pain free for the first time in more than a year, while Jimmy Anderson was as good as anyone in the world and Steve Finn was showing signs of getting back to his devilish best. Chris Woakes and Chris Jordan were both talented bowling all-rounders and there appeared to be plenty of depth to our bowling resources.

There was a freshness around the squad which I found exciting. In hindsight, it might have been naïve, but there was genuine collective belief we could make a significant and telling impact on the tournament. How wrong could we be?

When we landed in Sydney, there was a huge amount of excitement and energy in the group. I don't think anyone knew what our best team was, so the training was intense, competitive and enjoyable. We put in strong performances in some of the warm-up games and some players started to emerge as stand-out contenders. Finn in particular impressed, bowling with real pace and hostility barely a year after he was last in Australia, when he was a shell of his former self and returned home early in a terrible state after being described as 'unselectable' by our one-day coach Ashley Giles.

Finny had gone back to Middlesex, worked incredibly hard with their coaches Richard Johnson and Angus Fraser, and literally broken his action down to its most basic form before building himself back up again. He'd spent hours and hours in the nets bowling off one or two paces, sometimes just into the side of the net in a bid to groove his action and prevent his fragile confidence falling apart completely. Gradually, he built himself back up again and began to rediscover the confidence that had been so badly eroded over previous years of tinkering with his run-up, action and delivery stride.

It was great to see him returning to something close to his best. When on song, there are few more unpleasant bowlers to face and few more amiable and decent blokes to have in the dressing room. It was good to have him back.

After a string of relatively meaningless warm-up games which enabled us to acclimatise and work on fitness and tactics, it felt like the business was really beginning when we kicked off the snappily named Carlton Mid One-Day International Tri Series against Australia in Sydney. I'd bowled OK in the non-international warm-ups, but still felt the control I possess when at the top of my game was missing. My knee, at least, felt very strong.

We lost by three wickets to Australia with 61 balls to spare after being bowled out for 234. It didn't look good on paper. But there were some encouraging signs, with captain Morgs scoring a superb 121 from 136 balls while Woakesy impressed with the new ball by taking four for 40.

A few people questioned why I'd come on first change, but I was comfortable with letting Woakesy and Finny open up, the idea being that I'd come on and keep things tight while posing a wicket-taking threat at first change. Besides, I'd never really settled on opening the bowling in one-day internationals. I'd switched between opening and first change, which I admit I have found a bit odd. But I knew what I was trying to do now. However, that day the plan didn't quite work out as I was flogged for 49 off 6.5 overs as David Warner hit a match-winning 127.

We bounced back to beat India twice – once by a crushing nine wickets in Brisbane and then again ten days later by a less convincing three wickets – although Australia got the better of us again with a nail-biting three-wicket victory in Hobart after a superb Ian Bell hundred had seen us set them a challenging 304-run victory target.

Despite not really hitting our straps with either bat or ball, we managed to reach the final of the tri-series, where we played Australia at the WACA in Perth. We were really good in the field, limiting them to 278 for eight. I was pleased with the way I bowled, taking three for 55 off ten overs, although poor old Chris Woakes didn't fare quite as well with his ten overs going for a whopping 89 runs.

But, in a pattern which would soon become boringly familiar, we threw the final away by buckling under the pressure of the chase. We'd had Australia in quite a bit of trouble at Perth at 60 for four, when Mo Ali had Steve Smith stumped by Jos Buttler. But we allowed them off the hook as Glenn Maxwell and James Faulkner gave it a bit of a whack. With a target of 279 and with the fielding restrictions in place, we'd expect to chase that total nine times out of ten, but they blew us away at the top of the order. It was a disappointing way to end the series before the real business began.

I had mixed feelings about my own form. While on the one hand I was delighted with the way my knee was continuing to respond to the extensive surgery I'd undergone a few months earlier, I was disappointed at a return of just five wickets at 50.8 while leaking almost six runs an over.

With a serious lack of time in the middle, my batting – which had inevitably suffered after the shattering blow to my face I'd received playing against India at Old Trafford the previous summer – seemed to have regressed. Mooresy reassured me he was happy with the way I was bowling, but I knew I needed to contribute more with both bat and ball. The serious business was about to begin.

3

FROM HIGH HOPE TO NO HOPE

WORLD CUP MELTDOWN 6 JANUARY–14 MARCH

I had left the UK with every intention of letting my bowling do the talking over the coming weeks. I was feeling fit and raring to go after four months without any competitive cricket following the surgery on my knee. It was exciting that, for the first time in more than a year, I was potentially going to be able to bowl without experiencing the awful burning pain I had felt every time I'd delivered the ball ever since patella tendonitis was diagnosed in Australia the previous winter.

The schedule for the year ahead was unprecedented. With 17 Tests, 28 one-day internationals (31 if we reached the World Cup final) and five Twenty20 internationals awaiting us over the course of the next 12 months, game time certainly wasn't going to be an issue.

If all went to plan and we reached the World Cup final on 29 March, the players involved in all three formats could potentially expect to spend more than 300 nights away from home. In the past that amount of time away from home might have daunted me, and believe me life on the road is not as glamorous as it sounds, but with so little cricket under my belt in recent months, a group of young and hungry new team-mates and a recently operated-on knee to test out in the international arena, I felt invigorated by what lay ahead.

Every time I pull on an England shirt I feel as if I have something to prove, but the fact I'd been sidelined for so long and missed the seven-match one-day series in Sri Lanka, which had been factored in as a major part of our World Cup preparation jigsaw, made that desire even more acute when I got on the plane to Australia.

Aside from regaining form and fitness, I was also determined to recapture that sense of enjoyment and camaraderie I'd felt playing for England for the overwhelming majority of the eight years I'd been lucky enough to do so. I was convinced all the negativity swirling around could be confined to history if only we could get back to doing what we did best: winning.

I was focused on getting myself fully fit, reclaiming my place in the one-day side after a long injury lay-off, and helping to win matches for England by taking my share of wickets. It was clear from an early stage there was a very different dynamic within the squad compared with previous England one-day sides I'd been involved in. The boys were very chilled, very calm and, on the whole, very quiet. Players like Jos Buttler, Moeen Ali and Gary Ballance had come into the side in recent times. They are all lovely lads who were good fun to be around but very quiet and unassuming. They were certainly not big characters like Graeme Swann, Matty Prior or Kevin Pietersen. These were young guys finding their way in international cricket, and they were loving the experience of being involved. The group felt harmonious, together and focused.

While I hadn't been in Sri Lanka a month or so earlier, it was clear the boys all got on well. There was a nice, relaxed vibe. If anything, I was worried we might just be a bit too nice as a squad.

There had been a great deal of nonsense spoken towards the tail end of 2014 – much of it on social media by people who'd never been near the England dressing room – with completely over-the-top claims of cliques, disharmony and even, most bizarrely, bullying. It felt as if people were trying to sully what, for the vast majority of the England players involved, had been the most enjoyable and successful period of our careers. It was really disappointing. I will always look back with huge affection on the time I spent in the England dressing room under Andy Flower and Andrew Strauss between 2009 and 2012, when the team rose from the low of being bowled out for 51 by the West Indies in Jamaica to winning three Ashes series in succession, as well as beating India 4-0 at home to reach the top of the ICC's world rankings. I just didn't recognise the picture that had been painted by a tiny group of people seemingly intent on stirring up trouble.

Yes, we were a tough, determined group of professional cricketers who set consistently high standards and possessed a burning desire to win games of cricket for England. Honesty was an important part of the team culture, and it was important that we could be open with each other if things needed putting right. Just like any of the world's top sports teams, there weren't too many shrinking violets in the dressing room, but that didn't mean it was an unpleasant place to be around. It was certainly a successful place to be around for much of the time Flower and Strauss were in charge.

Having spoken to a lot of guys since, they were as disappointed as I was about the way the team dynamic had been so unfairly misrepresented. For those of us who had loved and treasured pretty much every minute of representing our country – while forging lasting friendships in the process – we weren't going to allow it to tarnish everyone else's memories.

While much of what had been said was complete nonsense, it was fascinating to see how the story had developed in the media. I've always been interested in how the media work – who knows, one day I might try to follow some of the many former players who've gone into it – but it was clear that people were increasingly moving away from the traditional media for their news.

Rather than print newspapers setting the agenda every morning, it was online where people seemed to be going for their information. Twitter seemed to be the platform of choice where people could shout the loudest. Whether the old establishment organisations liked it or not, it felt as if there was a changing of the guard. If you had a big following on Twitter, you had the platform to affect public opinion. And public opinion could shift incredibly fast, with one powerful message – true or false – on Twitter reaching a huge audience in a matter of seconds.

A lot of nonsense was being thrown out there, with some of the worst stuff aimed at my close friend Matt Prior – one of the most loyal team men you could ever hope to go into battle with. Matt showed a lot of class by keeping his own counsel at the end of 2014 and choosing not to respond. He was always a big believer in keeping things inside the dressing room, and I know some of the personal criticism thrown his way hurt him. He did not deserve it.

In general, I've embraced social media and believe it's a positive thing. I'm lucky enough to have nearly 900,000 followers on Twitter, while I also use Instagram and Facebook – as well as my own website – because they are a brilliant way to interact with fans and communicate things without your words being misinterpreted or twisted.

Most of the boys have Twitter accounts, although notably the two most recent England Test captains I've played under – Cook and Strauss – have steadfastly refused to go anywhere near it. Perhaps it's hard to be statesmanlike when you open yourself up to that world. Cooky is far happier on his in-laws' farm in Leighton Buzzard. He tries to switch off completely from cricket when he's not on duty.

'Sheep can't talk to me about cricket,' he once said.

Andy Flower was another one who just could not get his head around why we'd want to share our thoughts with the wider world and leave ourselves open to even more criticism than we already got!

But some of us are more than happy to indulge and, after some scepticism in the early days, the ECB also see the value in reaching a wider audience of fans and potential players. As our employers, they issue us social media guidelines. They're basically common sense, along the lines of 'don't swear' and 'don't criticise fans, team-mates or sponsors'. But we're generally trusted to put out what we see fit.

It's completely changed the relationship players are able to enjoy with fans, and vice versa, making real-time conversations and exchanges possible in a way they have never previously been. On the whole that's a good thing.

Of course there are downsides, one of them being that people can throw opinions out there which have absolutely no basis in truth but which get picked up and gather momentum incredibly fast. I suppose it's the same with the more 'old school' forms of media like newspapers, it's just that online things can go viral and escalate at an astonishing speed. Also, once it's out there on the internet it can never be deleted.

I enjoy the vast majority of exchanges I have with people on Twitter. Of course there is a small minority who see it as an opportunity to gain a little bit of attention by being abusive or intentionally provocative, but I've long since learned to ignore the trolls. I've had some absolutely appalling stuff thrown at me – even death threats – but the vast majority of exchanges are positive and harmless.

I know some former players scoff at the idea of social media, and there are some who trot out the 'it wouldn't have happened in our day' line, but times move on and in most cases I'm happy to move with them. A major part of the reason to be on social media is because it's fun. Of course there are also commercial reasons, because potential sponsors will look at your social media 'reach', and the bigger it is, the more attractive you become to them.

Every child who grows up playing sport dreams of playing for their country and I was definitely no different.

As professional sportsmen we're incredibly lucky to be able to make a good living from playing a sport we fell in love with as kids and have devoted our lives to. Every child who grows up playing sport dreams of playing for their country and I was definitely no different. Perhaps having a dad who played professionally for Gloucestershire, Nottinghamshire and England gave me a slightly more realistic, and less romantic, view of what it was like to be a professional sportsman, but it also made it more real for me. I always believed it was attainable, even as a skinny little teenager who struggled to hit the ball off the square. I worked out early on that if I could get my technique right, I had a chance.

People get very cross with sportsmen and women discussing money and I completely understand why. I thank my lucky stars every day for the job that I have and realise there are thousands of jobs out there which are more demanding and do not come with all the perks and opportunities we're afforded as professional players. I also realise that as a centrally contracted England player we get looked after incredibly well and have an amazing amount of support on all sorts of levels which you don't even get playing county cricket, let alone further down the leagues.

But the flip side of that is that it is still a job – an amazingly good job, of course – but a job all the same. I love every second of playing for England and would honestly play for free. But we have a limited window of opportunity to maximise our earning potential in a career, and I don't begrudge anyone trying to do that, as long as it doesn't interfere with the day-to-day objective of winning games of cricket for England – or whoever else pays your wages for that matter! One of the important things to remember is that success will bring rewards; so staying focused on the prize of winning games for England will enable all the other benefits to follow.

Why wouldn't you want to plan for you and your family's future by making sure you engage with commercial opportunities that present themselves during your career? There are so many things that are out of your control as a player, with career-threatening injury and loss of form a constant threat, that I think most fair-minded people understand sports men and women need to try to maximise their earning potential, within reason.

Social media fits into that picture and enables you to present yourself to the wider public on your own terms.

We are in the public eye so much as a result of our day-to-day jobs, with so many people ready to pass judgement on what we do, why not use what's available to us to inform fans what we really think? It's an exciting development and one that is only going to grow over time.

Some professional sports stars employ people to manage their accounts and even write their messages for them, but it can be pretty blatant when that's the case. I do have people I speak to and listen to who understand the media better than I do and can explain the potential pitfalls, but I always write my own tweets because they go under my name and I think it's quite obvious when they're just being put out there by someone's assistant.

Inevitably you'll mess up from time to time. We're only human after all. We all learned pretty early on the dangers of putting anything out there after a beer or two when your judgement isn't necessarily as sharp as it should be. If you do mess up, speed is of the essence. The longer you wait to clarify a comment or, in the worst cases, apologise, the more damage can be done.

I was given a timely reminder of this when I was woken up at 2am in my hotel room in Perth, midway through the World Cup warm-up games, by a phone call from my agent Neil Fairbrother.

'What's up, Harv?' I asked, still half asleep. 'Do you know what time it is?'

Neil, or Harvey as his friends know him, proceeded to tell me he knew precisely what time it was and that I needed to get onto Twitter to explain a tweet I'd sent out just before I'd gone to bed. Sometimes when you tweet something, you know it's going to get people talking. That's part of the fun, sharing opinions on anything from sport to fashion or politics. Generally I try to steer clear of talking politics, but for that night I'd put out what I'd considered to be have been a completely innocent tweet after hearing a fact about the minimum wage. It had read:

'I've heard if you earn minimum wage in England you're in the top 10% earners in the world. #stay #humble.'

I honestly hadn't thought anything of it until Neil woke me up sounding a bit concerned, telling me the tweet had 'gone bloody viral!'

I'd only intended the tweet to be a comment on how big the world was and how it was important to put concerns about money into perspective. I just thought it was an interesting fact. The #stay #humble hashtags were very much a reference to myself, but inevitably people jumped on it and immediately assumed I was having a go at Kev, which I absolutely was not.

Suddenly wide awake, I put out a clarification of what I'd meant and apologised for any offence caused:

'Clarifying my earlier tweet, I merely wanted to emphasise my amazement at just how big the world is.

'No offence meant and sorry if any taken. The hashtag was aimed at myself.' The apology definitely helped calm people down, but I was amazed to hear the next day that Radio 4 had discussed the tweet while Five Live and LBC Radio had held phone-ins about it! It was a very timely reminder of the perils of social media and I was disappointed that there was so much discussion around it so soon before the World Cup. I was also annoyed with myself for falling into the trap of giving people ammunition to attack me with. The usual suspects piled in.

Rhian Evans, our team media liaison officer who keeps across all forms of media to make sure we don't get any surprises when talking to the press, suggested I'd be better off speaking to the travelling pack of cricket journalists the next day, and I was more than happy to clarify my position further.

I fully expected the barrage of questions that came my way about the tweet, but I was a lot happier when the subject finally got back to cricket, my own form and fitness, and how the team might go in the World Cup.

I'd been delighted that I'd experienced no pain whatsoever in my knee and it appeared the operation could not have gone any better. Looking back I probably underestimated how long it would take me to recapture my match fitness and the control that I feel when I'm at the top of my game. It's hard to put your finger on exactly what match sharpness is. It's a combination of mental and physical fitness and just having the feeling of the game.

I felt I'd bowled OK in the early tour warm-up games and the Carlton Series without ever really hitting my straps. I was a bit frustrated at the amount of soft boundaries I was conceding and knew I had to bowl fewer loose balls. Peter Moores kept reassuring me, but I think we both knew I had significant room for improvement when it came to my control.

As a team, we'd shown some encouraging signs in the Carlton Series, reaching the final by beating India twice, even though we lost both our games against Australia in the round robin stage. As I've mentioned, the final itself was a disappointment, especially after we'd done well to restrict their score. Despite a serious lack of match practice I managed to club 24 from 20, including two sixes at the end, but the game was already well and truly over when I walked to the crease at 98 for seven.

It was an unsatisfactory way to finish our preparation for the World Cup, but with Steven Finn returning to something like his best form with the ball and Ian Bell, Jimmy Taylor and Joe Root all making valuable contributions with the bat, there were definitely positives to take out of the series. Our fielding had also been consistently excellent, with young players such as Taylor, Chris Woakes and Chris Jordan all outstanding in the field, while Buttler had looked good behind the stumps.

Some of the press were making a talking point out of Eoin Morgan's form. He'd scored a brilliant hundred in the opening Carlton Series game against the Aussies before proceeding to make scores of 0, 2, 0 and 0. These things can happen to a top-order batsman and I don't think anyone in our dressing room believed for a second his form wouldn't return.

Before the World Cup started, we had two more warm-up games, against West Indies and Pakistan. I was rested for our thumping nine-wicket win over the West Indies before returning for a narrow four-wicket defeat to Pakistan in a game we really should have won.

With a fair amount of cricket under my belt, I was able to work hard on my fitness, continuing to build up muscle to strengthen my knee while working on my general conditioning.

I had a little bit of down time ahead of the 50-over tournament beginning in earnest. As I've mentioned, there was clearly a very different social dynamic from the dressing rooms I'd been in in the past. The boys were very relaxed, fairly quiet and probably more laid back than previous ones. I thought the atmosphere was brilliant. There were fewer really dominant characters, with a number of inexperienced boys trying to make their way, and the social arrangements tended to be a bit more relaxed, too.

Early on the trip, we set up a WhatsApp group, which meant everyone would be included on where people were going out for dinner in the evening, so people could pick and choose if they wanted to join in. Someone might pipe up: 'Fancy a Nando's. Meet in lobby at 7pm.' If you wanted to go – great; if not, no worries. It made for a really inclusive environment and meant no one ever felt left out. I really enjoyed that way of arranging things. In previous dressing rooms, guys may have been more inclined to keep themselves to themselves. This way, everyone felt included. It suited the personalities of a lot of the new guys in the team. It was probably the biggest change in the team's culture and a clear sign of an important step forward.

You don't get a huge amount of time to socialise these days on tour, but with a lot of keen golfers in the squad, that was another great way for some of the boys to get closer. Belly and Alex Hales didn't know each other particularly well before we left for Australia, so they were partnered together on the golf course early in the trip. The pair of them were winning their match with three holes to play when Halesy's game fell apart. He missed a tiny putt on the last and they lost the match. Belly went out and bought a packet of digestives, which he crumbled into an envelope and addressed to Alex, who was handed it in the dressing room the next day. He thought it was a letter from a fan asking him to sign something, but inside were just these biscuit crumbs and a note from Belly saying: 'The biscuit who crumbles under pressure.' Halesy loved it. He was called the Crumbler for a few days afterwards.

It obviously would have been a useful boost to have beaten Australia in one of the three Carlton Series games, especially as they were set to be our first opponents in Melbourne, but the boys remained positive and tight-knit. The way the competition was structured – with four teams progressing to the knockout stages out of each of the two seven-team pools – everything was designed to ensure the so-called bigger nations progressed to the latter stages. It appeared as though it would take something pretty calamitous for us not to progress.

The way the fixtures had fallen would see us open the tournament against the hosts in front of more than 84,000 people at the MCG before taking on New Zealand, Scotland, Sri Lanka, Bangladesh and finally Afghanistan. Assuming we would beat Scotland and Afghanistan, in order for us not to qualify for the knockout stages we were going to have to have an absolute shocker by losing all four games against the Test nations: Australia, New Zealand, Sri Lanka and Bangladesh. While we may not have set the world alight in our preparation going into the tournament, even the most negative observer would have thought we'd have a better than even chance of qualifying.

We flew into Melbourne a few days before our first game genuinely believing we had a chance of proving a few doubters wrong by progressing deep into the tournament. In retrospect, to say we were overly optimistic would be probably putting things mildly.

As it turned out, things started off badly and got steadily worse.

There was some last-minute tinkering with the line-up, which was surprising considering we'd had so much time to prepare. Ravi Bopara had been a regular feature in the side during the Carlton Series, capable of clearing the ropes in the middle order and offering useful overs with his tidy medium pace. With almost 120 one-day international caps to his name, he was also one of the most experienced players in the squad, and one who had looked sure of a spot in the starting XI despite not having set the world alight on tour so far.

While other sides were starting to see the new ball as the best opportunity to attack and score runs, we were still looking at it as a part of the game to negotiate and not lose wickets.

But, on the eve of the game, Mooresy told us that Gary Ballance, who'd not played a match since September having broken a finger, would be batting at three – where Jimmy Taylor had batted in all the warm-up games. It was a huge ask for Gary, even though he had emerged as an excellent international cricketer. He had very little experience of batting three in one-day cricket at international or county level, and with such a long injury lay-off he would inevitably be a bit ring rusty. It was also slightly indicative of our mindset going into the tournament. While other sides were starting to see the new ball as the best opportunity to attack and score runs, we were still looking at it as a part of the game to negotiate and not lose wickets. While I had every faith in Gary, who has more shots than some people give him credit for, it wasn't necessarily the most attacking option we could have taken.

In the opening game against Australia, we suffered one of the most comprehensive defeats I'd ever been involved in with the England team. Their final victory margin of 111 runs looked big enough on paper, but in reality the gulf in performance between the teams was absolutely huge.

Australia batted first and absolutely murdered our attack. They finished on 342 for nine, which I later found out was the highest total England had ever conceded in 40 years of World Cups, with opener Aaron Finch smashing 135 from 128 balls and Glenn Maxwell chipping in down the order with 66 from just 40 balls. It was savage batting and, not for the last time in the tournament, I felt a sense of helplessness in attempting to stem the tide. I felt I bowled OK, picking up the early wickets of David Warner and Shane Watson, but still ended up going for 66 runs in my ten overs.

Poor old Finny took a hat-trick off the final three balls of their innings when he dismissed Brad Haddin, Maxwell and Mitchell Johnson in successive deliveries, but the celebrations were considerably more muted than they might otherwise have been. Australia had already chalked up 342 by then!

I think even the most experienced batting line-ups would have struggled chasing that total, but it was still hugely disappointing not to even threaten as we slumped to 73 for five after 18 overs. Whichever way you looked at it, it was game over. Jimmy Taylor, batting down the order at six, made an excellent 98 not out from 90 balls. But it only served to delay the inevitable and reduce the scale of the defeat on paper. In reality we'd been absolutely hammered.

Technically, the result wasn't a disaster, as it remained the case that if we beat Scotland, Bangladesh and Afghanistan we would still qualify. But there's no doubt the scale of the defeat shocked us. Australia were an outstanding one-day unit, and they would go on to win the competition, but to surrender in that manner was concerning to say the least.

The next day we boarded a flight from Melbourne to Wellington, where we were set to play New Zealand six days later. It was only a relatively short flight of around three and a half hours, but it felt much longer as one particularly obnoxious Aussie fan who'd had a bit too much to drink made it his business to berate us about the defeat for the entire flight. I was sitting about three rows in front of him, but poor old Ravi was pretty much next to him. It's a good job for that bloke that Ravi is so mild-mannered and good-natured. I know a few people who wouldn't have taken so kindly to his boorish abuse.

If you ask professional sportsmen where they're most likely to suffer abuse – apart from on Twitter – I'd wager most would answer 'at the airport'. The security check area is normally the worst because you're stuck in one position and it's pretty much open season for anyone who wants to have a pop. You'll have seen on Sky Sports News pictures of players walking through an airport wearing big headphones on their heads. A lot of the time there's no music playing, but headphones are a good way of blocking out the abuse!

It may have been a relief to get to Wellington, but on the pitch there was to be no respite.

Having won the toss and bowled against Australia in Melbourne, Morgs decided to give our batsmen first use of another pretty decent surface. But once again our top three of Belly, Mo and Gary Ballance fell cheaply to leave us 57 for three. Rooty and Morgs hung around for a while to give us a brief hope of respectability, but after reaching 104 for three in the 26th over, we collapsed in spectacular fashion as Tim Southee ripped through our tail, taking seven for 33. In the end, we were bowled out for just 123 in 33.2 overs. It was miles short of a challenging total.

We sat in the changing room before taking the field, knowing the chances of defending that score against a side containing world-class power hitters like Brendon McCullum, Martin Guptill and Ross Taylor were almost zero. But even so, allowing them to reach the total within 13 overs was totally unacceptable. McCullum batted like a man possessed, smashing seven sixes in an astonishing demonstration of hitting which saw him make 77 from 25 balls, 15 of which were boundaries. It was humiliating.

I bowled 2.2 overs for 27 runs, but McCullum was most savage on Finny, who went for an eye-watering 49 from two overs. For the second match running we'd completely lost control in the field. Woakes was the only bowler able to exert even a semblance of control. But it was car-crash cricket on our behalf. It was an even more comprehensive defeat than the one we'd suffered at Australia's hands and the press didn't hold back in their condemnation of our performance.

FROM HIGH HOPE TO NO HOPE

One journalist described it as 'one of the worst days in the history of English one-day cricket' and, in the cold light of day, it is hard to argue with that assessment. Another newspaper sought a degree of solace by pointing out it 'could not get any worse'. Unfortunately that wasn't true.

We were taking an absolute hammering in the press for our performances, while Mooresy was getting it in the neck for his selections and Morgs continued to struggle with the bat. We knew we had massively underperformed, but due to the way the tournament was structured, we still had a very reasonable chance of qualifying for the knockout stages.

There was no panic inside the dressing room and no finger-pointing; no one played the blame game. We knew we were better players than we'd shown so far and we reminded ourselves of that in the wake of the Black Caps defeat. However, what really worried me was that we'd lost two games where our opponents would have been walking off the field thinking 'that was easy'. For all the flack that Mooresy was getting as coach, we were the ones who were underperforming. I am a firm believer that coaches can do only so much and I can't stand it when I hear players saying they couldn't perform because the environment or culture wasn't right. That's just an excuse. As players you need to take ownership and responsibility for your own performance. As the tournament progressed, it became clear we weren't doing that.

As I said, the boys all got on really well all trip. My early tour concern that we were perhaps a little too nice as a group was beginning to be realised. I wanted to see little more dog in our team and a lot more fight.

Scotland were next up three days later in Christchurch. With all due respect to the Scots, we knew if we couldn't beat them we really did deserve to be on the next flight home. This time Scotland put us into bat and Mo and Belly got us off to the perfect start by putting on 172 for the first wicket in 30.1 overs. Mo, who'd established himself in the Test and one-day side the previous summer, batted absolutely beautifully against what was admittedly not the fiercest attack he'd ever face, to finish with 128 from 107 balls. He is a wonderful timer of the ball and incredibly graceful to watch and it was good to see him cashing in.

Belly made a slightly more pedestrian 54 from 85 balls, but the platform had been set for our total of 303 for eight. He received a fair bit of stick for his innings, with people saying he'd left too many balls and we should have pressed for a bigger total. In hindsight, the criticism could have been levelled at the entire team that we did not set our sights high enough when it came to what we considered a decent total.

But Scotland never really got going in reply, with Finny picking up another three wickets as they were bowled out for 184 in 42.2 overs. I'd returned to opening the bowling this time and, although I felt in reasonably good rhythm, I was frustrated to end their innings wicketless from seven overs. Much more importantly, we'd got the win and we returned to Wellington where we would face Sri Lanka six days later. We knew they would present an altogether tougher challenge.

The lengthy breaks between games during the tournament sometimes left us struggling to stay busy. The middle of a World Cup is not the time or place to let your hair down – as England's rugby players had discovered in New Zealand four years earlier – so you're a little bit limited in what you can do outside of nets and training.

We are professional sportsmen so we just had to get on with it, but we could definitely sense a certain amount of apathy towards the competition in some quarters of the media, though that was probably not helped by our underwhelming performances so far.

The main criticism was that the tournament simply went on for too long, stretching as it did across six weeks from start to finish. For the players it felt very stop and start. We'd play a game, have a day off, have another couple of days training, play, have a day off and so on. It was too spread out.

That's why the format of the next World Cup makes very little sense to me. The plan is to reduce the number of teams by two and yet the tournament is going to last two days longer. How on earth does that work?

I'm sure people will have thought long and hard about this, but it seems odd to me that teams like Ireland might not qualify for the next World Cup because they're cutting two of the Associate nations. I just don't get that. If you don't have smaller teams with fewer resources then you can't have major upsets, and you'll have no underdogs. Those countries bring excitement. I want to tune in to see Ireland beat the West Indies, and I'm sure there are plenty of people who'd like to see them beat England, too.

Just before this book went to print, I watched Japan beat South Africa in the Rugby World Cup and it was one of the most exciting and uplifting sporting occasions I can remember. It would be such a shame if cricket chose to get rid of those seeming mismatches and potential upsets. Sports fans need heroes, and underdogs often make the greatest heroes. I'll feel very sorry for Ireland if they're not in the next World Cup; they've made so much progress in recent years and it's in countries like Ireland and Afghanistan where the game of cricket can really grow. Why would you take underdogs out of a World Cup? Part of people's fascination with major competitions is the possibility of an upset. I'll never forget losing to Holland at Lord's in the 2009 Twenty20 World Cup. It was incredibly painful to be part of, but I have to admit it made a great story.

What a shame it would be if these sorts of stories were lost to the sport. The World Cup is cricket's showcase. We should be looking to broaden it, not make it smaller.

Sri Lanka were once considered minnows, but today they're one of the toughest opponents in world cricket at both Test and one-day level – and that's because they were initially given their opportunity in the World Cup. There was no chance of our underestimating them now, especially considering how poor we'd been so far in the tournament.

We trained well in the lead-up to the game and it was good to see our batsmen deliver in great style after Morgs won the toss and batted on another belting wicket. After coming in at 71 for two, Rooty scored an absolutely superb 121 from 108 balls (including 14 fours and two sixes) while Jos smashed an unbeaten 39 from just 19 balls to take our total to an eminently defendable 309 for six from 50 overs. The only negative was another low score for Gary Ballance.

We began Sri Lanka's innings buoyed up and filled with belief that we could claim our first win over one of the big boys. That belief didn't last long. Their openers, Lahiru Thirimanne and Tillakaratne Dilshan, set the perfect platform, reaching 100 off 19 overs when Dilshan was caught by Morgs off Mo. But even with him gone, there was a growing sense that the game was slipping away from us. That sense became reality as Thirimanne and Kumar Sangakkara picked our attack off with ridiculous ease to reach the target with almost three overs to spare. They didn't even look like getting out. All our bowlers suffered and that sense of helplessness engulfed me again as it became increasingly obvious we weren't going to be able to defend a total in excess of 300.

> We'd been absolutely annihilated for the third time in the tournament and ... were staring down the barrel.

Both Thirimanne and Sangakkara scored high-class unbeaten hundreds, and I'd rate Sangakkara's knock of 117 from 86 balls one of the best one-day innings I've seen. But the quality of the opposition's display provided little comfort to us. We'd been absolutely annihilated for the third time in the tournament and, with Bangladesh in Adelaide eight days later now a must-win game, we were staring down the barrel of what had been unthinkable a few weeks earlier: failing to qualify for the knockout stages.

You could hear a pin drop in the dressing room after the game. This couldn't really be happening could it?

With another lengthy break between games, there was no shortage of time to identify what we were doing wrong and where we needed to improve. Things hadn't worked out for Gary Ballance at three in the order, scoring just 36 runs from 71 balls in four innings. I felt for him, as I'd been incredibly impressed by him during his debut international summer in 2014. But it was asking a huge amount of him to bat in such a pivotal position having not played a one-day international for more than five months before the start of the World Cup. He started by facing an attack including Mitchell Johnson and Mitchell Starc in front of more than 80,000 people at the MCG and never really got going after that.

Mooresy had gambled on him at the last minute, and it hadn't paid off. I was convinced Gary would feature again in the one-day side, but for the time being it was best for him and the team that he missed out.

There had been a big clamour in the press for my old mate from Nottinghamshire, Alex Hales, to be given a run in the side. Many people had been surprised he hadn't featured already in the tournament and I was delighted when he was given the nod. Alex is one of my best mates, as daft as a brush but great company. He can also hit the ball an absolute mile with a really good range of shots and the ability to improvise. He'd played only seven one-day internationals before the Bangladesh game and was yet to fully convince, but I was confident he could deliver in a must-win game.

The week leading up to the game really dragged. We were desperate to get on with it and stop raking over the bones of our previous defeats. Whenever we go abroad, there is always a band of written and broadcast media who follow us around wherever we play. The same old faces tend to appear on every trip and generally the relationship between the players and press is pretty good.

Mooresy had made a big thing the previous summer about the importance of strengthening our relationships with the media, because ultimately they are the ones who reflect our views to a wider audience. I completely agreed with move. I didn't see any harm in being open and transparent with the media, most of whom are pretty decent. The vast majority, if not all, want England to win. We'd felt a bit disappointed with the way our 2013 Ashes victory over Australia had been reported, with our 3-0 series win seemingly overshadowed by the media focus on our supposedly negative style of play. There's no doubt that made things a little bit more strained, but I was fully behind the move to engage more with the media as well as with former players and pundits.

On tour, we generally hold a press conference every day when a player or member of the coaching staff is 'put up' to answer questions. These are quite formulaic affairs, with journalists pushing to get a headline by focusing on the most controversial current issue and players wary of creating a storm by saying anything that could cause upset or disrupt the team's dynamic. As a player, you're treading a little bit of a tightrope. In the spirit of openness, when it was my turn to do this, I thought I'd throw something out there almost as a distraction technique.

With so much talk about how badly we were playing and how we would be out of the tournament if we lost to Bangladesh, I decided that if anyone asked me about my batting – which hadn't been going well – I'd remind people that it wasn't so long ago I'd suffered a double fracture of my nose after being hit in the face by a Varun Aaron bouncer.

I'd been disappointed with my batting during the tournament but was convinced I hadn't become a No.11 bunny overnight as some people were trying to make out. I was seriously short of match practice and had been unable to spend the sort of time in the middle I needed to get my form back.

As it turned out, I was asked a direct question about whether my confidence had been affected by being hit in the face to which I gave an honest answer, which was 'yes'. Whose wouldn't be?

I went on to reveal that I had experienced the occasional nightmare with the ball coming right up to my face before I'd jolt back awake and that I was working with a sports psychologist, Chris Marshall, who worked under the ECB's head psychologist, Mark Bawden, to try to rebuild my confidence. I'd had a few occasions when, instead of that jolting sensation some people get when they're falling asleep and they feel like they're dropping off a cliff, I felt like the ball was flying into my face and I'd wake up bolt upright. It wasn't happening all the time, and I certainly wasn't having nightmares every time I went to sleep, but I'd found some of the painkilling medication I'd been on after the knee operation had brought on a few episodes.

I didn't see the problem with saying this. It was nothing to be ashamed of, after all. It also had the desired effect of diverting attention a little bit, even though I was subsequently heavily criticised by Shane Warne of all people, who said I shouldn't have let my opponents know I was having difficulties. You can't please everyone!

There was also a growing focus on our use of data in analysing our matches. People were talking about Mooresy being 'obsessed' with data analysis rather than instinctive coaching. It didn't wash with me at all.

As international cricketers you want to use all the tools available to you in order to gather as much information on opponents as possible. We all have ECB laptops and iPads with software packages that allow us to analyse our own performances and those of the opposition. We had our analyst, Nathan Leaman, with us and some players tapped into him more than others. We knew the data on things like where certain batsmen got dismissed most or how bowlers got most of their wickets was available to us if we wanted it, but it was certainly never rammed down our throats. Mooresy took the view that if we wanted to access it, then great; if not, no problem. He certainly never put pressure on anyone to go through the data, but once the press got their teeth into the story, it became far more of an issue than it ever was in the dressing room.

Eventually, game day arrived. It was now or never against a Bangladesh team that had improved from being whipping boys in all forms of cricket when they first received Test status in 2000 to being a very competitive one-day outfit who, on their day, were capable of beating the best sides in the world. We couldn't lay claim to being one of those the way we'd played over recent weeks and they probably sensed we were vulnerable.

Despite all the criticism and flak that was flying around, Mooresy and Morgs remained positive and upbeat about our chances, although Morgs did go as far as to say to the press that the form of his senior bowlers – me and Jimmy – was a 'concern'. I know Jimmy was as frustrated as I was that we hadn't been able to exert the sort of control we'd wanted. I certainly felt I was bowling OK, but the wickets weren't coming.

'Back your skills boys, back yourselves,' Morgs said before the game got underway, and when Morgs won the toss and bowled it was all-or-nothing time.

We started superbly, with Jimmy taking two wickets in his first seven deliveries to leave them 8 for two, with the dangerous Tamim Iqbal one of his two victims.

I bowled tidily, without much luck, and gradually Bangladesh began to build a creditable total. The underrated Mahmudullah scored a superb 103 while wicket-keeper Mushfiqur Rahim gave their innings real impetus by crashing 89 from 77 balls down the order. The Adelaide wicket was another belter, so our victory target of 276 really should have been within reach, especially considering some of the scoring rates already seen during the tournament.

Belly and Mo got us off to a decent start as we reached 42 from seven overs before Mo was run out in a needless mix-up. Hales was looking good, reaching 27 from 34 balls, but he was out to Mashrafe Mortaza.

Belly made another tidy if unspectacular 63 before getting out and when Morgs fell for his fifth duck in nine innings and Jimmy Taylor followed soon after, we found ourselves 132 for five after 29.4. A few nervous looks began to be cast around the dressing room and they only increased when Rooty – who'd looked calm and composed throughout – was out for 29.

Jos batted brilliantly alongside Chris Woakes, but when our wicket-keeper was out for 65 from 52 balls, the Bangladeshi players smelled blood. I was sitting in the dressing room barely able to believe what was unfolding in front of my eyes.

Chris Jordan was harshly adjudged run out when TV replays suggested he had probably made his ground and I strode to the wicket at 238 for eight, still needing 38 to win from just four overs.

'Looks like it's down to us, mate,' I said to Woakesy when I got out to the middle.

For a brief moment, it looked as if we might rescue victory from the jaws of defeat. Woakesy was batting beautifully, and when I managed to smash Taskin Ahmed over mid-wicket for six we needed 24 from 16 balls. We then took the target down to just 16 by the end of the 48th over.

Sadly, that was as good as it got. I played around a straight one from the first ball of Rubel Hossain's next over and Jimmy lasted just two balls before he was castled, leaving Woakesy stranded on 42 not out and the Bangladesh players in ecstasy. The unthinkable had happened. We were out.

> We were absolutely torn to shreds by the press, with most agreeing it was our worst-ever World Cup campaign. It was hard to argue with that assessment.

'Unbelievably disappointing,' was how Morgs described it after the game. He wasn't wrong. We were absolutely torn to shreds by the press, with most agreeing it was our worst-ever World Cup campaign. It was hard to argue with that assessment.

That week after the Bangladesh game was among the worst I've ever spent as an England cricketer. I'd set out in the hope of reclaiming form, fitness and a sense of fun as we embarked on our campaign. My fitness was good, my form OK, but the fun disappeared as the defeats mounted. We may have got on well as players off the field, but we had not delivered where it counted out in the middle.

I spent the majority of that week in my hotel room with the curtains drawn. It was awful. We just lolled around not wanting to speak to anyone or risk being spotted outside and subjected to abuse left, right and centre. Things got so bad I even took to playing online poker for the first time in my life. Thankfully, I was awful and packed up after a couple of days. But it was a really low time. We'd failed as a squad of players, let ourselves down, but we had to pick ourselves up and play one last meaningless game against Afghanistan before we could board the flight home. We were feeling very sorry for ourselves.

Before the Afghanistan game we had a very forthright meeting at the team hotel. As a group of players we were embarrassed by our performance and fed up with losing. We had no excuses. Yes, we lacked experience compared to the best sides in the tournament and that clearly showed the way we let the pressure get to us during some of the run chases. But we couldn't have asked for more preparation time. The Ashes had been rescheduled the previous winter in order to avoid us having to go straight from that series into a World Cup and we'd had plenty of time to acclimatise after arriving in Australia more than five weeks before the start of the tournament. As a group, management and players alike, we should have recognised earlier that the game had changed. Looking to preserve wickets at the top of the order and then aiming for fives and sixes an over wasn't enough anymore. Scores of 350 were par for the course and many teams were looking to score at seven or eight an over from the start.

Attacking the new ball had become standard. Put simply, we were too slow to adapt.

Mooresy was getting absolutely slaughtered in the press after supposedly saying he'd 'have to check the data' after we'd lost to Bangladesh. It was a comment he clarified several months later as actually having been 'I'll have to check later' when asked why England lost. But it gave those in the press who'd already criticised our supposed over-reliance on data another stick to beat us with. Sadly for Mooresy, the quote stuck.

I really don't know what the reaction would have been if we'd lost to Afghanistan. I shudder to think. But thankfully we showed enough professionalism to put our wounded pride to one side to win by nine wickets. But there were no celebrations. We had nothing to celebrate.

We flew home the next day.

4

THE END
OF THE BEGINNING

WEST INDIES TOUR 2 APRIL–7 MAY

We arrived back in the UK much earlier in March than we'd anticipated and the dull, late-winter weather matched my mood. The long flight back from Australia had given me a chance to ponder all sorts of things, among them my one-day international future. Inevitably, in the light of such a disastrous display, people were calling for a complete clear-out of senior players to make way for younger blood.

I was bitterly disappointed with how the World Cup had gone, although I believed I'd bowled considerably better than my meagre return of four wickets at 63.5 suggested. I was still only 28, had 119 one-day internationals behind me and my recently operated-on knee felt as good as it had done at any point in my career.

I firmly believed I had something to offer England's one-day side, indeed I still do and, despite what some people were saying, I had no intention of calling time on that part of my career. Whether the selectors would consider me was a different matter.

What was noticeable when we arrived home was how little attention the World Cup seemed to be getting in the UK. While we were in Australia, it felt like it was the epicentre of the world, but when we landed at Heathrow after the flight from Sydney, it was hard to believe a World Cup was going on. People were apathetic towards us, which was indicative of just how poor we'd been I guess, and when we walked through the airport we barely got a second glance.

What hadn't gone away was the pressure being heaped on Peter Moores. His 'check the data' quote had been seized upon as evidence of his inability to react instinctively to situations and coach what he saw, rather than what he read off a spreadsheet. It was absolute rubbish, of course, but it didn't stop people who'd never worked with him, or even spoken to people who had, tearing his methods apart. I didn't understand why the quote wasn't clarified earlier, as it allowed space for those who'd already decided he should go to fill the pages with criticism. By the time he eventually did clarify his comment several months later, the damage had been done.

Bealey had been out in Australia for part of the tournament, but it was good to be able to spend some extra time with her when I got back, even if I wasn't great company for the first few days. We were doing some work on my house, so I was able to get a bit more involved in that. But there was no hiding my frustration at our feeble World Cup show and I moped around Nottingham for several days in a fairly black mood.

Alastair Cook had been badly stung by being dropped so soon before the World Cup, so I wasn't hugely surprised to hear him say so publicly a few days after we got home, around the time the squad was announced for the upcoming West Indies tour. Cooky is definitely not the sort of bloke to intentionally go after a headline – in fact the mere idea of rocking the boat or making a fuss makes him cringe – but he clearly had stuff to get off his chest. He'd spent three and a half years plotting the team's World Cup campaign and felt he was the right man to lead us into the tournament.

In an interview in Abu Dhabi, where he was preparing to play for the MCC against Yorkshire, Cooky said the squad looked 'shell-shocked' at the World Cup and questioned the wisdom of making such a significant change of leadership so soon before the tournament. He reminded people England had actually reached No.1 in the one-day rankings under his captaincy and it was pretty obvious he remained frustrated by the decision to drop him.

The West Indies tour was looming fast and there were recalls for Jonathan Trott and Ben Stokes, while Durham pace bowler Mark Wood also got a call-up for his first senior tour along with the Yorkshire pair of Adam Lyth and Adil Rashid.

I wasn't surprised to see Woody given his chance. I'd been impressed with him both on and off the field in Potchefstroom, while Stokesy was a player I'd always rated really highly. Barely 12 months earlier, he'd scored an absolutely magnificent backs-to-the-wall hundred against Mitchell Johnson and the rest of Australia's attack at Perth. He had never stopped fighting during that 5-0 whitewash, which couldn't necessarily be said for everyone, and I thought he'd been a bit unlucky when he was dropped from the Test side the following summer after a run of low scores. He paid the price for our defeat to India at Lord's and I was also surprised to see him miss out on the World Cup squad. Given an extended run in the side, I was convinced that at 22 years old, the Durham all-rounder had a long international future in front of him.

Lyth and Rashid were both excellent county players who deserved their call-ups, but it was Trotty I was happiest to see make a return after an absence of more than a year.

I'm not sure even to this day people realise how much it hurt Trotty to leave the Ashes tour prematurely. Ever since he'd made his debut in the final Ashes Test against Australia at The Oval in 2009, scoring a second-innings century that all but guaranteed we couldn't lose the game, he'd been an absolutely integral part of the team. He was a self-deprecating guy who could be very funny, but he took his cricket incredibly seriously and prepared as meticulously as anyone.

He cared deeply about playing for England and, as it turned out, worried a lot about his performance and not letting the team down. Over the five years he'd been in the side in the lead-up to that Ashes series, he'd worked hard to become one of the outstanding batsmen in world cricket. He was the player in our team I'd have chosen to go out to bat for my life. Despite all his idiosyncrasies, he had a rock-solid technique and was ruthless off his legs. As good as anyone I've seen in fact. He had a very long attention span and just loved grinding out runs for England. I scored my first and, to date, only Test hundred in partnership with Trotty at Lord's against Pakistan in 2010. He was a great guy to bat with because he was utterly selfless. He was a massively valued member of the side. Anyone capable of averaging 50 batting at No.3 for as long as Trotty did has to be a class act.

So it had been unbelievably sad to see him struggle so badly on that Ashes tour. There is simply nowhere worse in the world to lose matches than in Australia, because they are so ready to rub it in your face.

Trotty, like a number of our batsmen, was expecting to get some serious heat from Mitchell Johnson, who thought he'd spotted a chink in his technique against the short ball during the one-day series at the tail end of the 2013 summer. The press made a huge deal of it.

By Trotty's standards, he hadn't enjoyed the most prolific summer, managing only two fifties in five Tests against Australia, despite making lots of starts and always looking the part. It was wearing him down. Seeing him as one of our key players, Johnson, who didn't feature in the Test series, targeted him in the ensuing 50-over games. When we got to Australia, it was clear he intended to attempt to exploit the weakness he believed he'd identified against the short ball.

Technically, Trotty had never had a problem at international level before and it clearly played on his mind that he was struggling against the searing pace Johnson was able to generate. He was also having difficulty coping with the additional media attention that inevitably went hand in hand with back-to-back Ashes series. It was suffocating. The early signs of just how tired he was began to emerge when he pulled out of a couple of the one-day matches with 'back spasms'. He had no history of back spasms. Obviously being able to handle the demands placed on you by the media is part and parcel of being a successful professional sportsman or woman. The level of media attention brings with it significant benefits from sponsors, but I do sometimes wonder at the level of scrutiny we are under. I've spoken to players from other countries and they're amazed by the amount of attention we get. The players who tend to have the longest careers are the ones who don't get fazed by criticism or comments that are thrown around, but inevitably some find it harder to cope with than others.

Trotty set himself incredibly high standards and, as it transpired, was allowing his own personal expectations to get on top of him. He put on a brave face, but inside it was eating him up. Normally, you'd get at least an 18-month break between Ashes series to overcome any issues which may have cropped up by playing some cricket away from the uniquely intense glare which only Test series between Australia and England generate. It really is unlike anything else in cricket. Being away from your family for such extended periods of time is an additional challenge which people don't always appreciate. Believe me, all hotels begin to look the same after a while and the novelty of room service soon wears off.

Trotty got runs in two of the three warm-up games leading into the series, but as it turned out he was really battling with the mental side of the game.

By the time we got to Brisbane for the first Test he was clearly struggling and it wasn't long after he came to the crease that Michael Clarke brought on Johnson. The very first ball was short, quick and superbly directed. It whacked straight into Trotty's glove and the crowd sensed blood. It took only another five deliveries from Johnson before he was on his way back to the pavilion when he fended down the leg side and was caught behind by Brad Haddin. Trotty's pained expression as he trudged off the field spoke of a man who was experiencing real inner turmoil. By the time the second innings came around, he was struggling so badly it looked to me as if he was on the verge of tears as he walked out to bat. It was horrible to watch. He later admitted he'd been 'at breaking point'.

It was no huge surprise after we'd lost in Brisbane that we were told Trotty would return home. The ECB doctors described his departure as 'stress related'. We all wished him well with his recovery. It must have been unbelievably tough for him to make a decision like that. I've been through periods in my career where I've felt really down. I think if you ask anyone who has spent an extended period of time playing international cricket they'd say the same. The spotlight is just unrelenting and it can get too much for some players who can become really introspective and withdrawn. It's not a nice place to be. It's an aspect of international cricket that a lot of people aren't that comfortable talking about. I remember Ashley Giles telling me once that his wife was so concerned by his state of mind she nearly flew out to see him on tour in Bangladesh. Graeme Swann tells a story of how he'd spent so much time speaking to his young son on Skype while on tour that when he eventually got home his little lad just kept pointing at the laptop because that's where he thought his dad was.

It was no huge surprise after we'd lost in Brisbane when we were told Trotty would return home.

It's normally performance-related when guys get low, but I think the lowest I've ever been on tour was in India in 2012 when I lacerated the fat pad on the bottom of my foot. It was excruciatingly painful. Sometimes I'd wake up in the middle of the night, needing to go to the toilet, and I'd literally have to crawl on my hands and knees just to make it to the bathroom. That wore me down over time. I don't want to sound too dramatic, but I've read a lot of military books and one way of motivating myself is to remind myself how tough those guys have it. They also spend extended periods of time away from home, but have the added concern of being shot at or mortared. We only have to worry about Mitchell Johnson bowling thunderbolts. It keeps things in perspective.

Having said that, I felt enormous sympathy for Trotty when he'd been forced to return home early from Australia. Plenty of people wrote him off as an international cricketer after that, so it was great to see him back in the fold for the West Indies tour 18 months later. It was testament to how highly he valued wearing the England cap that he was willing to throw himself back into that environment. He'd taken an extended break after the Ashes and another after the start of the campaign at Warwickshire before returning to action in June. He ended up enjoying a reasonable season and averaged in the mid-40s. Andy Flower spoke with him at the end of the summer and convinced him to go on the Lions tour to his native South Africa as captain. He excelled with the bat, and it seemed the natural next step for him to return to the Test squad in the West Indies. We were absolutely over the moon to have such a high-quality player back in our ranks.

With the World Cup still going on, weeks after we'd returned with our tails between our legs, the analysis of our failure to perform seemed to be ramping up as the West Indies tour approached.

Ravi Bopara, who'd been left bitterly disappointed by the last-minute call to bat Gary Ballance at three, made some interesting comments which drew some attention. He argued there was a 'culture of fear' in the team and we needed to 'stop being so English'. I wasn't totally sure what he meant by the last comment, but I guess it was a reference to the conservative approach we'd been taking to our one-day cricket. I definitely agreed with him when he said we needed to cast off the shackles and aim for 300 or even 350 as a minimum target to defend.

Really, Ravi reaffirmed what had been said in that final meeting before leaving Sydney. We had to be more carefree in the way we approached the game and really attack opponents from ball one. The old notion of keeping wickets intact for a blitz later on in the innings was dead in the water. We also needed to start playing with smiles on our faces again after a couple of years where things may have got a little too serious.

I think we were all surprised when we heard the incoming ECB chairman Colin Graves, who was set to take over from Giles Clarke in May, had given an interview saying there would be 'enquiries' if we didn't beat the West Indies. 'I'd certainly be disappointed if we don't win the West Indies series, because I am pretty sure the West Indies are going to have a mediocre team,' he'd told BBC Radio Leeds.

'A lot of their stars are going to be playing in the Indian Premier League anyway, not in the Tests, so we should win that series. If we don't win, I can tell you now there will be some enquiries of why we haven't.'

I certainly didn't agree with his assessment that the West Indies were a mediocre team. The assertion was that they'd lost a lot of their best players to the Indian Premier League. But players like Chris Gayle and Dwayne Bravo hadn't played regular Test cricket for a long time while Kieron Pollard had never featured in the Test side. On top of that, we hadn't won a Test series in the West Indies for more than a decade so I wasn't sure it was a fair analysis. It became clear when we got to the West Indies that they had definitely noted Colin's comments.

THE END OF THE BEGINNING

I'm sure Colin – who I'm assured is a really decent bloke and is very highly thought of by all the Yorkshire lads in the team – didn't intend to heap any added pressure on us. But the fact was that he did!

A week or so before we were due to fly out to St Kitts for the first of two warm-up games ahead of a three-Test series, I had a sponsors' media appearance booked in through Hardy's. I was nervous going into it. More so than usual. I knew the journalists would try to drag me back to the World Cup, where I didn't want to go, so I was keen to focus on Jimmy closing in on breaking Sir Ian Botham's record of 383 Test wickets in the West Indies.

I don't mind admitting I find it difficult facing the media after I've underperformed and the best advice I can give to any young cricketer – or sportsperson for that matter – is understand and accept the questions, but make sure you say what you want to say.

I didn't especially want to rake over the coals of how bad we'd been in Australia and New Zealand and was much keener on talking about one of my best mates potentially becoming England's all-time leading wicket-taker in the next few weeks. It seemed to work.

There was another change we had to deal with. Our bowling coach, David Saker, announced he was moving on a couple of weeks after we returned from Australia. I was gutted to see him go, although not surprised he'd landed the Renegades job back in Melbourne. It showed how highly thought of he was. Sakes had been involved with the squad for nearly four years and was an extremely popular member of the backroom staff. He'd been with us for our most successful period and contributed a huge amount to our success.

Sakes was a master storyteller who could always find a way of lifting spirits in the changing room. If the boys were down he'd look to pick us up. One of my favourite stories of his was when he was playing against England for Victoria in a tour match and he sledged Adam Hollioake. They had a proper set-to and Sakes told him to meet him outside the ground after the match to settle things man-to-man. At tea, his team-mates told him about Hollioake's track record as a tough nut and his love of cage fighting and boxing. After tea, Sakes went out and apologised to Hollioake and told him it was only sporting to keep things on the field of play.

A week before we were due to depart, Ottis Gibson was appointed as fast bowling coach for the West Indies tour on an 'interim basis'. As with Mooresy, this would be Ottis's second stint in the job and I was delighted to see him back. Paul Downton, who made the appointment, said Ottis was 'highly regarded in the fast bowling fraternity'. He was dead right.

I go back a long way with Ottis. We opened the bowling together in my first year at Leicestershire and he's always been a bit of a mentor of mine. He really helped me as a young kid. He always let me bowl with the wind, which sounds a really small thing, but as an 18-year-old that was a huge help coming from a senior player. We were quite similar in that we were both attacking bowlers who liked the game to move forward. Drying up one end and simply 'bowling time' wasn't in either of our natures.

I'd miss Sakes, who was a great guy and brilliant to have around the dressing room, but if he was going to be replaced by anyone I was more than happy it was Ottis.

They're really quite different coaches. Ottis is the more technical of the two whereas Sakes has taught me a lot tactically. Sakes always encouraged me to bowl defensively but with attacking fields.

He was a big believer in constantly hitting the top of off stump while trying new things with your field positions and getting inside the batsman's head. Sakes is probably the best tactical coach I've worked with and typically Australian, very much always looking at how you win the game. He believed by the time you got to international level you wouldn't require a huge amount of technical coaching. While that worked for me, for some bowlers it didn't suit them a huge amount.

Ottis takes the view that if you get your action right, the rest of the game will look after itself. Neither was right or wrong. They both have fantastic qualities and I've been lucky enough to have been able to pick up bits and pieces from both of them over the years. For me, the key to a top-quality coach is that they know the individual. It shouldn't be one size fits all.

You could sense Cooky's energy when we met up again as a squad before flying out to St Kitts. Despite a significant change in personnel, there was inevitably going to be a hangover effect from the World Cup among those of us who'd been involved. Cooky came in with a real energy to pick the guys up from that and try to move on as fast as possible. While we can be inclined to berate the amount of cricket played, one of the benefits of international cricket is that you do get another chance to put things right almost straight away. It may have been a different format, but if we did sit back and feel sorry for ourselves we'd inevitably carry on with that losing cycle.

It was evident during the World Cup that we hadn't talked enough as players and the young guys weren't speaking up as much as they should have been. We needed more edge and hopefully bringing experienced guys like Cooky and Trotty back into the group would help that. While you all want to be aiming for the same objective, I'm not one who believes every dressing room has to be all touchy feely, with peace and harmony reigning. Sometimes you require the opposite effect. You need that competitive edge in professional sport, and I think during the World Cup there were times when we just didn't have it. The most important thing is that everyone aims for the same outcome: winning games for England.

It's incredibly important that all the players feel they can contribute and speak up when there is something to be said. That can be quite a scary thing, but you only get better as a group when you do that. Almost all the very best sports teams in the world are led by the players. Think of Martin Johnson's World Cup-winning rugby team or the Australian national team throughout the 1990s. That was something the senior players tried to encourage. Guys like Stokes, Lyth, Woody, Adil and Jos all had something to contribute and needed to feel they'd be listened to if they did.

As we left for St Kitts, it felt as if we had a chance to begin repairing the damage that had been done. Even though it was a one-day tournament, it felt that our World Cup performance had further distanced us from fans already weary following an up-and-down year in 2014 which, on balance, contained more downs than ups.

We had a few days to acclimatise after arriving in St Kitts before the first of two warm-up games against invitational XIs who, if truth be told, we did not expect to provide us with overly difficult opposition.

We talked a lot about the type of pitches we could expect to play on, with the general expectation that they'd be slow and low. I'm reliably informed that West Indian pitches in the 1970s and 80s could be absolutely lightning. Sabina Park in Jamaica apparently used to resemble corrugated iron, and played like it as well. But, certainly since I started playing, they've generally tended to be slow and low, meaning you have to adjust your plans accordingly. With the dry, abrasive surfaces, the shine and lacquer tend to go off the ball quickly as well, meaning taking wickets with the new ball is even more important than usual. Our slip fielders practised lots of low catches to prepare for what was in store.

It's incredibly important that all the players feel they can contribute and speak up when there is something to be said.

The pitches also meant Cooky would have to set some different fields, and with nicks unlikely to carry to the slip cordon, we would look to bowl to an offside field predominantly in front of the wicket. Cutters and variations in pace were likely to be important means of taking wickets once the shine went off the ball. Potentially, it was going to make for some fairly attritional cricket, and in the searing heat our fitness was going to be tested.

I'd continued to work hard on my knee with the ECB physios after I'd got back from the World Cup. Although I wasn't experiencing any pain, it was important to keep working hard following such extensive surgery. I'd like to put on record my thanks to Ben Langley, Jon Alty and Craig de Weymarn who spent endless hours on the physio's bench manipulating my knee and keeping my spirits up in the days and weeks following the surgery. But playing Test cricket is a significant extra physical challenge compared with one-day cricket, so I still had something to prove.

As expected, the quality of the opposition for the first two-day warm-up game was not quite what we'd hoped for. The St Kitts Invitational XI won the toss and elected to bat, but lasted just 26.3 overs as we rolled them over for 59. I bowled nicely to pick up two for 16 from seven overs, while Stokes was probably the pick of our attack. But it was hard to gauge how well we'd bowled because of the paucity of the opposition. Cook scored a hundred and Root, Bell and Trott all made fifties as we scored 379 for six before declaring and reducing our opponents to 76 for seven in their second innings before running out of time to force victory.

It wasn't a particularly useful warm-up, although it was good to see Trotty and Cooky both in the runs. For Trotty especially it must have been hugely satisfying to make a very tidy 72 from 150 balls in his first innings for England since Brisbane 18 months ago.

We decided to mix up the sides in the second match, which began the day after the first had finished, in order to ensure our batsmen faced international-class bowling, and vice versa.

As it transpired, my knee was the least of my fitness concerns. Having gone wicketless in my first spell, I came back for a second and in my ninth over slammed my front foot down on the pitch only to feel an alarming burning pain through my ankle. The Basseterre pitch was so hard that every time you put your foot down it felt as if you were stepping on a plate sliding across a slippery floor. I panicked a little bit as the pain persisted, but the physios confirmed I hadn't broken anything. However, with my recent injury history, they decided I should err on the side of caution and not bowl again in the two-day match. It felt a bit stiff the next morning, but early concerns that it could affect my participation in the Test series were unfounded.

The match petered out in to a draw, with Stokesy again impressing with the ball, but it had a very low-key feel about it and we were all looking forward to getting the real action underway in Antigua the following week.

It was memorable for one reason, however.

As we came off at lunch on the first day, Mooresy called everyone together for a meeting. It was strange for him to want a chat as we walked off. He gathered us around and said: 'Listen guys, Paul Downton has been moved on. That's as much as I know. There's going to be an announcement to the media imminently. You just need to concentrate on your cricket.'

Paul Downton had been appointed to the role of managing director of England Cricket in October 2013, after Hugh Morris decided to step down after six years in the job. In fairness to Downton, the timing of his appointment couldn't have been much worse, coming as it did just a couple of months before what turned out to be one of the most disastrous Ashes tours in English cricket history.

He made some big calls after that series, not least the decision to tell Kevin Pietersen that he wasn't being considered for selection as an England player after the 5-0 Ashes defeat, before reappointing Mooresy when Andy Flower stepped aside. As a team we moved on very quickly from Kevin being out of the picture, but the controversy it generated saw Downton take a lot of flak. I hadn't really got to know him that well during his time in charge, but he was always very affable when he was around the squad and seemed like a very decent guy. However, new ECB chief executive Tom Harrison had decided it was time to go in a different direction. Downton was gone.

As players, you try not to pay too much attention to what's going on higher up in the corridors of power at the ECB, but I'm sure from the moment Downton moved on Mooresy would have begun to question whether the writing was on the wall for him.

Downton described Pete as 'the outstanding coach of his generation' in April 2014 when he re-appointed him following Andy Flower's post-Ashes resignation, and he reiterated that belief in an interview with Sky in March following the World Cup. It felt very much as if Mooresy was Downton's man and, just like in any big organisation, when new personnel are brought in at the top it can lead to sweeping changes. Those in charge want their own people in beneath them because they are accountable for their performance. Mooresy would have realised his position was under threat.

Inevitably, as soon as Downton's departure was announced, speculation began about his possible successor. The names of Andrew Strauss, Alec Stewart and Michael Vaughan emerged as the three clear favourites. The new role was re-named director of England cricket and given a tighter remit to focus solely on the England team.

For me, the choice was a bit of a no-brainer. Nothing against Stewart or Vaughan, who would have brought their own experience and expertise as former England captains and I've no doubt would have done excellent jobs, but it just seemed Strauss was destined for a role in administration. He'd done a lot of media work since retiring in 2012, but it always felt he'd be more comfortable making decisions and forging strategy on the inside of English cricket, not passing judgement from the outside.

On the other hand, Vaughan had carved out a successful career in the media, clearly relished the role and was making an excellent living from it. He indicated he was interested in the job and met with the ECB hierarchy, but it seemed he might have too many things on the go to focus on one solitary job.

Alec Stewart was the man I knew least well of the three. He seems like a really decent guy, but he was another one who'd carved a great role for himself in the media and was heavily involved with his beloved Surrey, where he was director of cricket.

Strauss was the standout candidate for me. Some people were pushing the line he would be too close to senior players in the team to make the sort of tough decisions he'd need to make. I thought that was nonsense.

I considered Straussy a friend, just as I consider the vast majority of players I've played with for England down the years as friends, but I didn't think for a second he'd allow friendships to get in the way of making tough calls. He'd shown time and again as England captain that he was prepared to be ruthless. He was always fair and willing to explain his decisions articulately, but he was fiercely driven and would always place the best interests of the team above those of the individual.

During the Trent Bridge Test against India the previous summer, I'd held a barbecue at my house for a few of the guys, and Straussy popped along with Ian Ward. He's the sort of person you can hand a Corona to and chat to him about anything. It's generally about golf to be fair, but he's a really good guy who was widely respected by the overwhelming majority of players who played under him.

He'd always backed me when he was captain, but he could be tough. In 2011, during the Sri Lanka series, there were some vocal calls for me to be dropped after I'd lost my way a bit after being asked to fill the role of 'enforcer'. It never sat comfortably. I was bowling too short and not taking wickets. I couldn't really have argued if I had been dropped, but Straussy said: 'You're the sort of bloke I want in the team, get your role clear and deliver.' I'd said to him and Flower at the start of that series that I didn't want that enforcer role and that I was at my best when I was hitting the top of off stump. Strauss agreed and in the India series that followed, I barely bowled a bouncer. I finished with 25 wickets at less than 14, including a hat-trick at Trent Bridge. Strauss's clear direction had helped get my career back on track.

His main quality as England captain was his ability to gather information and then make the right call. He was never dictatorial but he was always firm. Like all the best leaders, he never went up too high or came down too low emotionally. And he listened. Hugh Morris, one of the nicest blokes you'll ever meet, had done the job successfully for years before Downton and I saw no reason Strauss couldn't fill the role quietly, behind the scenes, in a similar way. He was the obvious candidate in my mind.

All the speculation that was swirling around must have been incredibly tough for Mooresy, but it was typical of the man that he didn't allow his own worries to affect the team or his enthusiasm and drive for the job. Several commentators seemed pretty adamant that whoever took the director of cricket role would appoint a new coach, but not once did Mooresy allow the talk about his future affect how he was around the team. He remained positive, energetic and full of ideas, never giving the remotest impression he was feeling the pressure. The respect for him within the dressing room grew even more because of how he conducted himself for the rest of that tour.

Back on the pitch, it was good for the boys to get 90 overs in the field in the final warm-up, because with three back-to-back Tests coming up it was likely to be a test of endurance.

Sadly, the day after we finished the second warm-up game, I was walking into the team hotel and one of the journalists asked if I'd heard the news. I said I hadn't and he told me that former Australia captain and broadcaster Richie Benaud had passed away. He was 85, so he'd had a good innings, but hearing that he'd died cast sadness across the entire squad.

I used to watch videos of my dad playing in the 1986-87 Ashes series and I'll always remember Richie's commentary on that. The word 'iconic' is overused, but it unquestionably applied to Richie. He had this way of sounding as if he was reciting poetry when he was commentating, making it relaxing and peaceful to listen to. There aren't many commentators whose voice becomes synonymous with their sport – Bill McLaren in rugby, Peter O'Sullevan in horse racing and Murray Walker in Formula One are three of the true greats who spring to mind – but Richie's voice symbolised cricket and we'll all miss him. It was agreed there would be a minute's silence before the first Test. I don't think I'd be exaggerating to say the whole cricket world felt sad to hear he'd left us.

With Richie very much in our thoughts, we moved on to Antigua to begin preparations for the first Test. While Test series against the West Indies are big events in themselves, and we were certainly not underestimating them in their own backyard, people weren't slow to remind us we had only five Tests to play before the start of the Ashes. Having been in the depths of despair at the World Cup just a few weeks earlier, I still believed we could get our act together in the Test arena in time to challenge Michael Clarke's men. Our Test form had steadily improved under Mooresy in 2014 and we'd played some of the most aggressive and positive cricket for several years in beating India 3-1 following our capitulation at Lord's in the second Test.

All the talk in the week leading up to the first Test in Antigua was around Jimmy's pending record. He needed four wickets to overtake Sir Ian Botham as England's highest-ever wicket-taker. The Antigua Test was also set to be Jimmy's 100th in an England shirt and all the attention had understandably left my old mate feeling under pressure to deliver. It was a good kind of pressure, but pressure nonetheless.

Jimmy had flown his family out to Antigua and a load of friends had also come out in the hope of witnessing a moment in history. Over the past few years, Jimmy had become good friends with Greg James, the Radio One DJ. He has a section on his show called the 'Going Home Song' where someone sings about going home. We play a game called odds-on, which effectively involves laying odds on the likelihood of someone being prepared to do something. In this case, Jos lost after Gary Ballance challenged him. His forfeit was to walk up to Greg, who he'd never met before, and sing 'My name is Jos and I'm going home' as loud as he could before running away. Poor old Greg – who's a massive cricket fan – couldn't understand what on earth was going on.

THE END OF THE BEGINNING

For Jimmy, having all his friends and family out there added to the sense of occasion, but also increased the sense of expectation. I was excited for him. We've played so much cricket together. Before the start of the Ashes I'd played only five Tests without him. He is unquestionably the most skilful bowler I've ever played with and over the years we've become extremely close friends. Partnerships are about complementing each other's skills and there's no doubt we dovetail, with Jimmy's ability to swing the ball at good pace while I hit the deck hard from a different trajectory on different lengths.

Jimmy's taught me a huge amount and guided me through my international career. In terms of number of wickets taken by a new-ball pair, I think we're third behind Waqar Younis and Wasim Akram and Curtly Ambrose and Courtney Walsh. Not the worst company to be in! Our success together comes from us complementing each other's styles and constant communication around how to get batsmen out. Jimmy's got that ultra-competitive instinct everyone enjoys watching. I have massive respect for him as a competitor and as a man, and it became abundantly clear later in the summer how much affection he's held in by the English cricketing public as well.

The night before the first Test, in keeping with a growing tradition Mooresy was keen to encourage, we were given a rousing presentation by former England captain Nasser Hussain, now a highly respected pundit on Sky Sports. We were in the team room at our hotel when we were told Nasser would be speaking to us. The whole thing started very amusingly, because Sky had put together a montage which Nasser thought was going to be a kind of tribute to his captaincy. As it turned out, they'd put together a piss-take version. They'd packaged all these clips on a video screen saying 'Nasser Hussain – England's legendary captain' and then showed him winning the toss and putting Australia in to bat at Brisbane in 2002 when they scored almost 500. The next clip said 'Nasser Hussain – a great player of spin' before showing him being caught and bowled off some part-time leg spinner. Next up was 'Nasser will always tell you to play straight on these wickets' before showing him being bowled while attempting to sweep. It nailed him!

Luckily Nasser very much saw the funny side of things and it went a long way towards breaking the ice.

He urged us as players not to get to the end of our careers and wonder 'could I have given more?'

He went on to speak passionately about how much it meant to him to play for England and some of the epic battles he'd faced against the West Indies. His pride in playing for England really shone through and you could tell the lads were hanging on his every word. He spoke about how, when he'd retired after 96 Tests, he could look himself in the eye knowing he had squeezed every last bit of talent out of himself. He had got the absolute maximum out of Nasser Hussain and only retired once he knew he had no more to give. He urged us as players not to get to the end of our careers and wonder 'could I have given more?' He also talked a lot about making the best of our time at the top, not underestimating the players we had in the dressing room and appreciating how special it was to be playing for England. It was a really powerful talk.

As it transpired, the pitch at the Sir Vivian Richards Stadium couldn't really have been less conducive to swing or seam bowling and we had to wait until the last day for Jimmy to finally break Beefy's record.

Six years after having a Test match abandoned on the first morning due to a dangerous pitch, it appeared the groundstaff had gone to the other extreme and prepared an absolute road. And just like a road, there was very little encouragement for pushing above the 70mph mark!

As expected, there looked to be very little in it for our fast bowlers. There was a little bit of straw grass on top but nothing significant, so we were surprised when West Indies captain Denesh Ramdin won the toss and put us in to bat.

Our middle order of Gary Ballance, Joe Root and Ian Bell was settled following our last Test series win the previous summer, so Trotty came back into the side at the top of the order alongside the captain. We still hadn't really settled on Cooky's opening partner since Strauss had retired at the end of 2012. A number of players had been tried, with none seemingly able to make the position their own. Nick Compton, Michael Carberry, Rooty and Sam Robson had all been given a run without nailing down the role. Adam Lyth was in the tour party and there was a train of thought that he should be given the chance to show his Test credentials ahead of the Ashes, but I felt it was only fair to give a batsman of Trotty's proven quality a second chance after all he'd been through.

Stokesy also came back into the side, providing that all-important balance of a five-man attack. Chris Jordan had done well against India so was given another chance, while the always reliable James Tredwell played in Mo's absence through injury. A number of commentators argued vociferously that Adil should have played. It was a tough call, but the selectors decided Tredwell's extra control gave him the edge.

It was Jimmy's 100th Test appearance, my 75th and Trott's 50th and we were presented with commemorative caps before play by former England captain Michael Atherton. It was a nice touch by the ECB and much appreciated.

Sadly, Trotty's return did not have a happy ending. After observing a collective minute's silence in honour of Richie Benaud, he made his way out to bat with Cooky. After an absence of a year and a half from the side, we were all hoping he could slot back in. Unfortunately, he lasted just three balls before edging Jerome Taylor to slip in the very first over of the match.

Cooky and Ballance both fell cheaply to leave us in trouble at 34 for three, but not for the first time, or indeed the last, Rooty played a part in digging us out of trouble in an excellent partnership with Belly.

The pair put on 177 for the fourth wicket to nullify the West Indies attack as the early life in the pitch subsided. Root eventually fell for 83, but Bell went from strength to strength, scoring his 22nd Test hundred. Stokesy chipped in with 79 off 95 balls and, having been put in, we were very satisfied with a first-innings total of 399 all out.

We bowled with a great deal of discipline when the West Indies batted. We had them in trouble at 99 for four, before Jermaine Blackwood dug deep to score an excellent 112 not out. Jimmy and I each grabbed a pair of wickets, while Tredders took four for 47 from

26 miserly overs as we secured a 104-run first-innings lead. Jimmy would have to wait until the second innings for his crowning glory. He was bowling really nicely, but it was clear the record was playing on his mind. How could it not be? I spoke to him between innings and reassured him it was only a matter of time. He knew that, of course, but it was understandable he wanted to get it over and done with.

In our second innings, Ballance bounced back from his World Cup woes with a very well-constructed 122 from 250 balls, including 11 fours and two sixes. It was a terrific knock from Gary and reminded everyone of his qualities in the Test arena after an excellent first international summer in 2014. Rooty scored another fifty, while Jos Buttler hit a quick-fire 59 not out from 56 balls enabling Cooky to declare on 333 for seven. It meant the West Indies needed to survive around 130 overs or score an improbable 440 runs in their second innings to win the match. The only real downside to our innings was another low score for Trotty.

I got rid of Kraigg Brathwaite with a snorting bouncer that he spliced to Rooty at short leg in my first over before tea on the fourth evening. When Joe snared Darren Bravo courtesy of an absolutely sensational catch from Jordan at slip before the close it left us needing eight wickets on the final day to take a 1-0 lead. We were firmly in the box seat.

Six years earlier we had been frustrated by a dogged rearguard from Daren Powell and Fidel Edwards which saw the last-wicket pair earn a draw by surviving for ten overs. Surely lightning couldn't strike twice?

We steadily chipped away at the West Indies on day five, with Jimmy finally drawing level and then passing Sir Ian's record when he tempted Marlon Samuels into a loose drive outside off stump before producing a classic leg cutter to dismiss Ramdin with an hour left.

It was an amazing moment. Everyone knew what that wicket meant to Jimmy, and I was so proud of what he had achieved. We looked up and it was good see Beefy smiling broadly and waving from the commentary box. Jimmy was understandably pretty overwhelmed and emotional, having deservedly etched his name into the history books. It was a very special time and one that everyone lucky enough to be on the field will remember forever.

Ramdin's dismissal left the door open at 294 for seven, with 18 overs left after a dogged seventh-wicket partnership with Jason Holder.

Holder still had 50 overs to survive when he'd come to the crease. The pitch was at its flattest on the final day and he batted with discipline and no little skill to reach his maiden hundred in only his fifth Test. As it became increasingly obvious we weren't going to be able to prise out the last three wickets, Holder went to his ton with a brace of lofted drives off Tredders and, with Kemar Roach digging in for 55 balls at the other end, Cooky offered his hand and shook on a draw with the West Indies 350 for seven from 129.4 overs.

It was intensely frustrating not to be able to force the win on that final day, but we left Antigua feeling as if we'd made most of the running in the Test match.

It was a huge relief for Jimmy to finally achieve the record and that evening I handed him a specially engraved bottle of Châteauneuf-du-Pape to mark the occasion. We'd both developed an interest in and love of wine in recent years, and I look forward to sharing a glass with him in years to come and remembering the special moment he passed Beefy's record.

WEST INDIES V ENGLAND (1ST TEST)

Sir Vivian Richards Stadium, North Sound, Antigua

13, 14, 15, 16, 17 April 2015

MATCH DRAWN

Toss: West Indies
Umpires: B.F.Bowden (New Zealand) and S.J.Davis (Australia)
Referee: A.J.Pycroft (Zimbabwe)

ENGLAND

* A.N.Cook	b Roach	11	c Benn b Taylor	13
I.J.L.Trott	c Bravo b Taylor	0	c Ramdin b Taylor	4
G.S.Ballance	c Bravo b Holder	10	c Blackwood b Benn	122
I.R.Bell	c Ramdin b Roach	143	run out	11
J.E.Root	b Taylor	83	b Holder	59
B.A.Stokes	c Holder b Taylor	79	st Ramdin b Benn	35
J.C.Tredwell	c Bravo b Holder	8		
† J.C.Buttler	c Ramdin b Roach	0	(7) not out	59
C.J.Jordan	not out	21	(8) ct Bravo b Roach	13
S.C.J.Broad	c Blackwood b Roach	0		
J.M.Anderson	c Holder b Samuels	20		
Extras	(B 7, LB 3, W 8, NB 6)	24	(B 1, LB 6, W 5, NB 5)	17
Total	**(110.4 overs)**	**399**	**(7 wkts dec; 86 overs)**	**333**

WEST INDIES

K.C.Brathwaite	c Jordan b Tredwell	39	c Root b Broad	5
D.S.Smith	c Buttler b Anderson	11	c Ballance b Tredwell	65
D.M.Bravo	c Buttler b Jordan	10	c Jordan b Root	32
M.N.Samuels	c Buttler b Broad	33	c Tredwell b Anderson	23
S.Chanderpaul	c Stokes b Tredwell	46	lbw b Root	13
J.Blackwood	not out	112	c Buttler b Jordan	31
*† D.Ramdin	c Buttler b Broad	9	c Cook b Anderson	57
J.O.Holder	c Ballance b Tredwell	16	not out	103
K.A.J.Roach	c Buttler b Tredwell	5	not out	15
J.E.Taylor	run out	0		
S.J.Benn	c Root b Anderson	2		
Extras	(LB 4, W 6, NB 2)	12	(B 2, LB 2, NB 2)	6
Total	**(113 overs)**	**295**	**(7 wkts; 129.4 overs)**	**350**

WEST INDIES	O	M	R	W		O	M	R	W
Taylor	20	4	90	3		14	5	42	2
Roach	29	6	94	4		14	1	53	1
Holder	25	11	69	2		17	5	63	1
Benn	26	3	85	0		26	3	115	2
Samuels	10.4	0	51	1		15	0	53	0
ENGLAND	O	M	R	W		O	M	R	W
Anderson	23	9	67	2		24.4	3	72	2
Broad	22	2	67	2		21	5	61	1
Jordan	23	8	46	1	(4)	18	6	48	1
Stokes	19	3	64	0	(5)	13	0	50	0
Tredwell	26	12	47	4	(3)	40	14	93	1
Root						13	6	22	2

FALL OF WICKETS

	E	WI	E	WI
WKT	1ST	1ST	2ND	2ND
1st	1	19	15	7
2nd	22	42	20	90
3rd	34	89	52	119
4th	211	99	166	127
5th	341	192	226	155
6th	357	227	281	189
7th	357	276	333	294
8th	361	292	–	–
9th	361	292	–	–
10th	399	295	–	–

CLOSE OF PLAY

Day 1	England (1) 341-5 (90; B.A.Stokes 71*, J.C.Tredwell 0*)
Day 2	West Indies (1) 155-4 (66; S.Chanderpaul 29*, J.Blackwood 30*)
Day 3	England (2) 116-3 (38; G.S.Ballance 44*, J.E.Root 32*)
Day 4	West Indies (2) 98-2 (40; D.S.Smith 59*, M.N.Samuels 2*)

Despite not being able to force the win, it re-energised us watching one of our team-mates achieve such a significant landmark. We knew we'd played some really good cricket and moved on to the Grenada Test in high spirits.

The pitch that greeted us there was another flat one, but there was some rain around on the first morning and Cooky decided our best chance of taking 20 wickets was to put them in after winning the toss. Fit-again Moeen Ali came in for Tredders, which was tough on him after bowling tidily as ever in Antigua. But we were pretty content to have them 188 for five from 70 overs at the close. Marlon Samuels reached 94 not out that night having exchanged a few verbals, but nothing out of the ordinary. That evening, Samuels gave a bizarre press conference during which he constantly referred to himself in the third person while repeating 'these English lads never learn'. It was all a bit odd.

Samuels made 103 before Jimmy had him caught by Bell at slip, then I picked up three wickets in four overs in what was my best spell of bowling since before the surgery. It was really pleasing to see my speeds consistently pushing 90mph and I felt in a lovely rhythm as I attacked the crease.

We bowled them out for 299 before Cook and Trott put on 125. Trotty was eventually out for 59, but it was good to see him back in the runs before Root produced his latest master-class of 182 not out to provide the bedrock of our first-innings total of 464. There was a slightly bizarre moment when Samuels stood and saluted Stokes after he'd holed out in the deep for 8. Most people found it amusing, but it's fair to say Stokesy wasn't one of them. Samuels has a bit of a history with us – with most teams in fact – and he's not high on many of our lists of opponents we'd want to go for a beer with. He's certainly not on Stokesy's. But the salute got him some attention, so hopefully that made him happy.

They made a better fist of their second innings and, at 202 for two at the close of day four with Brathwaite unbeaten on 102, a draw looked an absolute certainty. Jimmy had other ideas, however, dismissing Brathwaite for 113 before ripping out their middle order in double quick time. Jimmy ended up with four for 43, while Mo picked up three wickets, as the West Indies were all out for 307 just after lunch. It left us needing 143 to win. It was a fantastic effort to take 20 wickets on such a flat track and the bowlers, Jimmy in particular, rightly took plenty of plaudits.

But the game was far from won, and when Trott was bowled by a very sharp delivery from Shannon Gabriel in only the second over, we could easily have wobbled. Although he didn't appear to be the fittest, Gabriel was capable of bowling very quickly indeed in short spells. Ottis told us he'd been brought up in a seriously tough neighbourhood and cricket had provided an escape from a potential life of crime. It's always good to hear when sport has given someone a lifeline.

After Trotty's dismissal, Gary Ballance steadied the ship, batting superbly alongside Cook to guide us home in 41.1 overs and earn us a remarkable nine-wicket victory just after tea on the final day. In the process, Gary scored his 1000th Test run in only his 17th innings, making him the ninth fastest player to reach that mark. It showed what a class act he was and, more importantly, contributed significantly to our first overseas win since November 2012, when we'd beaten India in Calcutta. It was also our fourth win in five Tests and a phenomenal effort all round. We enjoyed the celebrations that evening.

WEST INDIES V ENGLAND (2ND TEST)

At National Cricket Stadium, St George's, Grenada

21, 22, 23, 24, 25 April 2015

ENGLAND WON BY NINE WICKETS

Toss: England

Umpires: S.J.Davis (Australia) and B.N.J.Oxenford (Australia)

Referee: A.J.Pycroft (Zimbabwe)

WEST INDIES

K.C.Brathwaite	b Anderson	1	c Root b Anderson	116
D.S.Smith	c Buttler b Jordan	15	b Anderson	2
D.M.Bravo	c Cook b Broad	35	c Buttler b Broad	69
M.N.Samuels	c Bell b Anderson	103	c Buttler b Anderson	37
S.Chanderpaul	c Ali b Stokes	1	c Cook b Anderson	7
J.Blackwood	lbw b Jordan	26	c Anderson b Jordan	10
*† D.Ramdin	c Buttler b Broad	31	lbw b Ali	28
J.O.Holder	c Buttler b Broad	22	run out	2
K.A.J.Roach	c Root b Broad	1	c Anderson b Ali	10
D.Bishoo	lbw b Ali	30	not out	15
S.T.Gabriel	not out	20	lbw b Ali	0
Extras	(B 5, LB 6, W 1, NB 2)	14	(B 8, LB 2, NB 1)	11
Total	**(104.4 overs)**	**299**	**(112 overs)**	**307**

ENGLAND

* A.N.Cook	b Gabriel	76	not out	59
I.J.L.Trott	c Blackwood b Bishoo	59	b Gabriel	0
G.S.Ballance	b Samuels	77	not out	81
I.R.Bell	b Gabriel	1		
J.E.Root	not out	182		
M.M.Ali	run out	0		
B.A.Stokes	c Blackwood b Bishoo	8		
† J.C.Buttler	st Ramdin b Bishoo	13		
C.J.Jordan	run out	16		
S.C.J.Broad	c Smith b Bishoo	0		
J.M.Anderson	run out	2		
Extras	(B 9, LB 2, W 1, NB 18)	30	(W 1, NB 3)	4
Total	**(144.1 overs)**	**464**	**(1 wkt; 41.4 overs)**	**144**

ENGLAND	O	M	R	W		O	M	R	W
Anderson	24	10	47	2		22	7	43	4
Broad	24	9	61	4		21	2	71	1
Jordan	25	4	65	2	(4)	21	6	69	1
Ali	13.4	1	47	1	(3)	24	9	51	3
Stokes	17	7	66	1		8	0	34	0
Trott	1	0	2	0					
Root					(6)	16	7	29	0

WEST INDIES	O	M	R	W		O	M	R	W
Roach	28	4	100	0		7	1	18	0
Gabriel	22	3	67	2		7	3	20	1
Holder	21.1	6	57	0		1.4	0	11	0
Bishoo	51	10	177	4	(5)	8	0	32	0
Samuels	21	4	38	1	(4)	12.3	1	54	0
Blackwood	1	0	14	0					
Brathwaite					(6)	5	1	9	0

FALL OF WICKETS

	WI	E	WI	E
WKT	**1ST**	**1ST**	**2ND**	**2ND**
1st	2	125	3	2
2nd	28	159	145	–
3rd	65	164	224	–
4th	74	329	238	–
5th	129	335	239	–
6th	223	364	257	–
7th	233	387	260	–
8th	246	426	282	–
9th	247	431	307	–
10th	299	464	307	–

CLOSE OF PLAY

Day 1	West Indies (1) 188-5 (70; M.N.Samuels 94*, D.Ramdin 6*)
Day 2	England (1) 74-0 (26; A.N.Cook 37*, I.J.L.Trott 32*)
Day 3	England (1) 373-6 (124; J.E.Root 118*, J.S.Buttler 4*)
Day 4	West Indies (2) 202-2 (75; K.C.Brathwaite 101*, M.N.Samuels 22*)

THE END OF THE BEGINNING

One-nil up in the series, we moved on to Barbados knowing we were assured of fantastic support on an island that always attracted a huge amount of travelling England fans. Despite making 59 in the first innings in Grenada, Trotty's second duck of the series in the second knock had left him flat. He lasted just three balls again in Barbados and you could sense things weren't right. Cooky continued his excellent form with 105, but our first-innings total of 257 was well below par.

However, Jimmy was on fire and produced another magnificent haul of six for 42 from 12.4 overs as we skittled the West Indies for 189 in less than 50 overs. I finished with one for 31 from ten, but Jimmy was the undisputed star of the show. It was another superb display from a man at the very top of his game.

Sadly, we couldn't back him up in our second innings and we folded feebly for just 123 with Jos (35 not out) and Stokes (32) our only batsmen to offer any serious resistance. Trotty made just 9 before Jerome Taylor trapped him LBW, and there was a resigned look about him as he walked back to the pavilion, despite the huge ovation he received from the fans, who recognised they were almost certainly seeing his last innings in an England shirt. It was a very disappointing effort from us in front of the massed ranks of England fans who never once stopped cheering us on. They deserved better.

In reply, we reduced the home side to 80 for four at one point, when Jimmy removed Shiv Chanderpaul to claim his 397th Test wicket. But Darren Bravo dug them out of trouble to make a really disciplined 82 as the West Indies won by five wickets to level the series. It was hugely disappointing.

In the changing room afterwards, Trotty asked to say a few words. He stood up in front of us and, holding his beloved England cap in his

WEST INDIES V ENGLAND (3RD TEST)

At Kensington Oval, Bridgetown, Barbados

1, 2, 3 May 2015

WEST INDIES WON BY FIVE WICKETS

Toss: England
Umpires: Umpires: B.F.Bowden (New Zealand) and B.N.J.Oxenford (Australia)
Referee: A.J.Pycroft (Zimbabwe)

ENGLAND

* A.N.Cook	c Ramdin b Samuels	105	c Brathwaite b Gabriel	4
I.J.L.Trott	c Permaul b Gabriel	0	lbw b Taylor	9
G.S.Ballance	b Holder	18	c Bravo b Permaul	23
I.R.Bell	c and b Holder	0	lbw b Taylor	0
J.E.Root	c Ramdin b Permaul	33	c Bravo b Holder	1
M.M.Ali	run out	58	b Permaul	8
B.A.Stokes	c Hope b Gabriel	22	c Chanderpaul b Permaul	32
† J.C.Buttler	not out	3	not out	35
C.J.Jordan	c Ramdin b Taylor	3	lbw b Holder	2
S.C.J.Broad	b Taylor	10	b Holder	0
J.M.Anderson	b Taylor	0	lbw b Taylor	2
Extras	(LB 1, W 1, NB 3)	5	(B 4, LB 2, NB 1)	7
Total	**(96.3 overs)**	**257**	**(42.1 overs)**	**123**

WEST INDIES

K.C.Brathwaite	c Jordan b Anderson	0	c Jordan b Ali	25
S.D.Hope	c Cook b Anderson	5	lbw b Jordan	9
D.M.Bravo	c Jordan b Ali	9	c Broad b Stokes	82
M.N.Samuels	lbw b Anderson	9	b Broad	20
S.Chanderpaul	c Jordan b Root	25	b Anderson	0
J.Blackwood	c Ali b Anderson	85	not out	47
*† D.Ramdin	c Buttler b Broad	13	not out	0
J.O.Holder	c Buttler b Stokes	5		
V.Permaul	c sub (A.Lyth) b Anderson	18		
J.E.Taylor	b Anderson	15		
S.T.Gabriel	not out	0		
Extras	(B 4, LB 1)	5	(B 5, LB 6)	11
Total	**(49.4 overs)**	**189**	**(5 wkts; 62.4 overs)**	**194**

WEST INDIES	O	M	R	W		O	M	R	W
Taylor	18.3	8	36	3		11.1	1	33	3
Gabriel	15	3	47	2		7	4	16	1
Holder	16	4	34	2		9	3	15	3
Samuels	27	5	53	1	(5)	4	1	10	0
Permaul	20	1	86	1	(4)	11	3	43	3
ENGLAND	O	M	R	W		O	M	R	W
Anderson	12.4	5	42	6		13	4	35	1
Broad	10	3	31	1		13	5	29	1
Ali	10	2	56	1	(4)	12.4	1	54	1
Root	9	1	34	1	(5)	8	4	16	0
Jordan	6	3	4	0	(3)	11	5	24	1
Stokes	2	0	17	1		5	0	25	1

FALL OF WICKETS

	E	WI	E	WI
WKT	1ST	1ST	2ND	2ND
1st	0	0	11	35
2nd	38	5	13	35
3rd	38	21	18	70
4th	91	37	28	80
5th	189	82	39	188
6th	233	107	62	-
7th	240	124	95	-
8th	247	162	98	-
9th	257	178	98	-
10th	257	189	123	-

CLOSE OF PLAY

Day 1	England (1) 240-7 (89.2; J.C.Buttler 0*)
Day 2	England (2) 39-5 (21; G.S.Ballance 12*, B.A.Stokes 0*)

hand, began an incredibly emotional speech explaining the reasons he would be retiring from Test cricket with immediate effect. With his voice quivering, he said he no longer felt he was equipped to cope with the pace of Test cricket. He felt it had moved on in the 18 months he'd been out of the side and he didn't feel he could catch up.

It was an incredibly honest admission and showed the quality of the man that he could admit that. Plenty have hung on too long. It was one of the most moving moments of my life hearing this man who had committed so much of his life to playing for England admit he didn't want to put himself through it any more. Several of us were in tears as we listened to Trotty's heartfelt speech. For the younger players in the dressing room, it was a reminder of how hard you have to fight to carve out a successful Test career.

With 3,835 runs in 52 Tests at 44.08, including nine Test hundreds, Trotty will be remembered as one of England's best ever No.3 batsmen and he can look back on his career with great pride. It shouldn't be forgotten he averaged more than 50 in 68 one-day internationals as well. We would miss him enormously in the dressing room. But you could almost see the pressure lift from him as he made his speech. He didn't need the mental anguish any more. It was time for the next phase of his life. I'm sure a few county bowlers won't be too happy, because I've no doubt he'll go on to score many, many more runs for Warwickshire in the coming years. It was very sad to say goodbye to a champion player.

There was a slightly unpleasant end to the series. As we left our dressing room to walk down to the pitch to collect the Wisden Trophy – which people seemed to have forgotten we'd won – it became clear there was a nasty atmosphere. We looked over at the West Indies team dressing room and they'd written 'mediocre' in bold letters on a big sheet of paper and taped it to their door. The West Indian players had obviously taken Colin Graves's pre-tour comments very personally indeed. When we got pitchside there was open hostility directed at us as the West Indies players, egged on by Samuels, hurled abuse at us. Ottis copped a lot of very personal abuse, which was totally out of order, while we were all taken aback by the extent of their anger.

It all got pretty heated. When someone is speaking on the stage at the end of a series, it's common courtesy to listen, but the West Indies players were shouting and hurling all sorts of abuse. For a while, it was quite an uncomfortable atmosphere as they vented their anger at us over the Colin Graves comments. I'm not saying they were quite in the Tony Greig 'we'll make them grovel' category of misplaced quotes, but they certainly didn't help relations between the teams. In the end, we were quite relieved to get away from the ground and back to our hotel without things getting out of hand.

With the match over inside three days, we had a couple of extra days with our families in Barbados to reflect on the series before returning to England. We were getting a lot of criticism for losing the last Test, and there was clearly a lot of pressure on Mooresy from large sections of the media. The West Indies coach Phil Simmons had made a point of saying his players had been motivated by being called 'mediocre' and it was frustrating we'd not been able to win the series outright.

However, I still thought we were making really significant progress in the Test arena. Yes, our one-day form needed serious attention, but we'd won four of our last six Tests and had a number of talented players coming through. Cooky had enjoyed a decent tour with the bat and had been full of energy around the squad. People were questioning Mo's performance with the ball in the two Tests he'd played, but he hadn't had a lot of bowling coming into the series and I was confident he could reproduce the sort of form he'd shown against India the previous summer once he got a few more overs under his belt. With Trotty retired, the opener's spot was once again up for grabs. It looked as if Adam Lyth would come in for the upcoming two-Test series against New Zealand. With the Ashes looming fast, it was going to be a big summer for him.

I'd continued to work really hard on my fitness and was happy with how I was bowling. A return of ten wickets at 32 was OK – slightly worse than my career average – but I was experienced enough to know that if I kept doing what I was doing then things would happen for me. I'm a big believer in judging myself on process, not results. When I was younger, I judged myself purely on how many wickets I'd taken. As I've grown older I've learned to analyse my performance more clearly after each match. Did I create chances? Did I bring the batsman forward? Did I use my bouncer aggressively? Did I go at under three an over? When you judge yourself by those standards rather than purely on the wickets column it becomes a lot easier to be happy with your performance. You are less of a hostage to fortune. Sometimes luck is with you, sometimes it isn't. It's an important lesson for young bowlers to learn. Recent history also shows the Caribbean is not an easy place for seam and swing bowlers to flourish.

Despite the disappointment of Barbados, we felt we'd bowled well as a unit, with Stokesy's presence in the side providing the balance of a five-man attack. Jimmy led the from the front with the way he bowled, and we left the Caribbean in high spirits and confident we had the basis of a team, under Mooresy, that had the potential to do something really special. All we craved was some continuity and a bit of time to build that trust in each other's ability to deliver their role that all the best teams have.

Even Vaughany's team that won the 2005 Ashes didn't click immediately, while in 2009 we took a team to the Caribbean that included Strauss, Flintoff, Harmison, Panesar and Pietersen, and lost. But it built our character and it grew our belief and our resilience in the field that helped us win the Ashes in 2009. That tour set the foundations for us to go on to become the best team in the world.

I'd left the Caribbean this time with precisely the same feeling I'd had in 2009. We'd drawn a series and claimed the Wisden Trophy, which hardly anyone even mentioned, and it felt like we'd bonded as a group.

There was genuine excitement about the summer ahead and a sense of harmony between players and Mooresy's coaching team. But what happened next shocked me.

Struck by a bouncer from Varun Aaron during the fourth Test against India in the summer of 2014. Getting hit like that had a real impact on my confidence for a while.

But I recovered from having my nose broken to appear in the next Test, to help secure a brilliant 3-1 series win. Alastair Cook, who'd been under enormous pressure, showed his true mettle that summer.

The Carlton Series in January 2015 was our warm-up for the World Cup. Although we reached the final, we lost to Australia three times in the tournament. Here Aaron Finch just gets home in time.

Before the tournament got underway, there was also time for a little bit of work with the sponsors, doing a spot for Hardy's Wine, and to see some of the sights in Sydney – not one for those with no head for heights.

Kumar Sangakkara looks on during our World Cup match against Sri Lanka – his was one of the best one-day innings I've ever seen. Defeat meant we had to beat Bangladesh to stay in the tournament.

After being outclassed by Australia in our first World Cup game, what happened in New Zealand was even worse, as the Black Caps chased down our total in less than 13 overs. Eoin Morgan, Jimmy Anderson, Steve Finn and I look suitably shell-shocked.

Headphones off as I arrived at Sydney airport after losing to Bangladesh. The smile for the cameras did not come easily – all I wanted to do was hide away in my hotel room.

Getty Images

Above: Having recovered from knee surgery, the last thing I wanted was for my ankle to give way, as I feared it had done during our warm-up match in St Kitts. Happily there was no lasting damage.

Right: There's always a different approach to life on tour in the Caribbean.

Below: Coach Peter Moores watches on during a training session. After Paul Downton lost his job, Moores knew his position was under threat, but he kept on focusing on the role and did a fine job.

Sir Ian Botham congratulates Jimmy Anderson after he had overtaken Beefy's long-standing record of 383 Test wickets during the first Test in Antigua.

Jason Holder is on his way – one of three victims during my best spell since my knee operation, at the Grenada National Stadium. We eventually recorded our first away victory in a Test match since 2012.

The tour was not a good one for me with the bat, and this dismissal in the final Test on our way to defeat summed it all up.

I was delighted when Jonathan Trott earned his recall to the England side in the West Indies, but things didn't work out for him, and after the final Test he announced his retirement from the side in an emotional speech to the dressing room.

For the series against New Zealand, Paul Farbrace was our interim coach, before the arrival of Trevor Bayliss, and the players appreciated his low-key approach.

Tom Latham is out LBW first ball on the last day of the Lord's Test to leave New Zealand 0 for two and in trouble.

Celebrating another success for Man of the Match Ben Stokes as we closed in on one of the best Test victories I've ever experienced.

An interruption for rain at Headingley couldn't put a halt to New Zealand's spectacular run charge in their second innings.

Kane Williamson celebrates bowling me out as New Zealand close in on victory in the final day of the Headingley Test.

5

THE SUMMER OF LOVE BEGINS

NEW ZEALAND SERIES 7 MAY–3 JUNE

We landed back from Barbados at Heathrow and within 24 hours some of the boys were already packing their bags again to fly off to Dublin for a one-off one-day international against Ireland at Malahide.

With speculation about his future as England coach reaching fever pitch, it was typical of Peter Moores that he should choose to accompany the experimental team across to Ireland when others would have stayed at home and tried to ride out the storm. Mooresy's attitude was that, as England coach, he had a duty to be with his players. With Eoin Morgan away on IPL duty, Jimmy Taylor skippered the side.

Along with the vast majority of the boys who toured the West Indies, I was given some time off to rest ahead of the New Zealand Test series, with the first of two back-to-back Tests getting underway at Lord's in two weeks' time.

Bealey and I were planning on having some building work done at our place and we wanted the name of the architect who'd done a job for Mooresy and his wife Karen, who live in a village just up the road from us.

Bealey dialled their home number and Karen picked up the phone. 'Have you heard what's happened?' she asked straight away.

'No,' Bea replied.

'Pete's been sacked. It's all over Twitter.'

I took the phone from Bea and asked Karen if she was OK.

I checked my phone and sure enough a number of newspaper websites and journalists were reporting that Andrew Strauss had been installed as director of cricket and Mooresy had been sacked with immediate effect. There was no official word from the ECB, but it wasn't looking good for Pete and I felt for him and Karen finding out about his future via social media while he was doing his job in a different country. It felt wrong.

I told Karen that until the news was official it could still be a mistake, but in my heart I knew it was almost certainly true. I felt for them both. They are good people and deserved better than this.

Speculation had already begun over who would replace Mooresy. I found it all really distasteful considering the poor bloke was still officially in a job. I was impressed by Sky pundit Paul Allott, a friend of Mooresy's from Lancashire, when he declined to comment on a possible successor when asked live on air. He pointed out in no uncertain terms that it was inappropriate to discuss who would take over when there had been no formal announcement. It was an honourable stance to take in a world which screams out for instant opinions.

Eventually, the ECB put out two statements, confirming what the world knew already: Strauss was in and Moores was out.

I remained delighted that Straussy had got the job as director of England cricket, but couldn't help feeling sad for Pete, who had never given less than 100 per cent in trying to make England a better team.

But, as we already knew, Strauss is not an emotional character swayed by sympathy. He'd weighed up the pros and cons and decided Moores had to go. Like it or not, in one decisive action he reminded everyone he was a man prepared to make tough calls. He wouldn't have taken the decision to sack Pete lightly; it was clear he believed change was essential.

'It was a very difficult decision for us to make,' Strauss said at his unveiling press conference days after his appointment. 'Peter Moores has been very popular in the England dressing room. He's got a very good record of developing players, but I felt that in some areas of international cricket he is a little bit exposed, around tactics and strategy.

'I think we saw that in the World Cup and also he was undermined by the fact he had done the job before. We got to the situation where every game was a referendum whether the coach should stay or not. That's not fair on him or the players. I felt it was the right call to make and my job now is to find the right coach to take England cricket forward. I've got a lot of work to do in the coming days and weeks to make sure that happens.'

Anyone who has played sport at the highest level knows how tough a business it can be. There is rarely room for sentiment or romance in an industry driven squarely by results and commercial imperatives.

Sadly for Mooresy, our results, in the one-day arena at least, had not been good enough and he ended up carrying the can for the players underperforming.

I loved working with Mooresy and held him in the highest regard as a bloke and a coach. His coaching record is impeccable, you only have to look at his county record where he wins the championship wherever he goes.

I first worked with him in the National Academy in 2005 when he was absolutely brilliant. He would make every single net session feel like an Ashes Test match and constantly challenge players to perform under pressure. He simulated scenarios and never let you relax or switch off in practice.

Anyone who has played sport at the highest level knows how tough a business it can be. There is rarely room for sentiment or romance.

After taking over from Duncan Fletcher in April 2007, he gambled on me and Jimmy Anderson the following winter by picking us against New Zealand in place of two England legends in Steve Harmison and Matthew Hoggard after England lost the first Test of that series. That selection took bravery and foresight. More than 700 Test wickets later, I like to think we've repaid the faith he showed in us as a pair.

He was pretty unfortunate to have been around during two of the most turbulent periods of recent English cricket history.

He was criticised during his first stint in charge for being a bit too prescriptive in his methods. I know Michael Vaughan wasn't overly keen on his management style and found him too intense. Some of the senior players, who'd been used to Fletcher's more reticent approach, found him overly eager and 'in-your-face'. However, there is no right or wrong way to coach, and some methods will work for some teams and not for others. Personally, I found him hugely energising to work with.

His first spell in charge ended at the beginning of 2009 when Kevin Pietersen told the ECB he couldn't work with him and as a result they ended up both being removed as captain and coach. His second coming five years later also coincided with a media storm, after Kevin was told by Paul Downton he was not going to be picked for England again following the Ashes whitewash.

He then had to set about the small matter of bedding in a new generation of players in the fallout from that disastrous series. For a host of different reasons, Kevin, Jonathan Trott, Graeme Swann – who shocked us all when he retired after the third Test in Perth – and Matty Prior's careers were either over or almost over when Mooresy took over the second time. His first summer back was tumultuous, on and off the field.

But Pete kept constant throughout that difficult 2014 summer and over the following winter, even as the wheels fell off so spectacularly during the World Cup. He was incredibly positive and determined to improve the England cricket team and the players in it. In 2014, he'd blooded the likes of Jos Buttler, Moeen Ali, Chris Jordan and Sam Robson in a summer that saw us turn our fortunes around after losing the second Test embarrassingly at Lord's before crushing India in emphatic style in the last three Tests to finish 3-1 winners. We played some wonderfully aggressive cricket in that series and I've no doubt it set the template for what was to follow.

Mooresy was also responsible for introducing a number of innovations that played a central role in us going on to win the Ashes. He brought us closer to the media and ex-players, which has helped us reconnect with our supporters. He was an innovative forward thinker who wasn't scared to look beyond cricket for answers.

We'll never know if we would have gone on to have the success we enjoyed over the rest of the summer if Straussy hadn't made the call that he did when he did, but the players Mooresy identified as the ones to lead the side into the Ashes were largely the same as the ones who eventually played. As players, we had to accept the decision and get on with the job in what was going to be a massive summer. The Ashes were less than two months away and, however much the squad craved stability, the decision had been taken to look elsewhere. Australians Jason Gillespie at Yorkshire and Justin Langer at Western Australia emerged as early front-runners for the job.

Straussy stated his intention to scour the globe for the best man to replace Pete, but in the meantime confirmed Paul Farbrace would take interim charge for the upcoming two-Test series against New Zealand.

Farby was a popular member of the backroom staff, with a relaxed attitude that put players at ease. He wasn't one for ranting or raving, and players appreciated his low-key approach. He didn't have much time to make his mark before a series some assumed we'd win comfortably, but we knew would be extremely tough against a side containing world-class players like Brendon McCullum, Trent Boult, Tim Southee and Kane Williamson.

It felt a bit disrespectful to the New Zealanders, but so much talk already seemed to focus on the Ashes. Every other question we'd be asked seemed to be about Australia or how we'd do in that series, overlooking the fact McCullum and his men would be looking to give us another bloody nose in the Test arena after humiliating us in the World Cup, where they finished up as beaten finalists.

It hadn't escaped our notice when Australia's in-form batsman Steve Smith piped up with some fairly punchy comments towards the tail end of our time in the West Indies. I looked online for the interview.

'I can't wait to get over there and play another Ashes against England in their conditions after beating them so convincingly in Australia,' Smith said. 'It's going to be nice to go in their backyard. If we continue to play the way we have been playing over the last twelve to eighteen months, I don't think that they'll come close to us, to be honest.'

In these slightly sanitised days of media training and paranoia around saying anything inflammatory, a small part of me admired Smith for stirring the pot a bit. But only a small part. The other part of me logged what he'd said and I promised to remind myself of it later in the summer. We decided to keep our powder dry.

In the meantime, we had New Zealand to consider. As captain, McCullum had made a name for himself as one of the most innovative and intelligent thinkers in world cricket. As a batsman, we had recent first-hand experience of his ridiculous natural ability. They were a dangerous side and we knew it.

The two-match Test series, followed by five one-day internationals and a Twenty20 game, would kick off what promised to be, if you were a fan, a fantastic summer of cricket. The Black Caps had held us to a 0-0 drawn Test series in New Zealand in early 2013, when we escaped defeat in the final Test in Auckland only courtesy of a brilliant backs-to-the-wall unbeaten hundred by Matt Prior in the last innings which saved us by the narrowest of margins.

That had been a really important tour for me for a number of reasons, not least because my sister Gemma – who was an England team performance analyst at the time – spotted a technical flaw in my bowling which had seen my speeds drop alarmingly and left me worried for my place in the side. I'd been really low on tour in India a few months earlier when fitness was my main concern. Now my lack of form was getting me down.

I was really struggling with my action and rhythm at the time, but couldn't put my finger on what was wrong. No one in the management set-up seemed to know either. Gem came to my room for a brew one afternoon and we put a few clips of me bowling on to my iPad. We watched a montage of wickets I'd taken over the past couple of years and, as they ran through, Gem spotted that my feet were crossing over in my delivery and not pointing straight down the wicket towards the batsman. As we re-ran the clips it was really clear that I wasn't getting my hips through in the delivery stride because I was blocking myself off with my feet and losing my front arm too quickly. It was a 'Eureka' moment and completely changed the way I approached my bowling.

Straight away, it felt easier to bowl. Rather than forcing things as I had been doing, and putting excess stress on myself as a result, I suddenly felt I could whip through my action as soon as I released the ball. Less effort for far more reward. Who wouldn't take that equation?

People say your best days as a professional sportsman tend to be around your late 20s and early 30s and I think that's because you understand your game so much better then while still retaining the physical attributes required for top-class international sport.

THE SUMMER OF LOVE BEGINS

By Gemma spotting that flaw in my action, I was able to institute a checklist that I can refer to if I'm not bowling well, which effectively breaks the mechanics of my action down into working parts that I can tick off.

Once I'd worked out what the problem was, I was able to fix it. I immediately gained four to five miles per hour on average and my confidence rapidly returned. Between then and the end of the West Indies tour I'd taken around 100 wickets at 25 apiece. Those numbers were set to improve as the summer went on. In many ways, I have my sister to thank for a defining moment in my career.

It was a big wake-up call for me and a realisation that I couldn't just take my action for granted, I had to think hard about it to keep it running smoothly.

With the New Zealand Test series approaching fast, a lot of the focus was on who would open with Alastair Cook at the top of England's order. Cooky had been given the resounding backing of Andrew Strauss, who described him as 'the right man to lead the England team'. He was absolutely right about that.

I also agreed with Strauss's move to appoint Joe Root as vice-captain ahead of Ian Bell, which England's new director of cricket described as a 'strategic decision'. Nothing against Belly whatsoever, but it had been clear from a very early stage of his involvement in the England dressing room that Rooty had the potential to be a future England captain. He has a cheeky-chappy persona and is good fun to be around, but he's also a fierce competitor who is more than willing to roll up his sleeves and get serious when the chips are down. His youthful looks belie a steely inner determination and, in cricketing terms at least, he is wise beyond his years. He had impressed everyone, management and players alike, on his first tour to India in 2012, when he made his Test debut. I vividly remember one team meeting where we were discussing how we should approach the Indian spinners. He immediately knew what he wanted to say and had no hesitation in sharing his opinion. It was impressive stuff. In a room full of gnarled old pros who could be quick to judge, it was clear he knew precisely what he was talking about.

> Find me an English cricketer who would say 'no' to the England captaincy and I'll find you someone who is not telling the truth.

Now 24, Rooty was maturing rapidly into one of the best batsmen in the world at both Test and one-day level. I'd already lost count of the number of times he'd dug us out of tricky positions and that ability to score runs when others were struggling would come to the fore again throughout the course of the summer.

I have no doubt Rooty will go on to be England captain in the future, possibly in all three formats. There had been talk about him taking over from Cooky when things weren't going well in 2014, but that was clearly too soon for him. There were all sorts of names being thrown about after the Ashes whitewash in 2013-14, and then again after we lost at Lord's to India the following summer, but I never doubted Cooky would come through.

Having been Twenty20 captain for the previous three years, friends even asked me if I would do the Test job if it came up. It was an impossible one to answer without sounding as if I was undermining my friend and captain, Cooky. Find me an English cricketer who would say 'no' to the England captaincy and I'll find you someone who is not telling the truth. Would I have done the job if someone had asked me? Almost certainly. Did I believe I was the best man to captain the England Test team? Absolutely not.

The workload faced by a fast bowler in the field makes it very hard to think about all the field placings and other bowling changes required. It's no coincidence that the overwhelming majority of successful captains down the years have been batsmen. Despite being asked the occasional question about it, I never seriously considered it as an option.

With Cooky getting Strauss's backing at the start of the 2015 summer, it felt like the right time to formally acknowledge Rooty's part in the England leadership team with an eye on the future.

My only hope is that the captaincy is not given to Rooty too soon, because it will almost inevitably have a detrimental impact on his batting form, as it has done for pretty much every player who has taken the job in recent times. Cooky, who scored hundreds in each of his first three Tests as captain before the almost inevitable dip in form, has done a phenomenal job at handling the enormous additional media, sponsorship and management pressures that go hand-in-hand with the England captaincy. I firmly believe he is the man to lead us in the short and medium term. But Rooty is clearly the man who will take over in the longer term. Just as Cooky had been given leadership experience when Strauss was captain, this felt like intelligent longer-term planning.

The second opener's spot, however, remained a problem. I totally understood the reasons for giving Trotty a go there in the West Indies, but sadly it hadn't worked out. Adam Lyth had fitted really well into the group and made a good impression on the tour without getting to play in the Test series. It seemed entirely right that he was given his chance to face the Black Caps at Lord's in the opening Test, when he would have an opportunity to stake a claim for an Ashes spot. It was a big ask for him, but I'd seen enough of him in practice in the Caribbean to think he could cut it at international level.

What I also immediately liked about Lythy was the sheer enjoyment he was so obviously getting just by being around the England set-up. I'm told he was very emotional when he got the call telling him he'd been selected to go the Caribbean, and it was plain to see he was living the dream just by being around the England squad. At 27, he was a little bit older than some when they make the breakthrough to international cricket, and those years he'd spent at the coalface for Yorkshire gave him a real appreciation of the chance he was being given.

It was an important reminder to those of us who'd been around the block a bit more just what an amazing thing it was to play cricket for England.

Some players could have grumbled for not getting a Test on tour. Not Lythy. He had a smile on his face from the moment we took off for St Kitts to the moment we touched back down at Heathrow. He brought a really positive energy. He was always upbeat.

THE SUMMER OF LOVE BEGINS

While the opener's spot still needed filling, I had a really good feeling about the Test side, despite our underwhelming performance in Barbados. Getting the balance right in any team is so important and it just felt like we had a good blend of youth and experience, with a nice combination of naturally aggressive-minded players and those who preferred a more cautious approach. Critically, with Ben Stokes in the side, Cooky had a five-man attack to choose from, with a fifth bowler he knew could give him ten to 15 overs a day.

The most successful England side I'd ever played in was the one that won 3-1 in Australia in 2010-11 before beating India 4-0 at home the following summer. The batting was built around the top-order workhorses – Strauss, Cook and Trott – who would take the shine off the ball and grind opponents down, before our brilliant shot-makers Kevin and Belly would come in and take attacks apart. With Matty Prior at seven, me at eight and Swanny at nine, it meant the batting had real depth, with a calmness at the top and then real power coming through in the middle and lower order.

Looking at the team now, there was a similar feel. Gary Ballance looked to have overcome his tricky time in the World Cup and Cook also was somewhere close to his best again after a lean 2014 with the bat. Root, Bell and Stokes provided that shot-making ability and sense of urgency in the middle order that can really take the game away from sides, while Jos Buttler had the potential to be a really exciting run-scorer at No.7. With Mo coming in as low as eight, there was quality running right through the team.

Any team that lost a spinner of the quality of Graeme Swann would struggle to find a replacement immediately. Look at how Australia struggled to replace Shane Warne. Mo, not a regular spinner with Worcestershire, had done a brilliant job the previous summer against India. He was only going to get better and he'd also been a great addition to the squad. There was still plenty of media noise about Kevin Pietersen, but as a team we'd moved on quickly and felt the middle order of Ballance, Root, Bell and Stokes had massive potential.

My own batting was still the focus of concern for some after another tricky series in the West Indies. It was frustrating for me that, as the second string to my bow, it seemed to be getting more attention than my bowling. My confidence had been affected by what had happened at Old Trafford the previous summer, but it was nowhere near as bad as some people were making it. I'd continued to work with ECB psychologist Chris Marshall and I felt it was a matter of time before the runs started coming again. I was still averaging 23 in Test cricket, which is not a bad return for a No.9.

I'd spoken to my old friend Michael Lumb after I'd been hit in the face and he reminded me of the time in 2010 when I'd broken his jaw and split his chin with a bouncer. He said it had taken him three months to get over it and it had really affected him psychologically. If it took a bloke with that amount of talent that long to get over it, it was always going to take me a while. It had undoubtedly been a shock having my nose broken in two places by a cricket ball hurled at almost 90mph. I'd never even been punched in the face before.

The frustrating thing was that I'd worked incredibly hard the previous winter to improve my batting and was having a pretty good summer with the bat in 2014 until the incident at Old Trafford. I've never considered myself a genuine all-rounder, even after scoring that hundred in 2010, but I did see myself as a lower-order batsman capable of changing the momentum of an innings by playing some shots and unsettling the opposition. I'm aware I'm not technically perfect, but I've got a good eye, long levers and the ability to put my hands through the ball. I love getting under the skin of opposition bowling attacks, because I know from personal experience how frustrating it can be if a lower-order batsman chances his arm and puts on more with the tail than you expect. I continued to work hard in the nets on getting my trigger movements right and getting fully into position. I never lost belief that my form would return sooner rather than later.

Ultimately, I was in the side as a bowler. Ever since Gemma had spotted the flaw in my delivery stride, I'd averaged 25.80 in 2013 and 26.70 in 2014 which, considering I'd played 12 months almost on one leg, I didn't feel was too bad a contribution.

The squad for the first Test against New Zealand was announced, with uncapped duo Mark Wood and Adam Lyth the two standout names on the list. Neither man had played a Test in the West Indies, but both had made a very favourable impression on the tour. Woody had definitely given some of our batsmen the hurry-up in the nets with his smooth, powerful action seeing him hit the 90mph mark fairly consistently from a short run-up. On top of that, he was a competent tail-end batsman who could chip in with some useful runs down the order. He was also a lot of fun.

Lythy was certain to make his debut, with Cooky the only other recognised opener in the squad, while it would be between Woody and Chris Jordan for the last bowling spot. Chris, another lovely lad whose claim to fame was that he'd been in the same school year in Barbados as the pop star Rihanna, had made some important contributions in the eight Tests he'd played since making his debut the previous summer without that real breakthrough match-winning performance.

He is an absolutely brilliant slip fielder and took some of the best catches I've ever seen in the West Indies. But with Woody seen as a fast bowler potentially in the Simon Jones mould, he made the cut for the final XI.

Back in 2013 we'd beaten New Zealand 2-0 at home ahead of the Ashes series and it was very much our aim to repeat that result when we set off for Lord's on the morning of the first Test.

We'd trained well in the lead-up to the match and were in high spirits that morning. I drove to the famous old ground in St John's Wood from our team hotel – the Langham near Regent's Park – with my usual passenger Jimmy and the weather set fair for a lovely day's cricket.

You'll often hear players talk about how special the first morning of a Lord's Test is. There really is nothing that comes close to walking out through the Long Room with the hushed anticipation of the MCC members and a full house outside. The day it doesn't see the hairs on the back of my neck rise will be the day I know it is time to retire. It's completely unlike playing somewhere like Edgbaston or Trent Bridge, where the crowds are generally far more vocal with an atmosphere sometimes more akin to a football crowd than a genteel cricket audience. Lord's is different. The history and tradition are tangible and there's something truly unique about playing there. The flip side is that touring sides also love playing there and often raise their performances accordingly.

The previous year we'd been frustrated by Sri Lanka, who held out to draw a match we really should have won, and we were absolutely determined to get our summer off to a winning start this time. The pitch was flat, as you'd expect, but there was a tinge of green to the surface which gave me hope there might be a little bit more in it for the fast bowlers than there sometimes is at Lord's.

Adam Lyth and Mark Wood were awarded their first caps on the outfield by Cooky before play that morning. Lythy had the dubious honour of being the 666th England player, with the number written on his shirt, while Woody was given number 667. Both men were clearly incredibly excited to be making their Test debuts, and it was evident how much this meant to Lythy to be representing England as he was once again close to tears when presented with his cap.

Both men are great characters to have around and brought a sense of levity to proceedings. They both cared passionately about playing for England, but neither took themselves too seriously and they played a key role in the new dynamic you could feel in the dressing room.

If I suspected Woody was a bit off the wall when I first encountered him in Potchefstroom, with his wheelie bin wind-up of Christine Ohuruogu six months earlier, spending time with him on tour in the Caribbean had absolutely confirmed it. He was one of those people who could make you laugh just by being himself. He'd given an interview a few months earlier when he'd described how he sometimes liked to ride an imaginary horse around the outfield, attempting to joust his team-mates while feeding himself Granny Smith apples. It was one of the most bizarre things I'd ever heard, but I found it hilarious as it only confirmed the impression I'd got of him in South Africa. He was a breath of fresh air, and I was excited about him being around. Most importantly, of course, he was also a bloody good cricketer. He was just utterly intrigued by the experience of playing at Lord's, as he'd never played there before during his county career, but he didn't seem overawed at all.

Woody promised to take his 'horse' for a trot on the hallowed Lord's outfield at some point during the Test, but in the meantime it was down to the serious business of beating a New Zealand side who had not lost a series since we'd beaten them in England in 2013.

McCullum had clearly taken the same view I had of the pitch, and decided to put us into bat after winning the toss. With a high-class battery of fast bowlers at his disposal, he had obviously judged his best chance of rolling us over cheaply was while that green tinge remained in the pitch. So under blue skies, Lythy walked out alongside Cooky for his first Test innings. I had everything crossed for him.

Eleven years earlier, Andrew Strauss had made a maiden Test hundred against New Zealand at the same ground and I'm sure Lythy would have given anything for a similar score. Sadly it wasn't to be as the left-handed opener lasted just 17 balls before feathering a Tim Southee delivery behind for just 7 to leave us 17 for one.

It got worse. Gary Ballance – who'd scored two hundreds in two previous Lord's Test appearances – never settled before driving loosely at Trent Boult and being caught at slip by Southee, while debutant Matt Henry surprised Cooky with a bit of extra pace which saw him glove an attempted pull behind.

When Belly was out for 1 to leave us reeling on 30 for four, we were rushing around inside the dressing room trying to find our kit as wickets fell at an alarming rate. All the pre-match talk of positive, aggressive cricket suddenly seemed a long time ago. We were in trouble, big time. You try not to second guess the press, but I could imagine a few of them chuntering about 'false dawns' and 'here we go again'.

THE SUMMER OF LOVE BEGINS

With Rooty and Stokesy at the crease, and batting to come, there was still hope of salvaging something from the wreckage of our innings, but at that moment it seemed to be about pure survival.

We always try to keep the balcony full to show our support for our team-mates, but that proved tricky at Lord's where there is very little space to squeeze everyone in. We'll do shifts to ensure people are always out watching, although some players find it too nerve-wracking and draining. Swanny definitely used to be one of those players.

But, with so much happening, we were all glued to the action. It became apparent fairly early on that the young pair were enjoying themselves, despite the gravity of our position. Rooty settled into his stride incredibly quickly, easing into a couple of early boundaries to reach 13 from nine balls. Stokesy warmed to the theme by thumping an imperious hook off Henry to long leg for his first boundary.

What followed was quite simply one of the most enjoyable partnerships I've ever watched. New Zealand kept pressing hard, but the more they came at the England pair the harder the ball seemed to fly away to the boundary.

I remember looking at Farby – who'd made a point of reminding us to enjoy ourselves before the Test – and smiling. This was enjoyable, that was for sure. Boundaries were coming at a fearsome rate and even the ultra-aggressive McCullum was forced into more defensive field positions to limit the flow of runs and retain the initiative New Zealand had grabbed so decisively in the first hour.

But as the fifty partnership was brought up in just 46 balls, we began to wonder if we were witnessing something special. You just don't bat like this on the first morning at Lord's, do you? It was brilliant to watch.

The pair rattled along at the best part of six an over. Rooty seemed to be having a dart at just about everything, while Stokesy was clubbing it with his big heavy bat and butcher's forearms. No sooner did New Zealand manage to string a couple of tidy overs together than Rooty responded with three fours in four balls from their off-spinner Mark Craig.

At lunch, we were 113 for four with the partnership unbeaten on 83 at close to a run a ball. We weren't out of trouble by any means, and it was still New Zealand's morning, but the difference in mood in our dressing room was vast. Rooty was bouncing around at lunch and you could tell Stokesy was up for the fight. Is he ever not?

We'd talked about showcasing our skills and you were not going to see a better example of it than that partnership. They received a huge ovation after lunch and simply carried on where they'd left off, smashing the New Zealand attack to all parts. Stokesy was particularly savage through the leg side, punching anything short through mid-wicket and mid-on. He looked determined and focused in partnership with Rooty, who was giving us yet another reminder of what an outstanding young cricketer he is. When the chips were down, two of our brightest young prospects were digging us out of a hole.

The power Stokes was able to get into his shots was astonishing. He is immensely strong and generates incredible bat-speed with a heavy blade. With broad shoulders and plenty of aggressive intent, he gives the ball an absolute caning. I think the speed at which the ball travelled to the fence took the New Zealanders by surprise.

The scoring eased slightly midway through the afternoon session before Stokes put his foot on the accelerator again after both men had reached their fifties. He took 14 from three deliveries from Henry, including a thunderously flat leg-side six I honestly thought was going to hurt someone in the crowd. It was primal stuff and we loved it!

Both men looked destined for hundreds as England reached 191 for four in the 45th over before Stokesy made a fatal misjudgement and shouldered arms to a ball which came down the slope and bowled him. Out for 92 from 94 balls, he had narrowly missed out on what would have been a deserved second Test century.

He was obviously bitterly disappointed as he walked off, but received an ovation from the Lord's crowd every bit as heartfelt as if he'd reached three figures. It had been a magnificent fighting knock just when we'd needed it and we stood and applauded him into the dressing room. If this was what England's future looked like, I wanted to be part of it.

Rooty had been left in Ben's wake a little bit but, with Jos now with him at the crease, he re-took the initiative to go back after the New Zealand attack. He looked set for his seventh century in only his 26th Test when he misjudged a cut shot and edged a catch behind for 98. Like Stokes, he received an ovation worthy of a hundred. From 30 for four, we had reached 251 for six thanks to our two young street-fighters and, while we still had some work to do, there was a massively energised feel to the dressing room which was reflected by the crowd.

Jos, batting nicely in partnership with Mo at No.8, reached his second Test fifty from 95 balls while Mo got to 49 as they began the final over of the day on 354 for six. Sadly for Jos, Boult bowled him an absolute pearler off the very last ball of the day to trap him leg before for a very well-made 67.

It was frustrating for Jos, who was absolutely gutted when he got back into the changing room, but it could not spoil what had been one of the most remarkable first days of a Test match I had ever been involved in. I'd watched engrossed from the pavilion as two of the most talented young cricketers I'd ever had the pleasure of sharing a dressing room with simply refused to roll over and be beaten. They had resurrected our innings in the most spectacular fashion to put us firmly in the driving seat after being put into bat. It was thrilling stuff and exactly the type of aggressive, no-fear cricket we'd talked about in Sydney after our World Cup exit. The difference? This was a Test match for goodness sake.

It was thrilling stuff and exactly the type of aggressive, no-fear cricket we'd talked about in Sydney after our World Cup exit.

I was later told no team had ever scored more runs in an innings after being 30 for four or worse. It really was quite something.

Jimmy and I were still shaking our heads when we climbed into my car to make the short drive back to the hotel.

'Was that for real?' Jimmy asked, deadpan.

The next morning, it was my turn at the crease. Boult welcomed me with a bouncer, which was no real surprise following my struggles with the bat in recent times, before having Mo caught behind in the next over for an excellent 58.

Woody walked out for his first Test innings with a broad grin on his face.

'This should be fun,' he said.

Sadly, I didn't hang around to keep him company as the highly impressive Boult bowled me a superb delivery that nibbled away just enough to catch the outside edge. I acknowledged the quality of the delivery as I walked past the bowler. Sometimes, you just get one that's too good for you.

Woody and Jimmy added 21 valuable last-wicket runs before Jimmy was caught and bowled by Henry. Our final total of 389 all out was probably somewhere around par on an excellent Lord's wicket, but it felt as if we'd scored 1000 after our horrendous start. However, if we thought we'd done enough to knock the stuffing out of New Zealand, we were soon made to think again as Martin Guptill and Tom Latham took the wind out of our sails with a big first-wicket partnership.

Woody looked to have got his first Test wicket in only his third over, when Cooky took a very good catch at first slip off Guptill, only for television replays to show he'd overstepped the crease and a no-ball was called. We were absolutely gutted for Woody, who for once wasn't smiling. He was absolutely devastated.

'Chin up Woody,' I said. 'At least you'll get two cracks at celebrating your first Test wicket! And if you carry on bowling deliveries like that you'll take plenty of them.'

Frustratingly, we dropped a couple of reasonably catchable chances as New Zealand's innings got going, with the usually reliable Ian Bell shelling one chance off Latham that a slip fielder of his calibre would expect to catch eight times out of ten. It was a pattern that was set to continue through the series.

Mo eventually made the breakthrough when he had Latham LBW with the score on 148, and we suddenly sensed a shift in momentum when I had Guptill caught by Gary Ballance two balls later.

But, in keeping with the match, New Zealand fought back. Kane Williamson weighed in with a magnificently controlled 132, while Ross Taylor and B.J.Watling both made excellent half-centuries. At 337 for two midway through the morning session on day three, with Williamson and Taylor going well, it looked as if New Zealand could be set for an absolutely massive total.

Thankfully, I managed to break the partnership when I bowled a rising delivery into Taylor's ribs which he could only manage to fend down the leg side where Jos took a stunning one-handed catch diving full length to his left. It was another key moment where one of our young stars had a massive part to play.

With McCullum now in alongside Williamson, New Zealand still had plenty of ammunition to fire, and when the New Zealand captain gave Stokesy a taste of his own medicine by crashing him into the Grand Stand for six to take them past our total, you could sense the crowd was fearing the worst. We were behind the eight-ball again.

Woody finally did get his first Test wicket when McCullum top-edged to Rooty in the deep and the Durham quick definitely had the smile back on his face as he picked up the further wicket of Corey Anderson in a hugely impressive spell.

I weighed in with a couple more wickets to finish with three for 77 from 26.2 overs while Mo and Woody also picked up three apiece as New Zealand were bowled out for 523, a first-innings lead of 134.

THE SUMMER OF LOVE BEGINS

We had mixed feelings in the dressing room. On the one hand we were deeply frustrated at allowing the Black Caps to build such an impressive first-innings total, but on the other we could consider ourselves lucky to be in the match at all while taking encouragement from the way we'd kept battling.

Cook reminded us of how we'd turned our fortunes around once in the match and we could do it again. The wicket was playing well and if we could make 350 second time around, McCullum's men would be the ones under pressure.

As it turned out we went even better than that, but not before being in serious trouble again at 74 for three with Lyth (12), Ballance (0) and Bell (29) all back in the pavilion. But cometh the hour, cometh the men. With Trotty out of the side, Cooky was the next man I'd have wanted batting for my life, and he got his summer off to the perfect start with a quite magnificent knock of 162 from 365 balls.

He put on 158 with Rooty (84) for the fourth wicket to wrestle back control before Stokesy came in and delivered a blow straight to the tourists' solar plexus with the fastest Test hundred in Lord's history. If his first-innings knock had been savage, this was positively Neanderthal as he clubbed his way to a century off 85 balls. His second fifty took just 28 deliveries. It was world-class stuff and a full vindication of the decision to move him to No.6 in the order, where he'd batted in Australia in 2013-14. His innings brought the house down and, after Cooky had laid the foundation, ripped the match out of New Zealand's grasp. The pair had put on 132, with England's captain contributing 24. Stokes's hitting was wonderful to watch.

We closed on the fourth evening on 429 for six, with Cooky unbeaten on 153 and a lead of 297.

That evening we began to hear rumours that Mooresy's replacement had been identified. The name doing the rounds was an Australian one, but not one of the ones anyone had touted. I knew of Trevor Bayliss from his time as Sri Lanka coach, while my old mate Lumby spoke very highly of him after a stint playing under him for Sydney Sixers in the Big Bash. But, to be honest, if he'd walked into the room there and then, I probably wouldn't have recognised him. I was interested to know more. But for now, there was a Test match to be won.

The final day was played on a Bank Holiday Monday and we turned up at the ground around 9.30am to see the crowds queuing around the corner.

The final day was played on a Bank Holiday Monday and we turned up at the ground around 9.30am to see the crowds queuing around the corner. It came as a bit of a shock to see the sheer number of people wanting to get into the ground, but it was indicative of the impact this extraordinary match had already had on the English cricketing public.

There was a huge buzz inside the ground that morning and when we were eventually all out for 478, we left New Zealand needing 345 in two and a half sessions.

Two years earlier I'd taken seven for 44 as we bowled them out for 68 in the fourth innings and I reminded myself of that as I got ready to bowl. With Jimmy needing just two more wickets to make it 400 career Test scalps, we couldn't have been more pumped going into the field.

When Jimmy had Guptill caught at second slip with his second ball and I trapped Latham in front with my first to leave New Zealand 0 for two, we knew a famous win was ours for the taking.

They were 12 for three when I had Taylor LBW in my third over before Williamson and B.J.Watling settled things slightly with a 49-run partnership. But Stokesy wasn't to be kept out of the action and produced yet another moment of pure theatre to bowl Williamson and McCullum in successive deliveries. The crowd were going absolutely potty.

He ran in for his hat-trick delivery with six slips, a leg gully and short leg, but Anderson left well and the danger momentarily passed. Anderson and Watling continued to frustrate us before Woody took yet another vital wicket when he had the New Zealand wicket-keeper caught behind for 59 to leave New Zealand 168 for six. We had 26 overs to take the remaining four wickets.

Root had Anderson LBW three overs later to put us on the brink, before Stokes beat Craig for pace to bowl him after he'd survived for 24 balls. Mo caught and bowled Southee moments later and we stood on the verge, only for Boult and Henry to take their side to within ten overs of safety with a dogged last-wicket stand lasting more than eight overs.

Just as the unthinkable began to creep into our minds, I tempted Boult into a rash upper cut and Mo took a wonderful diving catch down at wide third man, of all places, to win the match. I ran to Cooky and Mo in a moment of delight. It was unquestionably one of the best Test wins I'd been involved in, and Cooky had played a blinder with his captaincy and personal contribution with the bat. The fact we even had a third man in place to Boult was testament to our captain's clever field placing.

Stokes was obviously Man of the Match for an all-round effort Ian Botham or Andrew Flintoff would have been proud of, while I was quietly satisfied with a decent contribution with the ball. It felt like a defining moment in this team's evolution.

After the close we were unwinding in the changing room when McCullum walked in with his team and asked if they could share a beer. Of course we said 'yes'. It was a wonderful touch by the Black Caps' captain and his players, who must have been shattered by the defeat. We sat with them for more than an hour and chewed over a memorable Test match.

They had won over a huge number of fans with the way they'd played the game and shown that fierce, aggressive cricket does not have to mean abusive sledging. It was a brilliant advert for Test cricket.

The ICC has made a habit of coming down pretty hard on any kind of on-field dissent over the past couple of years. Every team had been warned about their behaviour during the World Cup and Phil Neale, our team manager, had passed on another ICC directive before the Lord's Test reminding us of our responsibilities as international cricketers. We were told in no uncertain terms that our behaviour was being watched, and that if we stepped out of line we'd suffer the consequences. As a fan, I don't want to see characters removed from the game by over-zealous officials, but it was understandable they were trying to protect the sport's image.

ENGLAND V NEW ZEALAND (1ST TEST)

At Lord's, London

21, 22, 23, 24, 25 May 2015

ENGLAND WON BY 124 RUNS

Toss: New Zealand
Umpires: M.Erasmus (South Africa) and S.Ravi (India)
Referee: D.C.Boon (Australia)

ENGLAND

A.Lyth	c Watling b Southee	7	c Southee b Boult	12
* A.N.Cook	c Watling b Henry	16	c Latham b Boult	162
G.S.Ballance	c Southee b Boult	1	b Southee	0
I.R.Bell	b Henry	1	c Latham b Southee	29
J.E.Root	c Latham b Henry	98	c Boult b Henry	84
B.A.Stokes	b Craig	92	c Taylor b Craig	101
† J.C.Buttler	lbw b Boult	67	c Latham b Henry	14
M.M.Ali	c Latham b Boult	58	lbw b Boult	43
S.C.J.Broad	c Latham b Boult	3	b Boult	10
M.A.Wood	not out	8	not out	4
J.M.Anderson	c and b Henry	11	b Boult	0
Extras	(B 16, LB 6, W 2, NB 3)	27	(B 2, LB 12, W 5)	19
Total	**(100.5 overs)**	**389**	**(129 overs)**	**478**

NEW ZEALAND

M.J.Guptill	c Ballance b Broad	70	c Ballance b Anderson	0
T.W.M.Latham	lbw b Ali	59	lbw b Broad	0
K.S.Williamson	c Ballance b Ali	132	c Root b Stokes	27
L.R.P.L.Taylor	c Buttler b Broad	62	lbw b Broad	8
* B.B.McCullum	c Root b Wood	42	(6) b Stokes	0
C.J.Anderson	c Buttler b Wood	9	(7) lbw b Root	67
† B.J.Watling	not out	61	(5) c Buttler b Wood	59
M.D.Craig	lbw b Ali	0	b Stokes	4
T.G.Southee	c Wood b Anderson	11	c and b Ali	20
M.J.Henry	c Root b Wood	10	not out	10
T.A.Boult	c Anderson b Broad	0	c Ali b Broad	10
Extras	(B 26, LB 34, W 6, NB 1)	67	(B 5, LB 7, W 2, NB 1)	15
Total	**(131.2 overs)**	**523**	**(67.3 overs)**	**220**

NEW ZEALAND	O	M	R	W	O	M	R	W
Boult	29	6	79	4	34	8	85	5
Southee	24	1	104	1	34	4	162	2
Henry	24.5	3	93	4	29	3	106	2
Craig	18	2	77	1	28	3	96	1
Anderson	5	1	14	0	3	0	13	0
Williamson					1	0	2	0

ENGLAND	O	M	R	W	O	M	R	W
Anderson	29	7	88	1	14	5	31	1
Broad	26.2	4	77	3	16.3	3	50	3
Wood	27	2	93	3	13	3	47	1
Stokes	21	2	105	0	11	3	38	3
Ali	26	4	94	3	8	3	35	1
Root	2	0	6	0	5	3	7	1

FALL OF WICKETS

	E	NZ	E	NZ
WKT	1ST	1ST	2ND	2ND
1st	17	148	14	0
2nd	25	148	25	0
3rd	25	337	74	12
4th	30	403	232	61
5th	191	420	364	61
6th	251	470	389	168
7th	354	470	455	174
8th	363	493	467	198
9th	368	515	478	198
10th	389	523	478	220

CLOSE OF PLAY

Day 1	England (1) 354-7 (90; M.M.Ali 49*)
Day 2	New Zealand (1) 303-2 (77; K.S.Williamson 92*, L.R.P.L.Taylor 47*)
Day 3	England (2) 74-2 (26; A.N.Cook 32*, I.R.Bell 29*)
Day 4	England (2) 429-6 (118; A.N.Cook 153*, M.M.Ali 19*)

What McCullum and his men were doing didn't seem false or forced in the least. They seemed genuinely decent fellas who were happy to play their cricket hard but in the right spirit. It was very refreshing.

The next day the papers were pronouncing it one of England's best-ever Test wins, lavishing praise on us for the way we had twice wrestled control back from New Zealand when all hope appeared lost. Stokes was the new hero, and the future suddenly looked bright once more.

I took a minute to consider what Mooresy must have been thinking, watching it all play out.

We had a quick turnaround for the second and final Test of the series at Headingley. Yorkshire's Liam Plunkett was drafted into the squad as cover and we headed up to Leeds full of optimism.

The start was delayed by rain on the first morning and I was pretty happy when Cooky won the toss and bowled at a ground traditionally friendly to seam and swing bowling.

New Zealand brought in 33-year-old wicket-keeper/batsman Luke Ronchi for his debut while we kept the same side that won at Lord's, and when Jimmy reduced them to 2 for two – including having Guptill caught by Belly to become the first Englishman ever to take 400 Test wickets – it looked like we were going carry on from where we'd left off in London. It was yet another special moment to see Jimmy go past 400 wickets and I embraced my old friend when the celebrations died down. It was an amazing privilege to be on the field at that moment but, being only a few overs into a Test match, there was no time for getting emotional.

New Zealand dug in to score 350, with Ronchi contributing an excellent 88, and I was left with mixed emotions after picking up five for 109 while going at well over six an over in the process.

So much depended on this match for Lythy. Playing at his home ground in the final Test before the Ashes, he knew back-to-back failures would cause huge questions to be asked of him. Make runs, he was in. It was a pressure situation but he responded magnificently, scoring a well-constructed maiden hundred as he put on 177 with Cooky for the first wicket. You could see what it meant to him when he reached three figures at his home ground. This was boy's own stuff and we all stood and applauded him as he soaked up the adulation of his home crowd.

'No one can ever take that away from him,' I said after he was finally dismissed for 107.

Our final total of 350 was disappointing after being 215 for one with Gaz Ballance and Cooky at the crease. But once they were out, our cards folded far too cheaply, with only a breezy 51-run ninth-wicket stand between me and Woody gaining us parity after we slumped to 267 for eight, with Southee ripping out our middle order.

On a personal level it was satisfying to have made a meaningful contribution of 46 with the bat, but we should have had a first-innings lead – and we knew it.

I struck two more blows early in their second innings, removing Latham and Williamson cheaply, but Guptill steadied the ship alongside Taylor as they put on 99 for the third wicket.

We pushed hard for wickets, perhaps too hard, and started leaking runs at an alarming rate as Guptill (70), Taylor (48) and McCullum (55) all made telling contributions in quick time. When B.J.Watling, playing purely as a batsman because of an injured knee, smashed 120 from 163 balls, we knew we were in trouble.

By the time No.9 Tim Southee hit 40 from 24 balls, we had long since lost control of the match. When McCullum eventually declared on 454 for eight in their second innings, having scored at almost exactly five runs an over, we knew survival was our only hope.

Lythy and Cooky made it through to the close on day four on 44 for none and we talked a good game in the media that night about still having a chance to win. Realistically, not losing was our only hope. Lyth was out early on the final morning, before a deluge of wickets saw us slump to 153 for seven when Mo was bowled by Henry in the 63rd over. The game was as good as up.

Jos made an excellent 73 and I weighed in with 23 but was unable to play a sufficiently long innings. Jos was the last man out when he was LBW to Craig, leaving us all out for 255 off 91.5 overs. It was desperately disappointing after the incredible high at Lord's.

We shared a beer again with McCullum and his men that evening. This time we were the ones feeling sorry for ourselves, but it was an important step forward in team relations that McCullum had initiated at Lord's. The series had been played in fantastic spirit and we all agreed the post-Test beers shared between the teams were a welcome development.

We were kicking ourselves for letting another series slip from our grasp. The euphoria of Lord's had not been diminished altogether, but this defeat meant it had faded a little. For now, we were pretty low.

Ashes talk ramped up again, but the Aussies could wait. There was still a five-match one-day series against New Zealand to play first and no one could possibly have predicted its significance.

ENGLAND V NEW ZEALAND (2ND TEST)

At Headingley, Leeds

29, 30, 31 May, 1, 2 June 2015

NEW ZEALAND WON BY 199 RUNS

Toss: England
Umpires: S.Ravi (India) and R.J.Tucker (Australia)
Referee: D.C.Boon (Australia)

NEW ZEALAND

M.J.Guptill	c Bell b Anderson	0	(2) c Root b Wood	70
T.W.M.Latham	c Root b Broad	84	(1) c Buttler b Broad	3
K.S.Williamson	c Buttler b Anderson	0	c Buttler b Broad	6
L.R.P.L.Taylor	lbw b Broad	20	c Stokes b Wood	48
* B.B.McCullum	c Wood b Stokes	41	lbw b Wood	55
B.J.Watling	b Wood	14	c Root b Anderson	120
† L.Ronchi	c Anderson b Broad	88	c Buttler b Anderson	31
M.D.Craig	not out	41	not out	58
T.G.Southee	c Lyth b Wood	1	c Anderson b Ali	40
M.J.Henry	c Buttler b Broad	27	not out	12
T.A.Boult	c Lyth b Broad	15		
Extras	(B 4, LB 14, NB 1)	19	(B 4, LB 6, W 1)	11
Total	**(72.1 overs)**	**350**	**(8 wkts dec; 91 overs)**	**454**

ENGLAND

A.Lyth	run out	107	c Ronchi b Boult	24
* A.N.Cook	lbw b Craig	75	lbw b Williamson	56
G.S.Ballance	b Boult	29	b Boult	6
I.R.Bell	c Craig b Southee	12	c Williamson b Craig	1
J.E.Root	c Ronchi b Southee	1	c Latham b Craig	0
B.A.Stokes	c Craig b Boult	6	c Ronchi b Williamson	29
† J.C.Buttler	c Taylor b Southee	10	lbw b Craig	73
M.M.Ali	c Guptill b Southee	1	b Henry	2
S.C.J.Broad	b Henry	46	b Williamson	23
M.A.Wood	c Ronchi b Craig	19	c Craig b Southee	17
J.M.Anderson	not out	10	not out	8
Extras	(B 19, LB 5, W 5, NB 5)	34	(B 12, LB 2, W 2)	16
Total	**(108.2 overs)**	**350**	**(91.5 overs)**	**255**

ENGLAND	O	M	R	W	O	M	R	W
Anderson	13	3	43	2	23	4	96	2
Broad	17.1	0	109	5	16	1	94	2
Wood	14	4	62	2	19	2	97	3
Stokes	17	4	70	1	12	1	61	0
Ali	11	3	48	0	16	0	73	1
Root					5	0	23	0

NEW ZEALAND	O	M	R	W		O	M	R	W
Boult	30	7	98	2		23	4	61	2
Southee	30	5	83	4		18	7	43	1
Henry	20.2	4	92	1	(4)	12	2	49	1
Craig	26	12	48	2	(3)	31.5	12	73	3
Williamson	2	1	5	0		7	1	15	3

FALL OF WICKETS

WKT	NZ 1ST	E 1ST	NZ 2ND	E 2ND
1st	2	177	15	47
2nd	2	215	23	61
3rd	68	238	122	62
4th	123	239	141	62
5th	144	247	262	102
6th	264	257	315	141
7th	265	266	368	153
8th	281	267	435	188
9th	310	318	-	230
10th	350	350	-	255

CLOSE OF PLAY

Day 1	New Zealand (1) 297-8 (65; M.D.Craig 16*, M.J.Henry 14*)
Day 2	England (1) 253-5 (88; I.R.Bell 12*, J.C.Buttler 6*)
Day 3	New Zealand (2) 338-6 (75; B.J.Watling 100*, M.D.Craig 15*)
Day 4	England (2) 44-0 (13; A.Lyth 24*, A.N.Cook 18*)

6

ENGLAND UNSHACKLED

THE AUSSIES TOUCH DOWN 4–30 JUNE

I was given notice shortly after the Headingley Test that I wouldn't be involved in the one-day series against New Zealand as the selectors looked to manage my workload with a packed schedule ahead. I was keen to play, of course, but I understood their reasons.

Andrew Strauss assured me I remained in England's white-ball plans but that it was in the best interests of the Test side that I took a rest. I fully accepted the decision though I explained that I was very keen to play in the next World Cup in 2019. I was just about to turn 29, but I was a 100 per cent certain I still had a few years left in which I could make a positive contribution to the one-day side.

Following our disastrous World Cup campaign, there had been a clamour for a clear-out of senior players from the underperforming one-day side. A completely fresh start was demanded by some.

Eoin Morgan had come in for an awful lot of stick. I thought a lot of it was harsh, considering how little time he'd been given to prepare before the tournament. But results had been so catastrophic it was inevitable he'd feel some heat. World Cups have a habit of seeing off

England one-day skippers, certainly in recent times, and it would have been the easy decision for Strauss to wipe the slate clean and start all over again with a new captain and team.

While Morgs hadn't been captain long enough for any serious judgements to be passed on his leadership credentials, his batting form was counting against him. He'd proved over the years that he was unquestionably an outstanding international one-day player – although it still baffles me why he hasn't been able to transfer that to the Test arena, despite a couple of brilliant contributions including a top-class hundred against Pakistan in 2010 – but he'd scored just 90 runs at an average of 18 during the World Cup at an unusually low strike rate of less than 65.

But, just as he did with Cooky in the Test arena, Strauss decided to keep faith with Morgs, giving him his public backing as the man to lead England's one-day revival. With so much desire for change, it would not prove to be an especially popular decision in the short term. But it was the right one, which showed leadership from Strauss amid all the knee-jerk calls for change.

The decision to retain Morgs as one-day captain also had consequences for me. Straussy phoned me one day while I was out walking the dogs. He told me he'd decided that Morgs should captain both the one-day and Twenty20 sides and he'd be relieving me of the Twenty20 captaincy with immediate effect. He thanked me for the four years I'd done the job and assured me it wasn't a personal decision, but one based on the best interests of English cricket as a whole. He also said his decision was final. I was disappointed, of course. No one ever willingly gives up the England captaincy in any format. But, in typical Strauss fashion, his reasoning was impeccable.

Strauss was firmly of the view that the one-day and Twenty20 sides needed to come closer together in terms of playing personnel, style and method. Quite reasonably, he believed it made sense to have one captain across the two formats to deliver the same message. He had a vision to create quite separate white and red-ball England teams and was eager to unify the Twenty20 and one-day sides under one captain: Morgs.

Having had stints in the IPL with the Bangalore Royal Challengers, Kolkata Knight Riders and Sunrisers Hyderabad, as well playing in Australia's hugely successful Big Bash competition with Sydney Thunder, Morgs was one of England's most experienced Twenty20 players. His innovative shot-making and explosive power made him something of a novelty when he burst onto the international scene. Now, with the entire one-day game having undergone a revolution in run-rates and shot-making, that novelty had become a necessity. He is a top bloke and if I was going to hand over the one-day reins to anybody, I was happy it was him. I wished Morgs well with the T20 captaincy and refocused my thoughts on honing my game for the Ashes.

While I wasn't going to be involved in the one-day team to play New Zealand, I was utterly fascinated with how the series would pan out. Our dramatic Lord's Test win had captured the public's imagination because of our no-fear approach and there's no doubt the way Brendon McCullum's men had approached the series had encouraged us to cast off our shackles, too. We got it badly wrong in the second Test at Headingley, but that defeat had received a fairer hearing in the media than previous losses. There seemed to be an understanding that if we were going to attempt to play this style of cricket, sometimes the wheels would come off in spectacular fashion. But it felt as if the press and the public were prepared to cut us some slack as long as we went out with all guns blazing.

Having been part of the brutally honest meeting in Sydney at the end of the World Cup, when the players admitted we were embarrassed at the manner in which we had lost, I was convinced the upcoming one-day series would see a massive shift in our approach.

I was sorry I wouldn't be part of it, but at the same time excited by the prospect of watching a young England team containing free-spirited players such as Jos Buttler, Ben Stokes, Alex Hales, Joe Root and Moeen Ali, as well as Surrey's exciting opener Jason Roy, strut their stuff. Ian Bell, Jimmy Anderson and I had all been given time off to rest and get ourselves in shape for the Ashes. Aged 33, Belly would call time on his one-day career at the end of the summer, although Jimmy and I both harbour ambitions to return to that format in an England shirt.

Paul Farbrace had started to feed a few messages through from Trevor Bayliss during the New Zealand series and I had no doubt that he would continue to do so through the one-day series. The pair had worked together for two years when Bayliss had been in charge of Sri Lanka and it was interesting to hear Farbs' view of our new coach. I'm sure Trev also found it helpful to be able to communicate with us through Farbs before he was physically in position to do so. The over-riding theme coming from our new coach was: 'Keep expressing yourselves and play your natural game.' Farbs was very much of that mindset, too.

In the build-up to the one-day series, I cast an eye back towards the Caribbean where Australia were making relatively light work of the

West Indies in their two-Test series. They won the first Test in Dominica convincingly by nine wickets, with their three-man pace attack of Mitchell Johnson, Mitchell Starc and Josh Hazlewood doing the majority of the damage as the West Indies were twice bowled out cheaply. I was pleased to see my old mate from Notts, Adam Voges, score his maiden Test hundred on debut in that game, too. Vogesy may have been 35, but clearly you're never too old to score your first Test hundred.

A week later, the Aussies repeated the dose with a dominant performance in Jamaica that saw Steve Smith score 199 to continue the remarkable form that had seen him rise to the top of world Test batting rankings. The West Indies capitulated in the second innings as Australia won by 277 runs. Their 2-0 series win, coming so soon after we'd drawn 1-1 there, was predictably seized on as evidence they would have too much firepower us for us in the Ashes. To me, it was just another reminder that we were about to go up against a formidable team. But at home, in English conditions, I firmly believed they were beatable. I'd already won three Ashes series and possessed none of the mental baggage some England players had built up around the Australians in the 1990s and early 2000s.

Before then, Morgs and his team had the Black Caps to face in a five-match one-day series. Only a few months earlier during our World Cup match, McCullum had absolutely destroyed our attack after we'd folded so meekly with the bat. The tourists went into the series as firm favourites.

They'd underperformed in the World Cup final, when Australia had beaten them by seven wickets with almost 17 overs to spare in what turned out to be a bit of a non-contest. But there was no questioning their credentials as one of the best one-day sides in the world. In McCullum they had the most innovative skipper in the game. During the Test series we'd observed them close up and their freedom of spirit had influenced the way we played. They look like they're having great fun and we asked ourselves 'what's stopping us from doing that?' We soon concluded, the answer was 'nothing'.

> 'For a long time now, we've been behind the eight-ball in one-day cricket and fallen behind by a long way,' he said. 'It's time for a catch-up.'

While I would love to watch every single ball bowled on television, the reality is that on the rare occasions I get a little bit of down time as an international sportsman there are always things to keep me occupied.

For starters, I had plenty of technical work to do in the nets, while I was also keen to work on my general fitness ahead of the Ashes.

It was interesting to hear Morgs interviewed before the series. He sounded bullish, no doubt emboldened by Strauss's public backing: 'For a long time now, we've been behind the eight-ball in one-day cricket and fallen behind by a long way,' he said. 'It's time for a catch-up.'

The first one-dayer was a day-night game at Edgbaston. I spent the afternoon working with Ottis Gibson and had seen the boys were going along relatively well at 50 for one from seven overs. Halesy and Rooty looked to have things reasonably under control. With a proper workout to be done and my own bowling to attend to, I didn't check in again for a couple more hours. When I got home, I turned on the television and almost dropped the controller when I saw the score. Adil Rashid was walking off the pitch with the crowd in a sense of delirium and the score reading 394 for nine with three balls remaining. No wonder they were going ballistic.

Liam Plunkett, who hadn't faced a ball yet, then proceeded to smash two huge sixes off Grant Elliott's last three deliveries as England closed their innings on 408 for nine from 50 overs.

'Have you seen the bloody score?' I texted Neil Fairbrother.

'Yes! And have you seen who got the runs?'

I looked down the scorecard and saw Rooty had hit 104 from 78 balls while Jos had gone even better in smashing 129 from 77 balls at an astonishing strike rate of 166.53. No wonder Harv was happy, Jos and Rooty were also part of his ISM stable. His boys had done good!

Jos's hundred had come off just 66 balls and was the second fastest England one-day hundred of all time, behind the one he'd scored against Sri Lanka off 61 balls the year before. Not bad for a bloke who'd only been playing regular international cricket for a couple of years.

Talk about turning the formbook on its head. We'd identified 350 as a minimum target too late at the World Cup, but by scoring 400 it really was making a statement that the boys had embraced one-day cricket's brave new world. I was absolutely made up for them and settled down on the sofa to see how our bowlers would respond under the lights.

I love playing at Edgbaston and I was suddenly really envious of the lads going out to bowl with the crowd going absolutely berserk. The atmosphere looked amazing and the boys looked really pumped up as they took the field.

McCullum and Martin-Guptill got going at a decent lick before Steven Finn bowled the New Zealand captain when he charged down the track at him. I was chuffed for Finny. He'd taken an absolute monstering from McCullum in the World Cup and he must have taken a great deal of satisfaction from that wicket.

Wickets continued to tumble at regular intervals as New Zealand struggled to keep up with the eight-an-over run rate, and Finny and Adil both finished with four-wicket hauls as England won by a thumping 210 runs.

It turned out England's total of 408 – beating our previous record of 391 against Bangladesh in 2005 – was only the 16th ever score in excess of 400. Notably, five of those scores had come in 2015. The winds of change were blowing hard.

Unsurprisingly, the manner of England's win received huge acclaim with talk of a new dawn for English one-day cricket. We'd heard that before, to be fair, but this did feel different.

The next game at The Oval produced yet more sensational cricket, but this time it was New Zealand's turn to bat first and run up a huge total. Ross Taylor was their destroyer-in-chief as he clobbered 119 not out from 96 balls to provide the cornerstone to New Zealand's total of 398 for five from 50 overs.

It was a massive target to chase, but at 100 for one from 15 overs the boys were going along nicely before Root and Hales both fell in the space of three balls.

Even as the wickets fell, the boys kept on backing themselves and a wonderful knock from Morgs, with support from the lower order, so nearly saw them home to a revised Duckworth-Lewis target of 379 from 46 overs. Morgs smashed six sixes and six fours in making 88 from 47 balls. Eventually England fell 14 runs short of the target but still received a great ovation from a crowd that had loved every minute of a thrilling match.

It was noticeable the next day that, once again, the coverage of the defeat was more positive than I would normally expect, with a lot of the commentators and reporters commending England's fearless approach.

I texted Cooky that evening. I knew he'd be tucked away on his farm and probably wouldn't reply but sent it anyway.

'This is pretty special isn't it, mate? Are you watching?' I asked. He definitely would have been. It was catching everyone's attention.

I also wanted to run a couple of ideas I had on how to get Steven Smith out past Cook. I wanted to see if he thought they might work, before I went away and practised it. As it happened, he did.

The one-day series continued to captivate, although England's total of 302 at the Rose Bowl looked relatively pedestrian by comparison with the first two matches. Morgs and Stokesy were in the runs this time. Kane Williamson and Taylor both scored hundreds in response and the Black Caps were cruising to victory on 242 for two in the 39th over before Northants all-rounder David Willey – playing only his second ODI after making his debut in the washed-out game in Ireland a few weeks before – had Williamson caught by Mark Wood to spark a mini-collapse that also saw him bowl Taylor to leave New Zealand 290 for six.

They did eventually get across the winning line with three wickets and six balls to spare, but once again England were praised for the style of cricket they'd played, albeit in a losing cause.

At 2-1 in the five-match series, England were staring down the barrel of a series defeat when New Zealand posted a whopping 349 for seven at Trent Bridge in the penultimate match. The boys appeared to have New Zealand under control at 271 for five in the 44th over, before Grant Elliott and Mitchell Santner cut loose at the end, giving Adil some serious tap in the final overs. In the not too distant past, chasing down a victory target of 350 would have been absolutely unthinkable. But this series, off the back of the World Cup, had shown that one-day batting would never be the same again. Previous assumptions about run rates and targets had been torn up completely.

I'd been lucky enough to play a round of golf at the Belfry that morning with my former team-mate Steve Harmison. We'd enjoyed a lovely round on a course that has staged some of the great Ryder Cup battles down the years. It was certainly too good for us. I'd kept tabs on New Zealand's innings via the ECB app on my phone while we were out on the course and we sat down to watch the closing overs of New Zealand's innings in the clubhouse after finishing off.

We had spoken at length on the walk round about the similarities in the build-ups between now and the 2005 Ashes series. Then, Michael Vaughan had settled on a five-man attack with four pace bowlers all offering different things to their captain. Harmy offered raw pace delivered from a great height, while Simon Jones was skiddy and could reverse swing the ball, Fred Flintoff was quick and at the batsman all the time, while Matthew Hoggard was a master swing bowler. Their spin bowler, Ashley Giles, was relatively unfancied by the media but went on to play a key role in the series.

But more than anything, that 2005 series – up there with the greatest in Ashes history – was teed up by England's ultra-aggressive approach to the one-day series that preceded it, with Paul Collingwood going toe-to-toe with Matthew Hayden of all people and Kevin Pietersen announcing himself in spectacular style.

Harmy and I marvelled at England's fearless approach to the current series as we went around the Belfry. We both agreed Farbs' input was important while Strauss's decision to back Morgs as captain had given him the belief he was in for the long haul. Most importantly, we finally had a group of players whose default position was to throw caution to the wind and go on the attack. We were loving the way England were approaching their cricket.

Despite our optimism on the course, our chat was quickly forgotten as we watched New Zealand make mincemeat of England's bowlers in the final five overs. When they reached 350, I'm sorry to say we both believed it was 30 or 40 too many. But what on earth did we know?

Not only did England chase down 350 to win, they chased it down with ease. Jason Roy and Halesy teed things up with a 100-run stand from 10.4 overs – with Halesy crashing seven fours and four sixes in the process of making 67 from 38 balls – before Morgs and Rooty both scored magnificent hundreds to see off New Zealand by seven wickets and with six overs to spare. Morgs' 113 came off 82 balls with 12 fours and five sixes while Rooty made 106 at from a relatively leisurely 97 balls. It was an astonishing result.

I listened in the car on the drive back from Sutton Coldfield to Nottingham and had a beaming smile on my face for the entire journey home. This was precisely the style of cricket we'd talked about playing in Sydney. Yes, it had come too late for the World Cup, but it felt like a tipping point had been reached. It felt as if English cricket had finally cast off its shackles. If scoring 408 in the first game wasn't astounding enough, chasing down 350 with six overs to spare was utterly out of this world. Finally, the one-day penny had dropped.

The media were lavishing praise on the team and there were brilliant scenes of a full house at Trent Bridge going absolutely potty as first Roy and Hales and then Morgs and Root just smashed the ball to all parts. It was fantastic to watch back on the Sky highlights that night. The atmosphere had been electric. I fast forwarded a few weeks in my mind to the fourth Test to be played at Trent Bridge. Wouldn't it be great to generate similar scenes among the crowd in an Ashes Test? I thought. Now that really would be something.

I pondered the conversation I'd had with Harmy. The more I thought about it, the more the comparisons between 2005 and this year made sense. I felt our attack had as much variety as the 2005 attack, with Woody similar to Simon Jones and Jimmy offering the swing that Hoggy had. I offered the height and hit-the-deck bounce of Harmy – although admittedly I didn't have his pace – while Stokesy was our street-fighter who could get among the Aussies in the same way Fred had. Mo, like Gilo, was underrated. But we knew his qualities.

Where our side differed to Vaughany's was that we hadn't been battle hardened the way they had by winning Test series home and away over an extended period. But it was less than three years since we'd won in India – which Vaughan's team hadn't managed to do – and there were enough of us in the dressing room with memories of that series. We also had guys in the team who had won multiple Ashes series and, despite the 5-0 hiding 18 months before, saw the Aussies for what they were: blokes like us.

That evening I received an email from the ECB Operations team inviting me to attend a camp in Spain a week or so later. It seems Straussy was planning a little team-bonding weekend. There were almost no other details other than we had to meet at Birmingham International Airport at 1pm the following Friday. We were told to bring training kit and leisurewear but no actual cricket kit. Bowlers were told to bring bowling boots and golf clubs. At least that showed there would be some down time.

The emphasis apparently was going to be on fitness and fielding. I also noted with interest the inclusion of Derbyshire left-arm quick Mark Footitt on the 14-man mailing list, while Adil Rashid was not named. Most concluded these were the players who would take on Australia, although Strauss made it clear Adil was still in contention for the Cardiff Test, despite not being included in the 14-man party that travelled to Spain.

The squad that would travel to Spain was as follows: Cook, Ali, Anderson, Ballance, Bell, Broad, Buttler, Finn, Footitt, Lyth, Plunkett, Root, Stokes, Wood.

I looked down the list and liked what I saw. These were boys I wanted to go into battle with.

An ECB press release gave Straussy the chance to outline the purpose of the camp: 'With Trevor Bayliss arriving in the country next Thursday, Trevor, Alastair and I felt it important that both players and management likely to be involved in the early stages of the Investec Ashes have a chance to meet him and fully understand his approach prior to meeting up for the start of the Test series,' Strauss said.

'With that in mind, we have arranged a preparation camp in Spain. This will involve a combination of physical and fielding sessions and planning meetings in an informal environment in order to provide the best possible lead up to the first Test in Cardiff.'

There was also the final one-day international left for the boys to play before we left for Spain, while I was due to play for Nottinghamshire in the County Championship. But news of the Spain trip had certainly got everyone talking.

People were also excited about the ongoing one-day series, which had been utterly spellbinding up to that point. The fifth and final match, to be played at Durham, was eagerly anticipated. Yorkshire's Jonny Bairstow replaced Jos behind the stumps after he picked up a hand injury at Trent Bridge. After assessing the conditions, Morgs won the toss and asked New Zealand to bat first at an overcast Chester-le-Street.

In bowler-friendly conditions, New Zealand's total of 283 for nine from 50 overs looked a challenging one in spite of the massive scores that had been routinely posted through the series so far. When rain hit, the target was reduced to 192 from 26 overs under the Duckworth-Lewis system and the game looked well and truly up for England as the top order chanced their collective arms and came a cropper. At 45 for five in the ninth over, the writing once again looked on the wall.

But, yet again, England refused to accept defeat as Bairstow (83 not out from 60 balls) and another relative newcomer Sam Billings (43 from 30 balls), produced what turned out to be a match-winning partnership.

With 17 needed from the final 12 balls, McCullum entrusted debutant Black Cap Andrew Mathieson with the penultimate over.

Jonny struck two crisp drives over extra-cover before Adil hit another four with a dab past short third man. Bairstow completed victory with a sliced drive past backward point, and the boys went absolutely bananas on the balcony. It was a fabulous way to end one of the most extraordinary one-day series ever played on these shores.

The following week I played a championship game for Nottinghamshire against Yorkshire at Headingley. From a personal point of view, things couldn't really have gone any better as I celebrated my 29th birthday by taking seven for 84 before making a rapid-fire 50 from 46 balls. But while things went to plan personally, for the team they went horribly wrong. We lost, heavily. Our defeat, by an innings and 8 runs, left us rooted to the foot of the Division One table and, as our coach Mick Newell admitted, in a relegation dogfight. It was tough leaving the dressing room after a defeat like that, knowing I wouldn't be available to pull my weight again until the end of August at the earliest. By then it could be too late. There was a lot of cricket to be played in every sense over the course of the next few weeks. However, it was a nice time to take a big haul and make a statement, because guess who had just landed in England? Michael Clarke's Australians.

A week after Nottinghamshire's defeat to Yorkshire, director of cricket Mick Newell announced that Peter Moores would be joining the club as a coaching consultant for the rest of the summer after the match against Worcestershire. I was delighted for Mooresy and the club that he'd been identified as someone who was in a position to take the club forward. Mick has done a phenomenal job in the 13 years he's been in charge and he admitted to questioning whether it was time for the players to hear a fresh voice and fresh ideas. It was a very mature approach and demonstrated an unselfish big-picture attitude that typifies Mick.

'A lot of those players have had to listen to me for a long time,' he told the press. 'You start to wonder if you're having a positive influence on the team. We felt it was a good time to shake it up and bring someone new in. It seemed a no-brainer. This team is looking for something and we hope it's the start of something to boost us. The players were a bit surprised, but I hope it inspires them. Players who want to improve will thrive under him.'

Mick would retain his hands-on duties, including selection, but Mooresy would take a significant role on the coaching and team-building side. As had been the case in every other job he'd taken in county cricket to that point – with Sussex and Lancashire, where he'd become the first coach ever to win the County Championship with two separate counties – his arrival would mark the beginning of a dramatic upturn in fortunes for Nottinghamshire. Remarkably, following that low against Yorkshire, and with Mooresy installed, Notts went on to finish third in the table, winning five of their last seven championship fixtures. Coincidence?

Aside from playing golf with Harmy, I also spent a lot of time while the boys were tied up with the one-day series working with Ottis at Trent Bridge on bowling around the wicket at left-handers. With one of the Ashes Tests being played in Nottingham, where the groundstaff are incredibly helpful, it made sense for me to do as much work there as I possibly could rather than at the Performance Centre in Loughborough.

With Chris Rogers and David Warner opening up for Australia and Mitchell Johnson and Mitchell Starc lower down the order, we knew the tourists would have at least four left-handers in their line-up. It made sense to work out precisely how I was going to bowl at them in Tests, rather than practising leg-cutters and Yorkers playing white-ball cricket.

I bowled around the wicket for hours on end, with Ottis observing and talking me through what he was seeing. The whole purpose of the exercise was to get my chest going towards the stumps and not the wicket-keeper, which can happen for a right-armer coming around the wicket. The ploy probably earned me ten wickets over the series. Those are the kinds of things people don't see – no spectators in the ground, trucking in on your own for hours on end, bowling at a cone while one bloke watches on – that can actually win you a series.

Those are the kinds of things people don't see ... that can actually win you a series.

The sessions I spent with Ottis were special, a good example of the technical side of coaching where he is at his best. Ottis knows my bowling as well as anyone.

When it had first been mooted that Straussy was going to take us away to Spain for a long weekend of team bonding, there had been a fair few grumbles. The trip was scheduled for the last weekend of June, meaning it would remove us from the final round of championship matches ahead of the Ashes. A few of the bowlers probably would have preferred one last run out before the Ashes to ensure they were fully in the groove. The camp meant Jimmy would go into the first Ashes Test in Cardiff starting on 8 July without a playing a first-class game in almost six weeks.

I was intrigued by the upcoming trip. I'd been away on pre-Ashes trips three times before. Two of them had been overwhelmingly worthwhile.

The other, in 2013, had involved a bizarre role-play exercise run by ex-SAS guys that saw us driving around Stoke all night after being tasked with tracking down a fake criminal and preventing a mock crime. But more of that later.

I trusted Straussy to deliver a camp that benefited the squad, but inevitably there was an element of trepidation about stepping into the unknown. In the end, the trip proved to be an absolute master-stroke. We gathered at Birmingham for the flight to Alicante in southern Spain. There were a few nervous exchanges on the flight because we really didn't know what to expect. Those of us who'd been on previous bonding camps had mixed experiences to say the least.

When we landed, we had a two-hour coach ride out to the resort where we were going to be staying for the next four days.

Straussy was already there and he let us know what to expect soon after we arrived. He was keen to stress that while he wanted the trip to be fun, it was also going to be hard work and required us all to buy into it. He made it clear that it definitely wasn't intended to be a holiday but it also wasn't going to be a beasting session. From the word go, things seemed purposeful and well organised.

On a previous occasion, in 2010, we'd been to Bavaria, when the boys had worked hard on their fitness and gained a hell of a lot of mental toughness from the trip and benefited enormously from it. Everyone that is except Jimmy, who had one of his ribs broken in a boxing bout with Chris Tremlett.

The boxing competition had drawn a huge amount of criticism after Jimmy's unfortunate injury emerged. I didn't have to worry about it too long as I'd lost in the first round to Steve Davies. At 6ft 7in tall and built like a prizefighter, we were all terrified of being drawn to take on Tremlett, but Strauss ended up winning it by ducking, diving and brawling his way to victory. I told you he was a tough so-and-so!

That Bavaria trip was hard work and taken very seriously by a group of players committed to being there. We did more than 1,000 press-ups in four days. I remember one point on that trip we'd been told we all had to address each other formally as 'Mr Strauss' or 'Mr Broad'. As we were marching, Paul Collingwood was overheard saying 'Straussy' by one of the Australian police who were leading the course and we all had to stop marching immediately, put our rucksacks on the floor and do a hundred press-ups as Colly – or Mr Collingwood I should say – counted them out. It was a brutal four days and the boys were absolutely shattered by the end. They'd wake us up at 4am and have us outside in the rain doing star jumps carrying bricks in our hands with spotlights flying around. Strauss said to me after that trip he had no idea it was going to be as hard as it was and if he'd known, he'd have tapered it back. Having said that, we got a massive amount out of that trip and it definitely had a positive long-term effect on the squad.

In 2009, we were taken to the First World War battlefields of Belgium where we laid wreaths at the Menin Gate Memorial to the Missing in Ypres and visited some of the many cemeteries in the area. It was an utterly humbling experience and, barring a couple of travel mess-ups involving Ravi Bopara and Fred, passed off without any significant problems. All of us agreed it had broadened our horizons and given a different view of what leadership actually involved.

Three years later, ahead of the 2013-14 Ashes series, we were taken on another pre-Ashes camp, but this one was a disaster. It was meant to be a big exercise in surveillance and counter-insurgency run by a bunch of former SAS soldiers. It turned into a complete farce. The organisation just wasn't there and we spent hours and hours in a classroom. Four days before we were due to embark on a three-month tour of Australia, we were sitting in a classroom in Stoke trying to work out how to use dodgy radios, some of which had run out of batteries.

We were all essentially on the same side, with a mission to stop this bloke committing a crime, but we all had different roles to play to achieve our mission.

As we attempted to track down this criminal, I was assigned the job of navigator to Stokesy, who was a designated driver. We literally spent three days driving around Stoke. We hardly even got out of the car. It was utterly miserable. Our bowling coach, David Saker, packed it in and went home halfway through. One evening it was arranged that we'd meet at 6pm for an evening drink to raise spirits. We got to the bar only to be told it couldn't serve alcohol until 7pm. Everything that could have gone wrong did go wrong.

There were a couple of amusing moments. But they were born out of farce rather than planned entertainment. One night Stokesy and I found ourselves parked up at 5am in some back alley in Stoke, supposedly setting up a surveillance position on a terraced house on a side road. We didn't know what the hell we were doing and I even managed to get myself told off for not using the phonetic alphabet correctly over the radio. My team was Team Hotel and we were given instruction only to use the phonetic alphabet during radio contact. In the end we were throwing all sorts of nonsense out there as long as it finished in Team Hotel.

'Team Blackhawk down alpha bravo potato onion samosa five niner golf course mike, Team Hotel, over' was one particularly memorable call. Kevin Pietersen was having a lot of fun over the mike along with the rest of us. It kept us amused as we drove round and round for hours on end. Eventually, we were given a polite reminder that we must adhere to radio etiquette.

'What the hell are we doing here?' Stokesy groaned at one point, easing back in the driver's seat of our black Ford Focus and putting his feet on the dashboard.

'I have absolutely no idea, mate,' I replied wearily.

As we were talking, an upstairs window of one of the terraced houses on the street we were meant to be observing opened and this bloke poked his head out of his bathroom window. He couldn't have been more than five metres away from us. Not having a clue we were there, he proceeded to light up a big joint and began happily puffing away.

Stokesy and I looked at each other and, without speaking, both decided to put our car windows up at the same time. We wanted to keep hidden, but the bloke spotted us and must have assumed we were police – rather than two England cricketers on some made-up surveillance course. He completely panicked, shutting the window in double-quick time before hastily turning out the lights. If you're reading this now, mate, don't worry I can't remember your address.

The sense of farce continued when we were all tasked with following our mystery suspect. The surveillance team had to track him and we followed him into a pub on the edge of Stoke. It was utterly surreal. At one point you had me, Stokesy, Boyd Rankin, Matt Prior, Alastair Cook and KP sitting in a pub in Stoke in the middle of the afternoon trying to listen in on this guy's conversation. God knows what the other punters must have made of it.

While we were inside the pub observing the suspect, Jonathan Trott had been posted outside to watch the exits like a hawk. His role was to track the criminal as he left the location and direct other surveillance units, who could then continue to track him. It was made clear to Trotty that this was a vital role, and he should keep his ear close to the radio at all times and listen out for instructions. As the criminal moved out of the pub, the message was sent that Trotty needed to be alert.

'Team Foxtrot, this is Team Hotel, over. Suspect is on the move. Repeat, suspect is on the move. Do you copy, over?'

Nothing.

'Team Foxtrot, this is Team Hotel, over. Suspect is on the move. Repeat, suspect is on the move. Do you copy, over?'

Again, nothing.

With the suspect gone, we moved stealthily outside, with the rest of the punters no doubt wondering what on earth was going on. Trotty was sat on the other side of the road, whistling away.

'Trotty? What happened? Where did he go?'

Trotty just looked at us blankly.

Didn't you hear the radio?'

Nothing.

'Trotty, the suspect is on the move. We called you on the radio to tell you.'

'Oh, shit. Sorry, boys. I was signing an autograph.'

We groaned, and the farce continued. To be honest, it felt like that camp just fell apart. There were things about it I questioned all the way through. We'd training incredibly hard leading into it and then just ate fish and chips and samosas for three days. We were meant to be athletes, for goodness sake. Blokes who had families were not especially impressed by having to spend their final three nights in the UK on a made-up surveillance mission in Stoke.

In fact, it was so bad, we didn't even bother to review it. No one had bought into it. It was just brushed under the carpet. Our coach, Andy Flower, even apologised to us later for how disorganised it had been.

Was it an indicator the wheels were falling off before the tour even began? I don't know. But it was a bit of a disaster.

This time, in Spain, it couldn't have been more different. Everyone was desperate to be there and from minute one the trip felt organised purposeful and full of energy. We had four-bedroom villas in a place called Desert Springs. I shared a villa with Cooky, Belly and Jimmy, while the management team of Trev, Farby and Straussy shared another one. The other lads were split between two other villas.

Some people were suggesting the trip would be a bit of a jolly and a couple of the Aussies made comments about it being a holiday, but that was nonsense. Yes, it was relatively relaxed, but it was also action-packed and full of purpose. Within half an hour of arriving, we were off on a ten-mile mountain bike ride, which for those of us who are not cyclists was bloody hard work.

The trip struck a good balance between fun and hard work. We did everything from fitness, running, cycling, football and golf with the odd meeting thrown in to discuss cricket. A lot of the focus was on fielding and especially our catching.

Cooky seemed really enthused at the prospect of the trip. He was very much of the view that we should harness the momentum that had built up during the one-day series against New Zealand and not look too far behind or too far ahead. He reiterated Trevor's message that we had a group of players whose natural instinct was to be positive and aggressive on the cricket field, so why try to change that?

It was brilliant to be able to get away from everything and bond properly together as a squad without any distractions. For a lot of the guys, this was going to be their first Ashes series and it was helpful for us more senior players to be able to explain what to expect. For an English cricketer, nothing comes close to the scrutiny and attention you come under when you're playing in an Ashes series. It is unlike anything else you experience as a player and light years away from county cricket. Those of us who'd played in a few were keen to articulate that to the younger lads in the squad. Every single tweet, comment or press conference quote is pored over and analysed with a magnifying glass. Things can escalate incredibly quickly. The aim certainly wasn't to overawe them, but it was important they knew what to expect.

On the first day we were there I had a good chat with Woody. We'd grown quite close in Potchefstroom when I think he appreciated a chat we had when I let him know he was one of the players being talked about in the England dressing room as a prospect. Still uncapped at the time, he thought he was miles away. So he was reassured to know he was on the players' radars. I'd been delighted to see him take nine wickets in his first two Tests against New Zealand and I was keen to offer him support and advice wherever I could.

For an English cricketer, nothing comes close to the scrutiny and attention you come under when you're playing in an Ashes series.

He was a bit down that some comments he'd made about Shane Watson to his friend Steve Harmison on the radio had been picked up. He'd given a wide-ranging interview covering everything from being a teetotaller to preferring football to cricket when he was a lad. At one point in the interview, he innocently recalled a story of the time he was called up as a teenage net bowler at Durham academy when the Aussies were in town and Mike Hussey instructed him to bowl a couple of bouncers at Watson. He added that Watson hadn't been very happy and called him a 'net hero'. It wasn't meant to be an attack on the Aussie, but inevitably it was written up that way.

Woody's entirely innocent comments generated a bit of a stroppy response from Watson the next day and the youngster was worried he'd stirred up trouble he hadn't intended. He was getting a load of grief on Twitter, with people saying he had no right as such a rookie player to have a go at a bloke who'd played more than 50 Tests. He hadn't meant it and it upset him a bit, but it illustrated the point that little things could get blown out of proportion.

I completely understood what he was going through. The day before we'd taken off, I'd made some comments where I'd said our best chance of getting Steve Smith out cheaply was if he batted at No.3, not No.5. My point was that, fantastic player that he is, he does have an unusual technique and tends to play away from his body. Against a moving Dukes ball in English conditions, I thought we might have a reasonable chance of dismissing him for less than 200 every time. It didn't mean I thought he was a bad player. Far from it.

Overall I'd been extremely complimentary about Smith, but of course the small part where I said his only weakness may be at three had been seized upon. People were interpreting it as me saying Smith had a dodgy technique and I'd be targeting it. Sometimes you can't win. Say nothing and you get lambasted, say something vaguely interesting and it gets blown up into a massive deal.

I'd learned not to worry about it over the years. The more you play international sport the harder you become towards it. Paul Collingwood was always very good at spotting when people were getting down, and I remember very early on in my career him telling me not to take it personally. He said the press weren't criticising me because they hated me, they were just doing their job.

I told Woody he couldn't win if he got involved in a slanging match on social media and the best thing to do was get his head down and play. I knew that in a few days everyone would have forgotten about it and moved on. He seemed to cheer up a bit. It was just good to be able to share experiences with the younger lads.

The trip was also a great opportunity for us to get to know Trev and for him to get to know us. His round of golf with Stokesy really was something to behold. Talk about different characters. It absolutely tears Stokesy up if he plays a bad shot. The fiery redhead side takes over and he starts smashing his wrists with his fists and whacking his clubs on the ground. He then spends the next couple of minutes cursing loudly to himself. Then he's fine.

If you know him, it is hilarious to watch. Poor old Trev didn't have a clue what to make of it at first.

'If you think that's bad, you should see him when he gets out,' one of the boys said to him. Trev just smiled.

We were all sizing each other a little bit and getting to know one another. It was a very different to the familiarity of Peter Moores and Andy Flower. I just tried to be myself.

Trev led a lot of the cricket meetings and impressed us with his understanding and willingness to listen. Cooky also took a prominent role in those meetings, while Straussy stayed very much in the background.

The one time he did push himself to the front – other than on the golf course and a strong performance at left back on a full-sized football pitch on the last day – was when he gave a presentation to us about the responsibility we had as England cricketers to English cricket as a whole. He reminded us of the things we could do to help grow participation in the sport. The style of cricket we were looking to play was definitely a reflection of that.

We enjoyed getting to know Trev. The day before we left for Spain, I had done a media event organised by one of our sponsors, Hardy's Wine. It involved a bit of a chat with some of the cricket media in one of the boxes in the Tavern Stand at Lord's. Nothing too heavy. I was standing with one of the guys from Hardy's and saw someone with his back to us talking to one of the ECB's media team in the room next door. I realised it must have been Bayliss, so I introduced myself and shook his hand. It was the first time I'd seen him in the flesh.

Michael Lumb had played under him for the Sydney Sixers and had given me a bit of the low-down on him. He spoke very highly of him and said he was outstanding to work under. He said he was relaxed, lets you play your own game and wants to play positive cricket. He also said he puts clear boundaries in place and he's not afraid to give you a rollocking if you deserve one, but he was fair. All in all he was very laid back, considered and thoughtful in Spain, exactly as Lumby and Farbs had described him. He wasn't going to be a ranter or raver that was for sure.

Our fielding during the New Zealand series had been poor. We'd dropped an unacceptable number of catches. We worked incredibly hard on our catching, with the boys in the slip cordon wearing their hands raw taking so many catches. They practised and practised until they were catching flies in their sleep. It was awesome to watch. Lythy had come into the side and was a very good slip fielder, while Cook, Root, Bell, Ballance and Stokes were our other close catchers. The work those boys put in out in Spain would pay massive dividends over the rest of the summer.

Everyone notices the runs and wickets you lose when players like Strauss, Swann and Collingwood retired, but the thing people sometimes forget is how good they were in the slips as well. Those guys took some unbelievable catches and we had to rebuild that cordon after they'd gone. The best cricket teams almost all have a settled slip cordon. Trev wanted to end the chopping and changing that had gone on. After letting their standards drop against New Zealand, the boys worked overtime to improve in Spain.

It was huge credit to Strauss that everything about the camp worked. The hard work and cricket discussions were mixed with fun and socialising. There wasn't much alcohol consumed, but the boys had time to let their hair down. On the third night we had a quiz night and the organisers, Chris Taylor (fielding coach), Rooty and Ben Stokes, decided it would be a good idea for them to come in fancy dress. Chris came as Spanish golfer Seve Ballesteros, Stokesy came as a chavvy Brit abroad – which he didn't really need to dress up for – and Rooty came as a matador. It was good fun. We'd all been asked to write a fact no one else would know about us which went into one of the rounds and there was a sports round. It was just an old-school pub quiz, really.

Unbeknown to Trev, Stokesy and Woody have a bit of a party trick where Stokesy pretends to knock Woody out. The routine sees Stokesy throw a full on punch and Woody somehow makes a slapping noise as the punch flies past his face before falling prone to the ground in a heap. It's incredibly realistic and does look exactly like someone being punched.

We were holding the quiz in the team room and when I walked in I noticed a gym mat on the floor near the stage. 'What on earth is that for?' I thought to myself.

Woody was sitting at the back of the room with his team when Stokesy walked in with his cap on back to front looking like a rude boy.

Suddenly, Woody piped up from the back of the room.

'Stokes, you look like a prick,' he shouted.

'What did you say?' Stokes shouted back.

'I said you look like a prick!'

Stokesy looked furious. He had a deadly serious look on his face as he stared straight at Woody, who proceeded to stand up shouting 'do you want some?' before charging full tilt at Stokesy who was standing at the front of the stage. Before Trev – or anyone else for that matter – knew what was happening, 'bang', Woody was lying on the floor in a heap after Stokesy had apparently knocked his lights out.

Now bearing in mind Trev had already witnessed Stokesy almost destroy a set of golf clubs with his bare hands after shanking a six-iron, he could have been forgiven for being a bit concerned at that point. His face was an absolute picture, along with those of the rest of the management.

After a brief moment of silence as everyone tried to work out what the hell had just happened, the room exploded into laughter as Woody jumped back on his feet completely unscathed. I looked at Trev and his face just said: 'What the hell has just happened here?'

Luckily, it all settled down when our physio, Mark Saxby, walked on stage dressed as a Spanish lady and danced a salsa with our batting coach Mark Ramprakash – a former winner of Strictly Come Dancing.

It was great fun and the boys had a fantastic night full of laughter. It contrasted to the first night when we'd gone out for a bowlers' meal with Trev and discussed intricate plans for each of the Australian batsmen. But that just about summed up the camp. We worked hard and played hard. It struck the perfect balance.

There were serious moments that night, too. Part of the thinking behind asking us to provide a piece of information about ourselves that no one else knew revolved around the notion of being open with each other. When I was asked, I think I shocked the boys a little bit when I told them I only had one and a half lungs as the result of being born three months premature. I explained that because I was so tiny when I was born, basically on death's door, one of my lungs never had a chance to fully develop. It's why I'm asthmatic now and carry an inhaler. It's never affected me playing sport – apart from on the bleep tests when I need the inhaler, and in Kanpur in India, which is about the most polluted place on earth – but the idea I've played my entire career with half a lung less than everyone is quite amazing when you think about it.

A couple of lads said: 'Mate, I never knew that.'

'That was the point wasn't it?' I replied.

The camp provided another indication of how a new more free-spirited culture was emerging. Yes, you still had your gnarled old senior pros like Belly and Cooky, who knew exactly what worked for them and what they needed to do to perform. But you also had blokes like Woody, Stokesy and Jos who were much more laid back. It was a great combination and pushed the older guys on.

On the flight back, you could really tell how much we'd warmed to each other on the tour. It was only a two-hour flight and me, Jimmy and Woody were in a row playing cards tucked up in economy. Trev was sat behind with Farby.

Trev was nodding off a bit.

All of a sudden, Woody spun round and gave this big 'G'day, mate! How's it going, mate? Put another shrimp on the barbee, mate!' Right up in Trev's face. The poor bloke was half asleep and had this lunatic screeching in his face.

'Er, yeah, I'm good, mate.'

It may sound trivial but it was another indicator the ice had been broken. Woody felt at home enough to do it and Trev would have enjoyed the fact our dressing room was just like every other cricket dressing room.

We returned buoyed by the trip. We were fit, healthy and together as a group. We knew how we wanted to approach the upcoming series and believed we had the players to deliver our game plan.

It was Ashes time. And we were ready.

7

CARDIFF

LIONS ROARED ON BY DRAGONS

25 JUNE–12 JULY

While we were away in Spain, Australia began their tour with a regulation win over a relatively young and inexperienced Kent team at Canterbury. Mitchell Johnson, Mitchell Starc and Josh Hazlewood had made up their three-man fast bowling attack in the West Indies – with Nathan Lyon the off-spinner and Shane Watson a rarely used fourth seamer – so I was interested to hear that Ryan Harris enjoyed a decent run-out following a lengthy injury lay off.

I admired Harris enormously as a bowler and a competitor. He was a late developer at international level, with fitness problems plaguing him throughout his early career, but over the past three or four years he'd managed to stay fit and shown he was undisputedly one of the world's leading fast bowlers.

He wasn't a big sledger, preferring to let his bowling do the talking, but he was relentless with the pressure he was able to exert through his metronomic accuracy while bowling at speeds in the high 80s and above. When fit, he had caused all our batsmen problems at home and away, and was the leading Australian wicket-taker in England in 2013 with 24 poles at 19.58. He wasn't too bad in Australia a few months later, when he finished second in the list behind Johnson with 22 wickets at 19.31. For a fast bowler to average under 20 in a modern series is a superb effort, so to do it twice in successive series was exceptional. We knew he was an extremely dangerous operator who Australia would be desperate to get match fit in time for the Ashes.

Shaun Marsh and Steve Smith both scored first-innings hundreds in Canterbury while Mitchell Marsh reached three figures in the second on what was apparently a very good wicket. But Harris getting through 30 overs in the match would have given the Aussies the biggest boost to their morale, four months after he'd undergone surgery on his right knee. After the match ended, he spoke optimistically to the media about his hopes of playing a full part in the Ashes, which were starting nine days later in Cardiff.

We had a few days at home after getting back from Spain on the Tuesday before heading to Cardiff.

We'd been far too busy in Spain to pay much attention to the media, but it was evident when we landed the amount of Ashes coverage had ramped up significantly now the Aussies were in town. You could sense the anticipation and I began to visualise what it would be like to walk out at the Swalec Stadium on the first morning. It got the butterflies in my stomach going just thinking about it.

There was a lot of interest in our new coach, Trevor Bayliss, who was relatively unknown to the majority of UK cricket fans. Much of it focused on the apparent contradiction that an Australian would be coaching the England cricket team during an Ashes series. I had no issues whatsoever with Trev not being English. In fact, I loved the idea that an Aussie could potentially help take the Ashes away from Australia. That is modern-day sport.

I made a tongue-in-cheek comment in the press when I said it would be 'beautiful' to see an Australian with three lions on his chest with an Ashes urn in his hand. Most people took it in the spirit it was intended; just a bit of fun. A few people interpreted it as being intentionally provocative and started ranting and raving. To me, it was all part of the game.

The issue of nationality for international coaches seems to get people fairly vexed. Personally, if they're the best person for the job, I don't care where they come from. It was a bonus that Peter Moores had been a passionate Englishman in charge of the England cricket team, but the most important thing by a distance is a coach's technical ability, their man-management skills and whether they command the respect of the team. If Trev was the best man for the job, he could have come from Timbuktu for all I was concerned. With all the success Australia have had over the years, I think the boys were just excited to bring some of that Aussie psyche into the dressing room.

Playing professional sport these days is such a global experience that sees you mix with players and coaches of other nationalities far more frequently than you ever did in the past. It's pretty much the same across all sports. Players just want to hear the message, regardless of what accent it's delivered in.

Duncan Fletcher and Andy Flower are both Zimbabwean and they were probably the two most successful England coaches of all time. David Saker, another Aussie, had been our bowling coach for the past few years, along with Pakistan's Mushtaq Ahmed as a spin-bowling adviser, so we were well used to having people from different nationalities around the dressing room. Trev's nationality provided nothing more than an opportunity for us to pull his leg every so often. He seemed more than willing to have a laugh and a joke about it, and the fact he was a proud Aussie never at any point compromised his determination for England to win. As professionals, we all knew the score.

The Australians were due to have one more three-day game, against Essex at Chelmsford, before the start of the series. With temperatures pushing into the low 90s across the UK, they must have felt more at home than normal during an English summer.

I'm a big believer that county matches against touring sides should not just be seen as an exercise in giving the tourists glorified net practice. They should also be an opportunity for aspiring county players to make a name for themselves in properly contested matches, with the home side also taking the chance to do the national team a favour by denting the tourists' confidence early in a tour. Alastair Cook first came to national prominence with a double hundred against the touring Australians in 2005, when he was just 20 years old. Historically, England games against state sides in Australia have barely been below international standard.

As time has moved on, and schedules have got tighter, these tour games seem to take on less and less prominence. I think that's a shame, especially as they give cricket fans who may not be able to get along to the international matches, for whatever reason, the chance to see international stars in their backyard.

Sadly, one Australian star the Essex fans wouldn't be seeing was Ryan Harris after it was announced on the final morning of the match that he had retired from cricket with immediate effect. It was sad news. I was genuinely gutted for the bloke. Having only recently recovered from knee surgery myself, I knew how much time, effort and emotion he would have put into his rehab and recovery. That's before you consider the physical trauma of undergoing significant surgery, which was something I'd probably underestimated.

At 35, time was not on his side. But he'd set his sights on this series being his swansong in international cricket and it was a huge blow for the Australians, and a personal tragedy for the player himself to have to pull out at this stage. The outpouring of praise in the wake of his announcement was testament to what a decent bloke he was and the genuine affection in which he was held. As international sportsmen, you want to play against the best opponents to test yourself. While a few people rightly pointed out Harris's absence was a bonus for us, I was genuinely sorry to hear he wouldn't be involved in the series.

Without Harris, who announced he would stay with the squad as support, the Aussies cruised to another easy win over Essex after the home captain Ravi Bopara won the toss and put the tourists in on a flat wicket in rocketing temperatures. Ravi was clearly under instructions to let the Aussies bat first come what may, but I thought it was a missed opportunity which could have seen the tourists battling it out in the field for a couple of days. Nothing against Ravi, who I'm sure would have preferred to bat, but in my view it summed up our overly accommodating approach to these games.

Aussie all-rounder Mitchell Marsh scored his second successive hundred of the tour to maintain the pressure he was placing on Watson for a starting spot. I had no doubt Watson would start the series but he was under the spotlight. He'd been a fantastic player for Australia down the years, adding balance to their side with his ability to bowl at a medium-fast pace with superb control. But he hadn't bowled a huge amount in recent Test series and, a bit like Jacques Kallis, he gave the impression of being a fairly reluctant bowler. Marsh, who was a yard quicker than Watson, was definitely one to watch and clearly had an eye on the all-rounder's spot in the tourists' line-up.

As is often the case, sledging was also high on everyone's agenda. It normally is before an Ashes series. It provides a talking point in every sense. I think the Aussies had worked out a couple of series ago that I enjoy being in the heat of battle and that getting stuck into me verbally actually has a positive effect on my game. But that wouldn't stop them targeting other players if they thought they were vulnerable. At their worst, the Aussies can be ruthless.

I have no problem with sledging. Everyone knows there are lines you don't cross.

I have no problem with sledging. Everyone knows there are lines you don't cross, so as long as you stay within the boundaries I think it's a legitimate part of a fielding team's arsenal to get verbally stuck into the batsman. It had been brutal in Australia in 2013-14, with our guys getting abused by fans and sometimes by the Aussie players who were just bringing drinks onto the field. Clarke had overstepped the mark once or twice and the whole series was played in a pretty hostile spirit.

But don't get me wrong, we're no angels with the verbals.

I fully expected the Australian players to come hard at us. We'd discussed what we expected would be their approach in Spain and the younger players knew they had to be ready for a verbal onslaught. The Australians had been heavily criticised after their World Cup final win over New Zealand when Brad Haddin, David Warner and James Faulkner all sailed pretty close to the wind with some of their antics in the field. Haddin had even said in the build-up he was uncomfortable with how nice the New Zealand team had been towards Australia and made it pretty clear he preferred a bit of good, old-fashioned animosity. It was typical of Haddin and part of the reason I admired him so much as a cricketer. He's a proper street fighter.

The Aussies have pretty much built their entire sporting culture around being aggressive on the field and trying to upset the opposition. I have no problem with that whatsoever. The key is to embrace it. We had to be ready for them to be aggressive towards us, because if we weren't prepared we could easily be unsettled. We'd all really enjoyed the spirit in which both series against New Zealand had been played. It showed it was possible to play tough cricket without having to resort to the sort of personal abuse you sometimes faced with Australia. But I didn't think for a second they'd change their habits and that was fine, too. As it transpired, we needn't have worried.

After so much time talking and preparing, it was a relief to finally get in the car and drive down to Cardiff to meet up with the rest of the boys ahead of the first Test. This was going to be my fifth Ashes series, but it felt every bit as special as my first back in 2009. The 5-0 series defeat in 2013-14 had unquestionably been the low point in my career – as it had for most of us – but I still retained overwhelmingly positive memories when it came to playing in Ashes series. Following that loss, I was hungry for revenge.

There was some controversy over Cardiff being awarded an Ashes Test ahead of grounds like Old Trafford and Headingley. I didn't really understand the politics and commercial decisions involved in how the Tests were allocated, but I always enjoy playing in Wales. The support we get down there from Welsh and English fans alike is fantastic and I was told ticket sales were buoyant for this eagerly anticipated Test. Glamorgan has produced some high-class cricketers down the years, with Simon Jones the most recent to play Test cricket for England, and if their ground was seen by the powers-that-be as the best venue to stage the first Test then I wasn't going to argue.

Despite the 5-0 drubbing last time, my record against Australia stood at six wins and six losses in 17 Tests.

The whitewash series had been a weird one for me in so many ways. After choosing not to walk during the first Test at Trent Bridge a few months earlier, the irony wasn't lost on me when I was portrayed as public enemy No.1 when I'd arrived in Australia – the country that invented not walking – I was routinely called a cheat and abused almost wherever I went. The local paper in Brisbane even slapped a picture of me across their front page on the first morning of the first Test urging fans to give me the silent treatment with the headline 'Broad Ban; Gabba fans silent weapon against smug Pommie cheat'. It got a little paper a lot of attention, I suppose.

I'd never experienced anything like the scale of personal vilification I came in for on that tour. I was booed by about 80,000 people at the

MCG and by the end of the tour I'd started to hum 'Stuart Broad is a w*nker' between overs to keep myself amused. I genuinely didn't mind the abuse. And my performances on the field didn't seem to be affected as I ended up with 21 wickets in the series at 27.52, just under my career average.

It was a source of personal pride that my bowling average across four series against Australia is better than my overall career average. Not too many players are able to say that. Growing up, I had watched the great Australian side of the 1990s routinely thrash England out of sight. With players like Warne, Border, Boon, the Waugh twins, Taylor, Healy, Gilchrist, Slater, Langer, Ponting, Hayden, Gillespie and McGrath – to name just a few – Australia seemed to have a never-ending conveyor belt of world-class players to call on. Every time one retired, another one just slotted in. Beating Australia has always been the pinnacle for every English sportsman. Losing to them has always been utterly galling.

People talk about me being a big-game player. I don't know if that's true. But I do like to think of myself as someone who will step up in high-pressure situations. Friendly games don't really do it for me. What's the point in taking five wickets if there's nothing at stake? Kevin Pietersen had a similar attitude when he played. He could score four noughts in a row in warm-up games but then walk out in front in front of a full house at the Gabba and smack a brilliant hundred when it mattered.

The thing I love about playing Australia is that you know you have to be on the money for every single ball. Relax for a second and they'll punish you. The team we were about to encounter in Cardiff would be no different. We had to be on our mettle 100 per cent of the time.

It's not that I switch off when there's no pressure, it's just I prefer it when there is. I've always been like that. I remember my dad telling me to wear striped socks when I had a county hockey trial as a kid to draw attention to myself and thus increase the pressure on me. It may sound like a weird comparison, but I always did well in trials when the pressure to perform was at its most intense. I've carried that into my professional career.

The key is being able to put things in perspective and not worry about the scale of the potential consequences. Paul Collingwood used to call it his 'f*ck it' stage. I remember in 2008 when he was horribly out of form and on the brink of being dropped, he went out and just whacked it against South Africa at Edgbaston. He scored a brilliant 135 in one of his best knocks for England. He'd stopped worrying about the consequences of getting another low score and just gone out and hit the ball. It was a liberating moment for him. I learned a valuable lesson speaking to Colly about that mindset.

As the first Test approached, I cast my mind back to two of my best performances in an England shirt. The first was in the final Test at The Oval in 2009, when I took five for 37 in Australia's first innings to help bowl them out for 160, which set up our victory. The second came in the fourth Test at Chester-le-Street in 2013, when I took six for 50 in their second innings – and 11 wickets in the match – as we took an unassailable 3-0 lead in the series. Those were undoubtedly two of my proudest moments in an England shirt. It gave me a warm glow thinking back to them ahead of the first Test.

The England selectors named a 13-man first Test squad during the Aussies' final warm-up game, with Adil Rashid as a second spinner alongside Moeen Ali. Steve Finn was also named. Adam Lyth had rubber-stamped his selection with his maiden Test hundred against New Zealand at Headingley and he'd be opening the batting with Cooky.

The Cardiff pitch tends to be fairly dry and spin friendly, and we had played two spinners there in the past, notably in 2009 when Monty Panesar and Graeme Swann had both played. With Monty playing such a memorable part in us saving that Test with his last-wicket stand with Jimmy, it's easy to forget he and Swanny took the sum total of one wicket for almost 250 between them in that Test.

But with the recent hot weather set to continue, it made sense for us to cover all bases. It also made sense to keep Adil around the squad to pick up more experience. The two spinners option provided an interesting talking point, but privately I wasn't sure if Cooky or the selectors would be overly keen to kick off an Ashes series by handing a young leg spinner – albeit a very good one – his Test debut. I'd been really impressed with Adil on tour in the West Indies and in the one-dayers against New Zealand, but Mark Wood had bowled exceptionally in his first two Tests and I always thought he was favourite to play.

We trained really well ahead of the Test. The boys looked razor sharp and ready for action. I was happy with my rhythm in the nets, the knee was feeling great and my last outing in first-class cricket had seen me take seven wickets for Nottinghamshire. Mentally I felt good. In fact, I couldn't have been in a better frame of mind for the start of what was going to be a massive series.

Cooky also seemed on top of his game. Although it was early days, he looked to have struck up a nice rapport with Trev, who made it very clear he wanted it to be Cooky's team. In the build-up to Cardiff, Cooky repeated his desire for us to maintain the momentum we'd built up in the one-day series.

'Do not go inside yourselves, boys,' he said. 'Keep expressing yourselves. Back your instincts. You won't be criticised for playing your natural game. Go out there and showcase your talent.'

It was great to hear that from our captain, and you could see the confidence it instilled in our younger players to know they had the freedom to go out and play. I was excited about the potential we had within the side.

The Test was starting on Wednesday, and on the Monday night we were called to a team meeting at our hotel and introduced to the greatest Ashes hero of them all: Sir Ian Botham. It was a great call by the management. Beefy was absolutely brilliant company. He recounted a whole load of his favourite Ashes memories, which seemed to revolve exclusively around him taking the Aussies out and getting them drunk the night before matches, and the boys loved every minute of being in his company. Woody was just completely star struck. He couldn't believe he was sitting in the same room as Ian Botham.

Apart from his fun stories, it was also interesting to hear his take on commentary as a former player criticising current players. He was keen to stress he didn't take things too seriously and he urged us not to listen to any of the comments or pay too much attention to what was said. He was great company and the boys were really excited to be in the company of a living legend.

The practice of warming up on the morning of a cricket match by playing football had been outlawed ever since Owais Shah had dived in on Joe Denly and injured him before he had been meant to be making his one-day international debut in 2009.

But during the New Zealand series, Farbs had suggested we started playing again as a slightly more fun way to warm up before the start of play. 'Go on, you're grown men,' he said. 'You know what's acceptable and what's not. Just go and play. If there are any bad tackles, we stop.'

It was another example of the coaches trusting us to be grown up about things and take responsibility for our actions. Farbs was confident we wouldn't abuse his trust by being silly and risking injury to one of our team-mates. It may sound like a trivial thing, but it immediately had a galvanising effect. It gave us a real sense of fun and enjoyment while fostering our competitive spirit.

Unfortunately, one of the photographers who follow us around took a picture of me, which seemed for all the world as if I was putting in a horrendous two-footed sliding tackle on Jos Buttler. I'd actually been lying down on my back completely stationary and Jos jumped over me, but the picture looked like Roy Keane's tackle on Alf-Inge Haaland. It appeared absolutely horrendous.

The fact all the boys knew it was an utterly innocuous moment didn't stop them mercilessly taking the mick out of me for the next week or so. Every Test venue we play at we always start a 'banter wall' in the toilet. The boys found newspaper cuttings and pictures of pretty much every terrible sporting challenge in history and taped them up there. Jos's head was replaced with a picture of Haaland and my face was put on Keane's body. I was savaged.

But, despite the stick, the football proved enormously popular. Every city we played in had a different cup named after it, and we ended up with scoreboards in the changing room and cup games and transfer systems. It became a huge source of fun among the boys over the course of the summer. I'm sure the Aussies looked at us a few times as we were running around laughing and messing about and thought: 'Are they potty?' But we didn't care, we were having fun and it was helping to bond the team. It was no surprise that Jos and Ben Stokes were among the best players, while me and Finny tended to stay at the back and know our limitations. Jos was eventually awarded the golden boot.

There was a sense of fun around the camp. With so many young players experiencing their first Ashes series and a new and relatively unknown coach, there was a very different squad dynamic to 2013.

There was a relaxed air around the place with no shortage of light-hearted mickey taking. As well as the 'banter wall', we also had a 'caption wall' in the dressing room, which Jimmy Anderson normally started, where a picture of one of the players or management, usually doing something stupid, would be posted. The lads could then write any caption they wanted underneath. Our fielding coach Chris Taylor was pretty big on that, too.

The day before the Test started, Rooty, Stokesy, Lythy and I decided to head off for a round of golf to take our minds off the serious business. We went to play at the Glamorgan Country Club where Cardiff City and the Wales national rugby teams train.

We'd never played the course before, so we were just finding our way around. We got to the 17th hole and there were trees all the way down making it a blind tee shot. Lythy piped up straight away.

'I saw this when we drove in,' the Yorkshireman said confidently. 'It's a dog-leg left, so the left handers need to hit a big fade with a rescue club and right handers a long draw. That will leave a short pitch onto the green.'

There wasn't a shadow of doubt in his voice, so we all took his advice unquestioningly. All of us nailed our tees shots – or at least thought we had – and drove the buggies up the fairway to where we thought we'd find our balls. As we turned left where the fairway opened up, to our horror we saw the Welsh rugby boys' cars parked up slap bang where our tee shots had landed. The fairway, in fact, veered right.

'Shit,' said Lythy. 'I could have sworn the fairway went left.'

We urgently checked all these big Range Rovers and Mercedes for any damage and made it very clear to Lythy he'd be the one breaking the bad news if there was any damage at all.

He'd already made us laugh on that round by announcing the reason he loved playing golf on such nice courses was nothing to do with the quality of the greens or the stunning scenery, but because it gave him a chance to make a few quid by finding all the top-notch lost balls. We'd seen him rooting around in the rough before shouting 'six quid!' when he found a brand new ball. Now, though, we weren't laughing at the prospect of potentially having inflicted damage on a 17-stone Welsh rugby player's car. Fortunately, we'd managed to miss them all, and we hurried off in the right direction thanking our lucky stars for the narrow escape and cursing the man we'd come to know as Lord Voldemort, after the Harry Potter character.

Notwithstanding Lythy's awful caddying skills, the round of golf proved an excellent way of keeping our minds off cricket and relaxing a little bit. We knew the next six weeks were going to be serious business.

I slept well the night before the first Test. I normally do. I was nervous, but in a good way. This was my fifth Ashes series and the Aussies knew I was not one for backing away from the contest. I was excited about at the prospect of what lay in store. I felt ready.

Driving into the ground that morning was absolutely fantastic. It was a warm, slightly overcast day, and the crowd lined the roads as we approached the stadium. As soon as I got into the ground I could sense the nervous energy. But, like my own nerves, it was a good energy. There was a real buzz about the place and an excitement you only get on the first morning of an Ashes series. The boys were all pumped.

I looked across at Jos, Mo, Lythy and Woody as we were warming up and remembered back to how I'd felt when I made my Ashes debut at the same ground in 2009.

To pass the time, before the anthems and all the formal stuff that accompanies the start of an Ashes series, I flicked through one of the programmes that had been placed on the benches in the changing room. It wasn't one of the official ECB programmes but one Glamorgan had put together as promotional material. I wasn't paying a massive amount of attention until I reached a page where five respected commentators and pundits had been asked for their views on who would win the series. I didn't recognise all of them, although former Glamorgan and England opener Steve James was among them. I've read plenty of what Steve writes and really like him as a pundit. As a former player, he understands some of the pressures involved, but I didn't agree with him this time. Along with every single one of the other experts, Steve had backed Australia to win the first Test and go on to win the series overall. Not one of them gave us a hope.

I understood we were underdogs, and that suited us to be fair, but for not a single one of those guys to back us was pretty surprising. I know we'd been whipped last time around, but we were at home and had three blokes in the dressing room who'd won three Ashes series and another (Belly) who'd won four. I found it quite amazing to see us written off so comprehensively.

BROADSIDE

You'll often hear sportsmen say they don't read the press or look at the media. Generally, that's not true. For a start, it's almost impossible not to these days with the amount of different platforms you can access. I know Cooky manages to lock himself on the farm to get away from all the noise, but even he will get a sense of what's being said in the media, while our team communications manager, Rhian Evans, keeps us posted with anything we need to know. The key is to use criticism, or lack of backing in this instance, to motivate you.

'I'll show them,' I thought.

Before the toss, we were introduced to the Australians on the steps down to the pitch. I'd been reading former heavyweight boxing champion Mike Tyson's autobiography at the time and I was interested in the part where he talked about beating some of his opponents before they'd stepped in the ring. I knew the Aussies respected me for my previous performances. When I'd left Australia following our whitewash in 2013-14, people had stopped me in the street to say so. The gist of what most them said was: 'Hey Broady, we might think you're a prick but you're a decent cricketer.' That was fine by me. I hadn't set out to be liked, I was much more interested in taking wickets to help England. I was just sad on that tour we hadn't performed as a team.

With that in mind, I decided to make sure the Aussies remembered my face and I made a point of staring straight into each one's eyes as we shook hands. They knew I wouldn't crumble under pressure, but would they? It gave me a huge boost of adrenaline. I felt nine feet tall and absolutely ready to go.

Cooky went out for the toss, which is always a huge occasion on the first morning of the Ashes, and had no hesitation in batting when the coin fell his side. The pitch looked very good to bat on and I was pleased when he came in to the dressing room and told us we'd be batting. As expected, Woody was included ahead of Adil and I congratulated him on making his Ashes debut. It was a huge moment for Lythy, too, as he knew he'd be walking out to bat alongside Cooky in a matter of minutes.

There'd been a little bit of rain around that morning and the start was delayed by a few minutes and, following a some fireworks and patriotic flag waving, we were finally able to get down to business.

'Express yourselves, boys,' Cooky said. 'We know what we're about. Go showcase your skills.'

'Express yourselves, boys,' Cooky said. 'We know what we're about. Go showcase your skills.'

As the pair strode out to bat, I settled in to watch the opening overs, hopeful I wouldn't be required to change fully into my whites all day. The first day of an Ashes series can be frantic though, so I knew I needed to be prepared for anything.

While Mitchell Starc had emerged as a very fine international left-armer and Josh Hazlewood was an excellent fast bowler with huge potential, it was Mitchell Johnson who we considered the biggest threat. How could he not be? The bloke had taken 37 wickets in the previous series at an average of 13.97 and played a part in ending the career of one of England's best-ever batsmen.

In the very best sense of the word, Johnson was a menace and we knew we had to play him considerably better than we had the last time around or we'd be in trouble again. Some of the spells I faced from him in Australia last time will live with me forever. In many ways, I feel a sense of pride at having survived some of them. He was capable of generating pace unlike anything I'd experienced before. While it can be an incredibly unsettling experience to bat against him, I am a massive fan of his. He is a superb athlete with a wonderful approach to the crease and a low-slung action which sees him release the ball at an unusual trajectory and at high speed. He loves a little verbal battle in the middle and is a fierce competitor. The crowd has got on his back in a very big way in the past but, as I'd experienced, he should take that as a compliment. As Sir Alex Ferguson once said, no one boos you if you're no good.

We'd spoken at length about how we were going to counter him, and the main message we took into the series was to play the ball and not the man. We had to get past the image of Mitchell Johnson bowling thunderbolts in Perth to simply watching the ball out of his hand and onto the bat. In English conditions, he was going to find it harder to generate the same sort of searing pace he had on the quicker Aussie wickets. The slate was clean from Australia last time. It was also noted that, without Ryan Harris, Australia wouldn't necessarily get the control from the other end they had in previous series. Starc – who was expected to take the new ball in Harris's absence – was very much a strike bowler in the same mould as Johnson. He was a wicket-taker but he could also leak runs.

With so many players making their Ashes bow, we were not carrying as many scars from the last series as many people seemed to want to make out. It was clear among the squad that we were not intimidated by the Australians. Woody and Lythy were chomping at the bit, while Mo, Jos, Stokesy and Gary all seemed relaxed about what lay in store.

To our slight surprise, Hazlewood, playing in his first Ashes Test, took the new ball alongside Starc, with Johnson coming on first change. As we sat on the dressing room balcony we could sense the crowd were waiting for Johnson.

But first of all, Lythy had the small matter of negotiating his first over in Test cricket. The crowd were expectant and as Starc turned at the top of his run, the noise was fantastic.

His first ball was a bit of a loosener, an 87mph loosener, but a loosener nevertheless. Lythy allowed it to travel harmlessly through to Haddin behind the stumps. First ball safely negotiated.

The next ball was fuller with a hint of away swing at 89mph, but wide enough for Lythy to shoulder arms and allow it through to the keeper. Ball two out of the way. Breathe a little easier, mate.

The third ball kept low and squeezed past Lythy's outside edge and narrowly missed off stump before travelling through to Haddin. Already, it was clear the pitch did not have an enormous amount of pace in it.

There had been a plenty of discussion about what type of wickets would be prepared for the series, with some of the Australian media suggesting groundsmen would all be under orders to prepare slow, low wickets to negate Johnson's threat. I thought that was nonsense. We had two blokes with almost 700 wickets between us in Test cricket who employed swing and seam to take our wickets. Why would we want slow and low pitches? We had been assured the pitches would be traditional English-type wickets with some carry but also enough grass to encourage the bowlers.

I have no problem with wickets being prepared to play to the home side's strengths. When you go to India, where spin is king, you wouldn't expect to play on a green seamer and when you go to Australia you expect fast, bouncy tracks to suit their quicks and wrist spinners. That's totally fair enough, but the issue was getting a lot of air time nonetheless.

All Lythy was thinking about was getting through his first over. Starc's fourth ball was very full and wide of the off stump, allowing Lythy to leave well alone.

The fifth ball kept even lower than the third, scuttling through to Haddin on the second bounce. We could hear the murmurs in the crowd. I look at Jimmy and raised an eyebrow.

Starc's final delivery of the first over was wide again and Lythy shouldered arms again. He'd done it. He'd survived his first over in Ashes cricket.

'Well done Voldemort,' someone piped up at the back of the dressing room.

Cooky worked his second ball from Hazlewood into the off side to get us off the mark, to the joy of the crowd, before Lythy scored his first runs in Ashes cricket with an outside edge between gully and backward point.

The next ball was full and on his legs. Lythy stepped across his stumps and clipped it crisply through the leg side for four.

'Great shot Voldemort!' came the cry from the back of the dressing room. But, no sooner had we stopped applauding his first boundary in Ashes cricket, than he was on his way back to the pavilion as Hazlewood produced a well-directed full delivery on off stump, which Lythy only succeeded in edging to David Warner in the gully.

Gary Ballance stood up and walked out to the crease. He'd had his problems during the World Cup, but during the tour to the West Indies he had looked like he was back to the form we'd seen the previous summer. However, the spotlight was back on him following a couple of scratchy innings against New Zealand and, in any Ashes Test, there is going to be pressure. I was convinced he was an international cricketer, but I wasn't a selector.

He got off the mark with an edge down to the third-man boundary in Hazlewood's second over before Michael Clarke made his first change after just four overs. Johnson was on and the crowd noise stepped up in volume.

Cooky and Gary negotiated Johnson's first over without too much trouble, although it was interesting to see him immediately hitting speeds into the 90s. The crowd were loving it. This was real Test cricket.

Cooky thumped Hazlewood through square leg in the next over and, with Johnson unable to make a breakthrough in his first four-over burst, we reached 42 for one by the end of the 13th over.

With the pitch not giving much assistance to the Aussie quicks, Clarke turned to his off-spinner Nathan Lyon in the 14th over.

Again, eyebrows were raised in our dressing room. It's not that often you see a spinner bowl this early in a Test. Within two balls, Clarke's plan had worked as Cooky edged behind to Haddin when attempting to play square of the wicket. In many ways it was a typical Lyon wicket. The off-spinner probably doesn't get the credit he deserves, but we certainly respected him in our dressing room.

He has an ability to generate over-spin on the ball, which means he gets more bounce than most off-spinners and it's that bounce which is his biggest weapon.

Cooky's dismissal saw Belly stride out at No.4 and within four balls he went down the pitch to Lyon only to miscue horribly into the leg side. The crowd were on edge. People would no doubt criticise Belly for his shot selection but, if we were going to stick to our attacking beliefs, they'd have to accept a few dodgy dismissals, too.

Belly had survived, but not for long. In Starc's next over, the left armer produced a beauty. The ball, which was full and straight and tailing in just slightly, thudded into Belly's pads as he was beaten for pace. Umpire Marais Erasmus was in no doubt as he raised his finger. Gary advised against a review.

At 43 for three, with Starc bowling beautifully, we were in a spot of bother. Perhaps not quite as bad as we had been Lord's against New Zealand, but considering the circumstances of the match, this was a far more pressurised situation.

Rooty arrived at the crease. The form he'd been in over the past year, after being dropped for the final Test of the 5-0 whitewash in Sydney, made him the perfect man for a crisis. We needed our young talisman to dig us out of another difficult spot.

Starc had his tail up and his very next delivery almost saw Rooty trapped in front as the ball angled into his pads again, only to catch the inside edge before thudding into his knee roll. Erasmus said 'not out' and the Aussies decided against a review only after consultation between Clarke and the bowler.

You could feel the tension in the dressing room. There was no chatter, no joking. We knew this was a critical phase of the game.

The next ball was full again but wider of the off stump and Rooty jabbed down on the ball as it passed his bat. It caught his outside edge and flew to the Australian wicket-keeper's right-hand side where he flung himself at the ball only for it to thud into his glove and out again. It was a catch Haddin would have expected to take more often than not. Rooty lived to fight another day. It was a missed chance that would define the Test match.

Joe and Gary began to settle into the task. Rooty was more fluent, playing a couple of trademark front-foot punches through the covers.

The crowd were enthralled. A bugler played the *Addams Family* theme tune as Johnson returned for another spell. The moustachioed gun-slinger smiled. In years gone by, the constant stick he'd received from the Barmy Army had got to him. Now he lapped it up. He seemed more at ease with himself.

So did Rooty, who after a nervy start rattled along to 30 off just 20 balls. He was taking the attack to Australia just as he had against New Zealand. He fist pumped Gary in the middle after slapping Hazlewood over backward point for four.

The pair made it through to lunch on 88 for three and the crowd rose as one to applaud them in. It had still been Australia's morning, but Rooty's impish innings had raised our spirits after a tough first hour. Haddin's missed chance had also been a massive moment in the match.

'Good stuff boys, keep going,' said Trev at the break. The pitch was docile and we had plenty of batting to come. With the sun emerging from behind the clouds, there were runs to be had.

Rooty and Gary were quickly back in their stride after lunch. Another wicket-less Mitchell Johnson spell came and went and, while he wasn't bowling badly, the boys could manage his pace through the air, with the wicket not especially helpful to quick bowling.

Gary never looked completely at ease, but he dug in determinedly and the pair negotiated the first hour after lunch. Rooty continued at nearly a run a ball, allowing Jimmy and me the luxury of moving to the back of the dressing room for a game of cards.

Both men passed fifty with Rooty very much the dominant partner. Eighteen months after being dropped against the Australians, he was on a mission to demonstrate he'd put that tour firmly behind him. We reached tea at 190 for three and we applauded them back into the dressing room. Johnson had been repelled, for the moment, and the Aussies had begun to look a little short of answers as the session wore on. We knew they'd come back hard, but the balance was very much back in our favour.

Gary was out shortly after tea, LBW to Hazlewood, for a gutsy 61 before Rooty reached a richly deserved hundred when he punched the same bowler through square point to reach three figures off just 118 balls. It was his seventh Test century and, as far as I was concerned, his best. Given the circumstances of the match, he'd played another blinder.

Stokesy got in on the act with a typically aggressive fifty, including a couple of engrossing overs against Johnson when the pair went at each other like a couple of rutting stags. We reached 280 for four before Root departed for 134 when he edged the impressive Starc low to Watson at slip. It was the end of a brilliant knock. The Aussies' celebrations were muted. They knew how costly Haddin's earlier drop had been.

As Rooty deservedly took the crowd's acclaim, cries of 'Roooooooooot' rang out around the ground. Up on the balcony, we joined in. He deserved the ovation. It had been a master class.

When Starc bowled Stokes for 52 a few overs later, the Aussies had a sniff again at 293 for six with an hour still to play.

Mo joined Jos at the crease as the crowd's earlier delirium fell to a hush. In another tense moment, we had two of our most chilled-out characters at the crease and Mo immediately lifted the pressure by scoring seven runs from the first three balls he faced from Starc before Jos whacked a beautiful cover drive off the final ball of the same over to reclaim the momentum again.

It was a shot hit with such authority it couldn't fail to send a message to the Australians that this was a new England.

Mo just looked utterly unfazed by the occasion. He left his fifth ball from Lyon only to get down on one knee to slog-sweep his sixth over mid-wicket for six. It was brilliant counter-attacking batting. In a few balls after Stokesy's departure we'd smashed 17 runs. It was a statement of intent. You punch us, we'll punch you harder.

Johnson returned late in the day to more pantomime jeering and proceeded to charge in again. But again he was repelled and one superbly timed pull shot from Mo brought up the fifty partnership and brought us all to our feet. It was a shot hit with such authority it couldn't fail to send a message to the Australians that this was a new England. The destroyer from Down Under was human after all.

I had my pads on by now, but obviously hoped I wouldn't be required that night. Unfortunately I was, as Jos fell just before the close after he chipped Hazlewood straight to Johnson at mid-on to depart for 27.

I got out to the crease and the Aussies were silent. Nothing. They were giving me the cold shoulder. I knew their game. Hazlewood bowled me an aggressive final over, but I survived to get us through to stumps at 343 for seven from 88 overs. What a day.

I got back to the hotel that evening and crashed out. Physically I'd not been required to do much, but the amount of nervous energy we'd all expended had been enormous. Tomorrow was another big day. What is it they say about the first hour being crucial?

I rose bright and early and made the short journey with Jimmy from our hotel in Cardiff Bay to the ground on the outskirts of the city centre. There were a few rumours knocking around that Starc, Australia's best bowler on day one, had an ankle problem. What would be would be. I had a decent net in the morning and felt good as I walked out to bat with Mo.

'You all right pal?' I asked him.

'Loving it!' he replied with a big grin on his face. He was, too.

I got away with a nicely timed punched drive down the ground off the second over of the day from Hazlewood before the young Australian responded by bowling a short ball that smashed into my helmet as I ducked. Momentarily, I wasn't sure what had happened, before realising I'd been hit again. I knew it wasn't as bad as the previous summer, but inevitably there was concern.

Six years ago, I'd made my Ashes debut on the same ground against an Australian side containing a wonderfully talented left-handed opening batsman, Phil Hughes. In November 2014, the 25-year-old had tragically died when he was struck on the back of the head by a bouncer in a Sheffield Shield game between South Australia and New South Wales. His death had devastated the cricketing community and, understandably, prompted serious questions about helmet design and the use of the short ball in cricket.

I don't think any cricketer who has ever been hit on the head by a delivery, and almost every single player who's played top-level cricket will have been at some point, did not think 'there but for the grace of God go I' when they first heard the shocking news. His death had been described as a 'freak accident' at the time, and there's no doubt deaths in cricket are incredibly rare. But people get hit on the head all the time in matches and in the nets – Australia's opener Chris Rogers had even missed a Test in the West Indies with post-concussion symptoms a couple of months earlier.

Phil's death had made the Australian team hyper-sensitive to the issue and their concern was noticeable as I received treatment from our physio. I felt OK, if a little shaken up, and I was keen not to show the Aussies that I was in any trouble. I shook myself down before inspecting my helmet. It was split straight down the middle.

'Blimey,' I thought to myself. At least it had done its job and saved me from any significant injury. Our physio Craig de Weymarn was happy for me to continue, with a new helmet, and I settled down to face the next delivery.

My ticker was going, though. Anyone who hasn't faced a cricket ball being delivered at or around 90mph and aimed at their head, will not be able to understand how intimidating an experience it actually is. It would be denying the obvious to suggest one of the reasons people love seeing great fast bowlers in action is because there's an element of danger. Modern equipment provides a certain level of protection, but as Phil's death had illustrated, it does not guarantee safety.

Hazlewood charged in again and I swished and missed at the next delivery outside off stump.

'Calm yourself,' I thought. But my heart was still racing.

The next ball Hazlewood dropped slightly short again and I climbed into it, connecting sweetly as the ball sailed in front of square leg for six. The crowd loved it and so did I.

We kept the scoreboard rattling along. With the Aussies maintaining their predictable short-pitched strategy to me, I was given a reprieve when Vogesy thought he'd got his fingers under a catch at short leg off Johnson. Television replays showed it had hit the floor first and the original 'out' decision was overturned. The crowd booed. No need for that. Vogesy wouldn't have known. We cracked on.

With Mo batting beautifully, we took the score to 395 for seven before I attempted a slog-sweep off Lyon and edged behind to Haddin for 18. We finished 430 all out, with Mo adding a precious 77 from No.8 in the order. It was a fabulous effort following our parlous position on the first morning.

The bowlers got together in the dressing room and made our intentions very clear.

'We are delivering today, boys,' Jimmy said, as the leader of the attack. 'This is our time.'

We shook hands and took to the field. The adrenaline was pumping and the crowd were roaring. Ashes cricket. I love it!

We had around 40 minutes to go at the Australians before lunch. From my very first delivery, I felt in the groove. Everything was working in order, my run-up and delivery stride felt smooth and the ball was coming out of my fingers perfectly. It was a great feeling.

I had two good appeals for LBW turned down in my first over, and Jimmy and I exerted plenty of pressure in our opening spell. They reached lunch at 26 for none, but Jimmy struck soon after the break when Cooky took an excellent catch to his right at first slip to dismiss Warner. The crowd went ballistic.

Our skipper took a nasty blow in the most uncomfortable of places when a Steve Smith edge bounced awkwardly on him, and the Aussies were in a strong position at 129 for one before Mo came up with the priceless wicket of Smith when he beat him in the flight and had him caught by Cooky at short mid-on.

As Clarke walked to the crease, Cooky didn't even need to say anything. I knew I'd be on next over. My team-mates believed I had a bit of a hold on the Australian captain after dismissing him in Brisbane in the previous series. I don't know about that, but I was happy to engage in another tussle.

I felt I was bowling beautifully, but without luck. My plan to go around the wicket to Rogers was working and I was giving Clarke the hurry-up.

Woody was also bowling nicely at the other end and he eventually made the breakthrough when Rogers edged behind to Jos on 95 to leave them 180 for three. Immediately the crowd noise lifted as my former team-mate Adam Voges walked to the crease.

The pair settled things down and took the score past 200 before Mo picked up his second vital wicket of the innings when he also beat Clarke in the flight and had him caught and bowled.

We immediately mobbed Mo. We knew what an important wicket it was. The cricket became quite attritional that evening. Each side knew a big mistake could be costly. Woody and Watson had a good old tussle after their overblown little spat in the media and the crowd were clearly engrossed. It was another critical phase.

It was Stokesy who won out when Jimmy pulled off an excellent diving catch at short extra-cover to get rid of Voges and leave the Aussies five down ten minutes before the close. They got through to stumps on 264 for five, but we felt we'd edged the day.

After being hit on the head earlier on, the medics wanted to be doubly sure I was OK at the close. I had to go through a series of tests and was told in no uncertain terms that if I failed one of them then I would not be allowed to bowl the next day. I was absolutely terrified of the prospect. Fortunately, I passed with flying colours.

We had our families staying with us, as is normal during a home Test match, but once more I wasn't especially great company that night. I was utterly shattered again. It can't be underestimated the mental toll these games take. Two days into the series and I was already in need of a rest.

I managed to get a good night's sleep and, invigorated by a massage when I got to the ground, felt buoyant again as we took the field. Cooky gave us another rallying cry before we walked out and I could sense something was in the offing.

Woody had bowled quickly the night before and he opened up the bowling with me that morning. It was no secret Shane Watson had a weakness for playing around his front pad and we had planned to keep a relentless line around middle and off to try to entice him into attempting to play a straight delivery through mid-wicket.

Four balls into my first over of the morning ... bingo! A full-pitched delivery jagged back into Watson as he walked into the ball and tried to play through the leg side. The ball thudded into his big front pad below the knee roll and I instinctively knew it was out. Umpire Erasmus agreed. Watson, looking a little sheepish, called for a review which showed it was clipping the stumps and off he walked. The Aussies were still 135 behind with four wickets left. The dangerous Haddin was in next, but the wind was in our sails.

Woody was getting properly stuck into nightwatchman Lyon, bowling with great rhythm, pace and aggression. With the crowd noise filling our ears, it was no surprise when he arrowed one into the batsman's pads to trap him plumb in front: 265 for seven. Come on.

Crucially, we managed to string together five maidens to maintain a vice-like grip around the Aussies' throats. We were slowly suffocating them and they knew it.

We knew precisely how dangerous Haddin was. I'd lost count of the times he'd dug his side out of difficult positions down the years and he struck a few crisp fours off Stokesy to temporarily relieve the pressure before Jimmy had him caught behind.

I got rid of Johnson before Jimmy wrapped the innings up when Rooty took another very good catch off Starc and Australia were all out for 308. We led by 122 runs and the ovation as we walked off felt like we'd already won the Ashes. It was amazing.

In the dressing room, Trev made his first really decisive move of the summer. Anxious that we didn't let our foot off the gas, he implored our batsmen to stay on the attack. Over the years, we had on occasion been guilty of lacking conviction after taking a first-innings lead. Trev was clear what he wanted us to do.

'Go and get me some runs, boys,' he demanded. 'Do not ease off here. Keep attacking. Go and get me some bloody runs, please.'

It was brilliant stuff and just what we needed to hear. You could see Belly's chest puff out as the coach implored our batsmen not to allow the initiative to slip. Even with 100 Tests to his name, Belly could still do with a gee-up sometimes. All the batsmen took it on board. We were not going to ease off.

Lythy walked out looking ten feet tall. He batted well after Cooky and Gary fell cheaply to leave us 22 for two. With Trev's words ringing in his ears, the Ashes debutant pushed on alongside Belly as the pair again decided the best form of defence was attack.

Lythy smashed Lyon into the stand to take us to 70 for two and the crowd were once again ecstatic. Lyon got his own back a couple of overs later, and Lythy went for a well-made 37 to bring Rooty to the crease with our lead closing in on 200.

After a lean spell, it was great to see Belly back in the runs. There really is no one better to watch in international cricket and he went on the attack early with some trademark cover drives. The pair put on 97 in quick time to stretch our lead further, with Rooty adding 60 to his first-innings 134 and Stokes then chipping in with 42 including nine fours. When I was out trying to force the scoring along, we led by 357 with two wickets left.

We probably already had enough, but Woody proceeded to play an absolute gem of an innings, smacking 32 from 18 balls including four fours and a six to rub salt into Aussie wounds. We were all out for

289 from 70.1 overs just before the close, leaving Australia needing an improbable 412 to win the Test match. Weather permitting, we had two full days to bowl them out.

Bealey and I had dinner in Cardiff that night, and I allowed myself a solitary glass of wine. There was much work still to be done, but I knew we were in an extremely strong position.

The next morning the sun beamed through the curtains in the hotel room. 'Perfect,' I thought as I peered out on to Cardiff Bay shimmering beneath the window.

There was a real buzz of excitement around the ground. One more push and we'd be 1-0 up. Could we do it today? Of course we could.

> There was a real buzz of excitement around the ground. One more push and we'd be 1-0 up. Could we do it today? Of course we could.

We warmed up again with our now-customary game of football and I could sense the energy. This was what we'd trained for.

It was noticeable how early the stadium would fill each morning. The crowd were packing in for every minute of live action they could get. Once again, the atmosphere was fantastic. The pitch remained bone dry and without much assistance for the quicks. Nathan Lyon had extracted plenty of turn in our second innings, but the fact 30 wickets had fallen in three days suggested it wasn't a batsman's paradise.

Jimmy and I opened up and both found some rhythm early on. Rooty was disappointed to drop Rogers at third slip in Jimmy's second over. Then I was convinced I'd had Warner caught behind in my third over. I've not had a great record down the years on reviews, but I was confident he'd nicked it. Umpire Dharmasena thought otherwise and Cooky immediately called for a review only for the replay to show the ball had narrowly missed Warner's bat and flicked his pad on the way through to Jos.

We were keeping things incredibly tight and it came as no surprise when I caught Rogers' edge and Belly held on to a good catch at second slip. Australia were 19 for one and we were on the move.

Warner came at us in the only way he knows, going on the attack in an attempt to unsettle us. He has a funny way of commentating to himself as you're bowling. It's pretty strange, but it's best to ignore him. Ever since the incident with Rooty in the Birmingham nightclub in 2013, when the Aussie had totally overreacted to Rooty dancing around in a coloured wig on the dance floor and decided to punch him without a word of warning, it's fair to say he wasn't that high on any of our Christmas card lists.

But fair play to the bloke, he can hit a cricket ball and he can hit it a long way. He is part of the new breed of cricketer, raised on Twenty20 and with an instinct to attack, attack, attack. He's good to watch, for sure. He seemed to have mellowed a bit and towards the end of the series we'd get to see his softer side, but Warner remained a fierce competitor and a spiky character.

He raced along to his 15th Test fifty (with 12 hundreds as well) before Mo grabbed his third key wicket of the match, trapping Warner LBW, to leave the tourists 97 for two on the stroke of lunch.

'Keep going, boys,' Cooky urged at lunch. 'One big burst and we're through them here. Keep attacking. Don't give them a sniff.'

I'd felt in lovely rhythm all through the match without getting the rewards I felt I deserved, but all that changed after lunch when I picked up two vital wickets.

First, Smith edged to Belly in my first over, before Clarke was lured into a loose drive to Stokesy at backward point to depart for just 4. That wicket gave me huge pleasure against a batsman I've fought plenty of battles with down the years. The Aussies were 106 for four.

Four balls later and we were in danger of running through them when Woody had Voges caught behind. Woody, who'd bowled beautifully all Test match, went running around like Usain Bolt whooping and hollering with delight.

'Ride the horse, Woody,' someone shouted. 'Ride the bloody horse!'

We were on the brink. It was a matter of when, not if.

Haddin fell to Mo to leave them 122 for six before Woody had Watson plumb in front again. To our surprise, Watson decided to review again, but it only delayed the inevitable as replays showed the decision was correct.

Left-handers Johnson and Starc both played some crisp shots in a bright and breezy eighth-wicket stand of 72, before Root had Starc brilliantly caught by Lyth at slip, after Cook had managed only to parry the ball up in the air and the game was as good as won.

Rooty and Lyth combined well again to finally dismiss Johnson for an excellent 77 and, with the crowd in a state of near delirium, Mo wrapped up our 169-run victory when Hazlewood skied a catch to long-off. Guess who took the catch? Man of the Match Root, of course.

'Roooooooooot!!' the crowd cried as we walked off. He'd had quite a game.

We were absolutely sky high. Written off before the Test, we'd produced close to a perfect performance. After Rooty and Gary Ballance dug us out of trouble on the first morning, we'd taken a grip of the game and won in precisely the style we wanted. Showcase our skills? Too right we did.

That evening, as we enjoyed each other's company in the dressing room over a beer, Beefy popped his head around the door.

'All right if I come in lads?' he asked.

'Err, yeah,' we replied.

Sir Ian congratulated us on our win and shared a glass of white wine with us. He also presented the Wales Cup to the winners of the football warm-ups. It was a lovely time to be in the dressing room. Woody kept saying: 'It's Ian Botham! It's Ian Botham!'

A few of us went back to the hotel for a nightcap but nothing too heavy. I ordered a cocktail, but Bealey spilt it and I didn't bother ordering another. I was happy enough with another drink. I was utterly exhausted and turned in just after midnight.

It might have been the perfect start to the series. But it had only just begun.

ENGLAND V AUSTRALIA (1ST TEST)

At Sophia Gardens, Cardiff

8, 9, 10, 11 July 2015

ENGLAND WON BY 169 RUNS

Toss: England
Umpires: H.D.P.K.Dharmasena (Sri Lanka) and M.Erasmus (South Africa)
Referee: R.S.Madugalle (Sri Lanka)

ENGLAND

Batsman	Dismissal 1	R	Dismissal 2	R
A.Lyth	c Warner b Hazlewood	6	c Clarke b Lyon	37
* A.N.Cook	c Haddin b Lyon	20	c Lyon b Starc	12
G.S.Ballance	lbw b Hazlewood	61	c Haddin b Hazlewood	0
I.R.Bell	lbw b Starc	1	b Johnson	60
J.E.Root	c Watson b Starc	134	b Hazlewood	60
B.A.Stokes	b Starc	52	b Starc	42
† J.C.Buttler	c Johnson b Hazlewood	27	c Haddin b Lyon	7
M.M.Ali	c Watson b Starc	77	c Haddin b Johnson	15
S.C.J.Broad	c Haddin b Lyon	18	c Hazlewood b Lyon	4
M.A.Wood	not out	7	not out	32
J.M.Anderson	b Starc	1	b Lyon	1
Extras	(B 17, LB 3, W 5, NB 1)	26	(B 7, LB 6, W 6)	19
Total	**(102.1 overs)**	**430**	**(70.1 overs)**	**289**

AUSTRALIA

Batsman	Dismissal 1	R	Dismissal 2	R
C.J.L.Rogers	c Buttler b Wood	95	c Bell b Broad	10
D.A.Warner	c Cook b Anderson	17	lbw b Ali	52
S.P.D.Smith	c Cook b Ali	33	c Bell b Broad	33
* M.J.Clarke	c and b Ali	38	c Stokes b Broad	4
A.C.Voges	c Anderson b Stokes	31	c Buttler b Wood	1
S.R.Watson	lbw b Broad	30	lbw b Wood	19
N.M.Lyon	lbw b Wood	6	(11) not out	0
† B.J.Haddin	c Buttler b Anderson	22	(7) c Cook b Ali	7
M.G.Johnson	c Ballance b Broad	14	(8) c Lyth b Root	77
M.A.Starc	c Root b Anderson	0	(9) c Lyth b Root	17
J.R.Hazlewood	not out	2	(10) c Root b Ali	14
Extras	(B 6, LB 11, W 3)	20	(B 4, LB 3, NB 1)	8
Total	**(84.5 overs)**	**308**	**(70.3 overs)**	**242**

AUSTRALIA	O	M	R	W		O	M	R	W
Starc	24.1	4	114	5	(3)	16	4	60	2
Hazlewood	23	8	83	3		13	2	49	2
Johnson	25	3	111	0	(1)	16	2	69	2
Lyon	20	4	69	2		20.1	4	75	4
Watson	8	0	24	0		5	0	23	0
Warner	2	0	9	0					

ENGLAND	O	M	R	W		O	M	R	W
Anderson	18.5	6	43	3		12	3	33	0
Broad	17	4	60	2		14	3	39	3
Wood	20	5	66	2	(5)	14	4	53	2
Ali	15	1	71	2	(3)	16.3	4	59	3
Stokes	14	5	51	1	(4)	8	2	23	0
Root						6	1	28	2

FALL OF WICKETS

WKT	E 1ST	A 1ST	E 2ND	A 2ND
1st	7	52	17	19
2nd	42	129	22	97
3rd	43	180	73	101
4th	196	207	170	106
5th	280	258	207	106
6th	293	265	236	122
7th	343	265	240	151
8th	395	304	245	223
9th	419	306	288	242
10th	430	308	289	242

CLOSE OF PLAY

Day 1	England (1) 343-7 (88; M.M.Ali 26*, S.C.J.Broad 0*)
Day 2	Australia (1) 264-5 (70; S.R.Watson 29*, N.M.Lyon 6*)
Day 3	England (2) 289

8

LORD'S
SILENCE IS GREEN AND GOLDEN

12–19 JULY

Our first Test win at Cardiff had received enormous acclaim from fans and media alike. Some went as far to say it was one of the biggest sporting upsets of recent times. I didn't agree with that, because I never had any doubt we could win, but it was nice to be on the receiving end of congratulations rather than brickbats. We wanted the fans to get behind us, and Andrew Strauss had been keen to make the point in Spain that we had a responsibility to play an attractive, attacking style of cricket to help draw more people to the game. Hopefully we'd done that.

One of the keys to maintaining performance at the highest level of sport is to not get too high when you win or too low when you lose. It was something Straussy was always very good at as a player and captain, and something I've got better at as I've grown older. We were content with our performance at Cardiff, but we were not going to rest on our laurels. We were certain the Aussies would come back hard at us.

We also had a clearer idea of how Australia intended to approach the series now. We'd been impressed by the way New Zealand had conducted themselves earlier in the summer, when their captain Brendon McCullum had extended the hand of friendship by asking to share a beer with us after we'd beaten them at Lord's. It was a nice gesture and we'd readily accepted. We thought it was something worth trying to carry over into future series.

Following the presentation ceremony at Cardiff, Alastair Cook had asked Michael Clarke if the Australians would like to come to our dressing room for a beer. Clarke indicated he'd go and ask his team-mates. Not long afterwards we got a message back. It was a polite but firm 'no'. We were a bit surprised, but it didn't unduly worry us. One of the boys suggested we grab a couple of beers and walk into the Aussie dressing room and plonk ourselves down next to them anyway. In the end, we decided that might be a bit disrespectful after they'd just lost a Test match. The last thing we wanted was a diplomatic incident, but it was a shame. The New Zealand series had been played in a really mature manner, without any of the silly stuff that can sometimes accompany international sport. But it was up to the Aussies: it was their prerogative. Our main motivation for wanting a beer with them was simply that it was a nice thing to do. But the Aussies weren't keen so that was that as far as we were concerned.

In between Tests, Jimmy Anderson gave an interview when he was asked a direct question about the issue. He gave a very calm, reasoned reply in which he said it was the Australian prerogative and he had no issue with it. But, as often happens with these things, it got made into a much bigger deal than it actually was. Suddenly, our ambivalence became 'England fury at Aussie drink snub', which was stretching it. We were surprised by the level of media interest, and it certainly irked the Aussies a bit.

A few of their cheerleaders piped up, with Matthew Hayden calling Jimmy a 'clown', while Peter Siddle also pointed out Jimmy had not been keen to share a drink when he'd asked on the last tour. It was all much ado about nothing and, as can happen in Ashes series where the attention is heightened, a tiny insignificant story had been magnified out of all proportion.

What was more interesting to us than their refusal to share a beer was the Aussies' apparent unwillingness to engage with us in any verbal exchanges. About the closest they came to sledging at Cardiff had been when Mitchell Starc put his fingers to his lips as if to say 'be quiet' to Ben Stokes after he bowled him in the second innings.

We'd expected the Aussies to come at us hard in the series, just as they had in the previous Ashes when Michael Clarke set the tone by telling Jimmy to 'get ready for a broken f***ing arm' when he was batting in the first Test at Brisbane. But, far from the avalanche of sledging we expected, it became obvious during the first Test that the Aussies were going to take a completely different tack. They were going to ignore us.

Down Under, in 2013-14, they'd set out to intimidate us. They didn't want us thinking they were ordinary blokes. It fed into their decision not to have a beer with us this time. I could understand what they were trying to do. Mitchell Johnson had enjoyed an incredible series that winter, when he had morphed into some kind of modern-day gladiator no one knew how to combat. They'd bullied us in the Carlton one-day series before the World Cup and then destroyed us at the MCG in the tournament opener. They thought they had a hold on us – an aura if you like – which they'd not had since Warne and McGrath had retired.

It seemed they wanted to keep us at arm's length in order to maintain that element of mystique. Allan Border started it back in the 1980s, I'm told, and Clarke thought it was important to keep their distance.

> It had been especially gratifying that so many of our young players who'd never played Ashes cricket before made significant contributions to our win in the first Test.

Our strategy to bring Johnson back down to earth was simple; bat a lot better against him. His first-innings figures of 25 overs and nought for 111 at Cardiff suggested we'd done precisely that. It provided the team with a huge psychological boost for the rest of the series, knowing we could nullify his threat. If he'd taken six for 50 in that Test, the series could have panned out very differently. To keep him wicket-less in the first innings was a massive statement by us and it shouldn't be underestimated how much of a lift that provided.

It had been especially gratifying that so many of our young players who'd never played Ashes cricket before made significant contributions to our win in the first Test. Moeen Ali, Adam Lyth, Jos Buttler and Mark Wood all enjoyed solid Test matches with bat, ball and in the field. Players can get stage fright on day one of an Ashes series, but the lads showed they were not overawed by the occasion. We'd prepared well and the only thing that was unexpected was the lack of verbals from the Aussies. Who'd have predicted that?

Because the first Test finished inside four days after starting on a Wednesday, we had an extra day of rest before the Lord's Test began the following Thursday. Four days still isn't a great deal of time to get your mind and body rested and recovered for another tough encounter, but the extra 24 hours definitely helped.

In the lead up to Lord's, we placed heavy emphasis on how the Australians would respond following their defeat. Words like 'backlash', 'revenge' and 'wounded animals' were the order of the day. In hindsight, we got it wrong. Rather than worrying about how fired up the Aussies would be, and how tough an adversary we could expect, we should have focused on ourselves and how we could maintain our level of performance. It would prove a significant error on our part and a painful but vital lesson learned for the rest of the series.

The pitch at Cardiff had come in for a fair amount of criticism, even though it had produced a result in four days. It was pointed out that in many ways it had not been the traditional type of wicket you'd expect in the UK, with very little bounce or sideways movement. It was actually quite sub-continental by its nature, with spin playing a big part in the outcome of the match. The Aussie media were whinging about it being designed to negate Johnson, but I don't think that was the case at all.

It meant attention inevitably turned to the Lord's wicket, where their highly experienced groundsman Mick Hunt had produced a very good track for our magnificent Test match win against New Zealand earlier in the summer. That pitch had just enough grass for the ball to carry through well to the wicket-keeper, although in the past Lord's wickets have tended to get slower and easier to bat on as the match progressed. I remember Fred bowling more than 50 overs in the second innings against Sri Lanka in 2006, as they batted for something like 200 overs to save the match. South Africa did something similar to us again in 2008 when I bowled 26 wicket-less overs in the second innings.

It is also a ground where touring teams love to play. The Aussies, in particular, seem to relish it. Our victory there in 2009 had, almost unbelievably, been the first time we'd beaten Australia there for 75 years, since 1934. When I heard that, I was utterly gobsmacked. Can you imagine there being an Australian ground where they didn't beat England for 75 years? They'd have shut the place down and bolted the doors within a decade! But, as a country, we're very obliging hosts and on the whole make tourists feel very welcome. We may have beaten them again in 2013 but, historically, Lord's is a ground where the tourists have prospered.

The first morning of an Ashes Test at Lord's takes 'special' to another level. I remember in 2013 Rooty having tears in his eyes as he walked through the Long Room for the first time in an Ashes Test. It is so evocative and the moment got to him. Lythy had been similar in his debut Test a few weeks earlier, while Woody had appeared completely mesmerised by the whole experience. He found every aspect fascinating. As a kid, you want to play for England at Lord's. As players, it is important we never forget we are living that dream. As Nasser said to us before the Antigua Test, it would not be long before we would be wearing suits and doing very different jobs. I reminded myself of that on the first morning at Lord's.

Cooky's captaincy in Cardiff had been excellent. He was decisive and inventive. Something that had irritated us in 2013, and caused a degree of friction between us and the media, was the constant criticism of his field placings, and accusations that he was defensive all the time. It felt like no matter what he did, he was getting it in the neck.

We won that series 3-0, but it wasn't enough to keep people happy. However, going through those kinds of experiences helps you grow stronger and makes you learn. In the three years Cooky has been in charge, he has had to put up with a lot of nonsense, much of it from outside the dressing room, but he has improved, just as anyone would do, and he showed his authority and imagination in Cardiff. Most of his field placings had come off, while he was backed up with one of our best fielding displays in years. After working so hard on our catching in Spain, it was great to see that effort paying dividends. Trevor Bayliss was at pains to stress that this was Cooky's team and he would boss it and make the key decisions. Trev was there to provide support and guidance, but he wanted Cooky running the show. He definitely did that in Cardiff. Lord's would be another test for all of us, in every sense.

On the first morning, as we were warming up, we were provided with further evidence the Aussies intended to carry on giving us the cold shoulder. I'd played a lot of cricket at Nottinghamshire with Peter Siddle and Adam Voges, and consider both of them good friends. So, as I was marking out my run-up on the outfield before play, I tapped Siddle on the shoulder to say hello.

'All right Sids, how are you doing, mate?' I asked with a big grin.

'OK,' he said stone-faced, before walking off. I saw him again not long after as he was bringing drinks down the pavilion stairs. I made a bit of a joke saying something about how heavy he was making them look and jokily asking if he'd spent enough time in the gym recently. He completely blanked me and walked straight past.

I went up to the changing room and told the other boys what had happened. It was really odd. Sids is a great lad and someone I definitely consider a mate. I'd even been to the Grand Prix with him the previous year, and he looked after my dogs when he was in Nottingham. I had no idea what I'd done to upset him.

Then Jimmy said that exactly the same thing had happened with him and Mitchell Johnson the day before. He'd said 'good morning' to Johnson when there were only two of them in the corridor, but Johnson just looked at the floor and walked straight past him.

With the amount of international sport that's played these days, we come up against each other more often and you get to know your opponents inside out. Back in the day, someone like Glenn McGrath would just roll into town every four years, take his haul of wickets, and then disappear again. Inevitably, there was a bit of mystique around him. Nowadays we know what makes our opponents tick. Added to the sheer volume of cricket played, there is also ample video footage to really understand the strengths and weaknesses of players you come up against. But it also means you can become mates with opponents as well as adversaries.

I'm fairly sure the Aussies would not have spoken to me, even without the team instructions not to do so. In Australia in 2013-14, I relished being portrayed as the pantomime villain of the England team and the more abuse I got, the more I enjoyed myself, but this was different. This was clearly a directive their players had been given not to speak to us.

Looking at the Lord's wicket on the first morning, it was immediately apparent there was less grass on it than we had hoped for. There was certainly less grass than the last time we played there against New Zealand. There was the tiniest tinge of green, but it felt bone dry to the touch. It certainly didn't appear to be the traditional English wicket we and our management had asked for. So when Australia won the toss, Michael Clarke surprised no one when he said Australia would bat, leaving us hoping there might just be a little more life in the pitch than we thought.

Our team remained unchanged from Cardiff, after Mo passed a fitness test on a slight side strain, but Australia made two very significant changes. First, Shane Watson was dropped and replaced by Mitchell Marsh, who would be making only his fifth Test appearance. Watson had gone into the first Test under pressure and looked horribly out of sorts in Cardiff, where he'd fallen LBW in both innings in almost identical fashion. He'd also gone wicket-less in 13 overs.

Brad Haddin, who'd dropped such a vital catch in Cardiff when he'd let Joe Root off the hook, was also omitted for 'family reasons' and replaced by debutant Peter Nevill. In one fell swoop the Aussies had lost two players with 125 Test caps between them and replaced them with two players with four. On paper, it looked a significant loss.

I thought back to an article I'd read by my former captain Michael Vaughan ahead of the series in which he had urged England to be ruthless in the same way Australia had been to us last time around. He pointed out in the piece that Ashes series had contributed to ending the careers of several England players. We needed to do the same to

Australia in this series. It was quite a brutal piece, but I agreed with the sentiment. There was every chance we would see both players again in the series, but to see a cricketer of Watson's calibre dropped after just one Test did feel like a victory for us. I watched from the balcony as Nevill received his first baggy green cap from former captain Steve Waugh. That must have been a wonderful moment for him.

There had been some speculation about Mitchell Starc's fitness after the Australian left-armer hobbled his way through our second innings at the Swalec Stadium. He was known to have an ankle problem, but looked to be bowling well in the nets and it was no surprise to hear him named in the tourists' starting XI.

There was some cloud cover about on the first morning before play so, despite what looked to be a batting-friendly wicket, it was up to us to do some damage with the new ball. Early wickets were going to be vital if we were going to unsettle the Australians and make them regret batting first.

Cooky's team talk before we went out reminded us of what had won us the Test match in Cardiff. He was going to set attacking fields again, and needed his bowlers to maintain a nagging line which didn't give the Australian batsmen width. He repeated the belief that they'd come back hard at us and urged us to maintain the attacking intent we'd shown over recent months.

'Let's get among them,' he cried as we left the dressing room and walked down through the pavilion and the Long Room – so packed with MCC members we could hardly squeeze through – and out onto the field. It doesn't matter how many times I do that walk in my life, I will always cherish the experience. The full house welcomed us warmly out on to the pitch. It wasn't quite the raucous atmosphere we'd experienced at Cardiff, but it was still buzzing. Lord's sort of hums on the first morning of a Test.

Jimmy opened up to Rogers and it took the left-handed Aussie opener just three balls to get off the mark with a streaky edged four over Belly and Rooty when he flashed hard at a ball outside off stump. Two balls later the former Middlesex player – who earlier in the summer had been banned from selling Ashes tickets at Lord's after being caught up in a slightly messy row over hospitality packages – drove confidently to the boundary again. Australia were 8 for none after five balls. Jimmy shook his head and walked back to his mark muttering under his breath. His next delivery swung significantly, but Rogers was able to leave it alone outside off stump.

I conceded a no-ball with my first delivery but otherwise kept it tight to Warner, who appeared to be biding his time on what looked an excellent batting surface. Jimmy and I plugged away, but it was obvious early on there wasn't going to be much in it for us in terms of lateral movement or pace off the pitch. Within three overs, the clouds had gone and the ground was bathed in glorious sunshine.

Rogers looked in very good touch as he rattled along to 21 from 23 balls, including a nicely timed boundary punched into the leg side from the last ball of my third over.

Cooky made an early change, bringing Woody on after Jimmy had bowled just four overs, but the result was the same. Woody's fifth delivery saw him drop short and Warner rolled his wrists on a strong pull shot through mid-wicket. The pair brought up their fifty partnership in the 12th over and, with every passing delivery, the signs got more ominous.

Woody generated plenty of pace in another impressive spell from the most inexperienced bowler in the attack. Just as he had in his three previous Tests, he was consistently hitting speeds in the high 80s while occasionally pushing 90mph. He gave both batsmen the hurry-up and very evidently relished being out in the middle at Lord's, representing his country in the Ashes. So many talented players down the years have not succeeded because the pressure of the occasion got to them. Fear of failure can become overwhelming and inhibit performance. The opposite looked to be true of Woody, who was patently loving every single minute. His talent was evident and his action was strong, generating pace from a short run-up which culminated in an explosive delivery stride and quick arm similar to Simon Jones. Like Jones, he was also capable of generating reverse swing, although he wasn't quite in the former Glamorgan quick's class just yet.

Jos is excellent at geeing up his bowlers, just as Matty Prior had been before him. Matty saw it as his duty to bring energy to his team in the field, set the example by running between overs and ensuring a constant supply of vocal support from behind the stumps. Jos was no different, and he urged us to stick to our plans and keep running in hard. I know some commentators think the wicket-keeper should be seen and not heard, but, as a fast bowler, I appreciate the encouragement from the behind the stumps.

Worryingly for us, not only were we not taking any wickets, we were not beating the bat much either. You could count the number of false shots the Aussie openers played in the first hour on one hand. The ball was finding the middle of their bats as the easy-paced pitch confirmed our bowlers' worst suspicions; this was a road.

The tourists reached 68 without loss at drinks after 14 overs and we gathered in a huddle. Cooky was staying positive, we all were, but the early signs were that it was going to be a long day at the office.

Cooky threw the ball to Mo after drinks. Just as Nathan Lyon had come on to bowl before lunch for Australia on the first morning at Cardiff, now it was our turn to hope spin could do the trick where pace had failed. Immediately, Warner's body language changed and he crunched Mo through cow corner for an ungainly but effective four from the off-spinner's first ball. The second ball saw the Aussie charge down the pitch again and bludgeon the ball through the same area for a second successive four. He was making his intentions 100 per cent clear. He was going after Mo.

There was a murmur of disappointment from the Australian fans as Warner failed to score from the next delivery before scampering a single. Rogers returned the favour to leave Warner on strike and we couldn't believe our luck when he charged down the wicket again to the last ball of Mo's first over and attempted another huge hoick into the leg side, only to miscue it straight up in the air for Jimmy to make a difficult spiralling catch in the covers look easy. The breakthrough had come courtesy of a brain freeze from Warner. As he trudged back to the pavilion, he must have known he'd let a golden opportunity to go big slip out of his grasp. There's a fine line between being positive and being reckless. He'd just crossed it.

Steve Smith bounced out to the crease. We hadn't reminded the Aussie No.3 of the comments he'd made ahead of the series that we 'wouldn't get near Australia' following our Cardiff win. I decided to be the bigger man and leave it alone, but I couldn't help feel a sense of satisfaction that we'd made his cock-sure prophecy appear foolish.

I'd also been stung by the reaction to comments I'd made about Smith before the series. I had been incredibly impressed by the way he turned himself from a cricketer who bowled a bit of leg spin and could chip in with handy runs down the order into one of the world's most prolific run-scorers. He had shifted up from seven to five and now to three in Australia's order and was the Aussie batsman – along with Clarke – whose wicket we prized most. Since scoring his maiden Test hundred in the final drawn Test at The Oval in 2013, he'd gone on to score another eight hundreds in 17 Tests before he walked out at Lord's. Anyone with a record like that deserved respect.

But while respect was due, you have to look at ways of getting even the best batsman out. Otherwise what's the point in walking out onto the field? I'd said in an interview before the series that, in English conditions with the Dukes ball nipping around and possibly swinging, our best chance of getting him cheaply was if he batted No.3. It was stating the obvious really. Smith moves around the crease more than almost any other top-order batsman I've played against. Typically batsmen who flourish in English conditions stay still until as late as possible and don't go hard at the ball. So, if we were going to have to bowl to Smith, I said I'd rather bowl to him when the ball was new and still doing a little. It was common sense.

I took a lot of stick for making those comments, with people accusing me of underestimating Smith. That wasn't the case at all. Critically, here at Lord's, my analysis was irrelevant because hardly a ball had deviated off the straight all morning. They didn't feel like English conditions at all. He must have known as he walked to the crease there was an opportunity to go big.

And go big he did. Mo bowled a very nice spell, but Smith came down the pitch superbly after settling in to play the shot of the morning when he drove beautifully through the covers with a high elbow for his first boundary. He struck another four straight back down the ground in Mo's next over to move into double figures. The Aussies cruised to 104 for one at lunch.

The silent treatment continued from Clarke's men during the intervals. To be honest it became a little bit painful. Even at lunch there was absolutely no conversation between the teams. Nothing. It was all slightly unnecessary. A few of us made the point of how funny it would have been if Swanny had been there, because he'll talk to anyone, he doesn't care how awkward it is. But we accepted they were going to behave like this and just got on with it. I found it all strange, and a little sad really. As it transpired, nothing would change until after the final Test.

There was nothing flashy, nothing spectacular but there was almost a sense of inevitability as they serenely moved along.

The afternoon session was something of a horror show for us. Jimmy and I bowled a tight line early on after lunch, but we were both really struggling to extract any kind of movement out of the pitch. On the rare occasion the ball did catch the edge of the bat, it didn't threaten to carry to the slips as a combination of soft hands from the batsmen and the slow pitch took the sting out of the delivery.

Smith looked ominous. Unlike Warner, he was in no rush to come after the bowling. He settled deep in his crease to Mo and worked him around rather than trying to thrash him over the rope, while he rarely looked troubled against our quicks. He also rotated the strike superbly. Rogers also appeared fairly relaxed in moving past fifty. There was nothing flashy, nothing spectacular but there was almost a sense of inevitability as they serenely moved along.

Rooty and Mo found themselves bowling in tandem midway through the afternoon session. Rooty is better than a part-time off-spinner, but it was indicative of how unresponsive our quicks were finding the wicket that we had two spinners on barely three hours into Australia's first innings. At one point, Jimmy and I shared a glance. I think we knew what the other was thinking.

Smith reached an untroubled half-century from 111 balls and it was impossible not to sense the crowd's frustration at a wicket that refused to respond, no matter what we threw at it. Then, all of a sudden, Stokesy got one to spit a little and catch Smith's outside edge as he prodded forward. The ball flew low to second slip, only for Belly to spill a difficult but very catchable chance. The crowd groaned. Like Haddin's off Rooty in Cardiff, it would prove a costly drop.

With Australia 191 for one just before tea, Cooky threw the ball to part-time off-spinner Lythy. He was absolutely delighted to get a bowl and he let out this little yelp at the prospect. It's hard to describe in words, but we'd started noticing that he makes this noise, almost involuntarily, when he's really happy. It's a bit like an excited yell and it comes out if he hits a good shot or scores a goal in football or if we bowled a good ball.

His 'woohoo' became quite familiar over the course of the series. Whenever we did anything good we'd just hear 'woohoo'. We wanted to hear another one before tea, but Australia reached the interval untroubled and we had to make do with: 'Well bowled, Lord Voldemort. Maybe you can nick one after tea.'

Cooky threw me the ball after the break and asked me to really run in for him. We both knew we needed a breakthrough soon or Australia were in danger of getting away from us. I maintained a really tight line and almost drew an edge from Rogers in my first over, but the ball slipped past his outside edge. I beat him again in my second over with a carbon copy of the first, but again the outcome was the same and I had to settle for some 'ooohs' from the crowd and a 'woohoo' from Lythy.

Smith looked more and more comfortable with every passing over. He was moving well at the crease and knew there were no demons in the pitch. Rogers moved into the 90s with an adroit late cut which suggested the Aussies may have been learning their lesson. A few hours earlier, Warner had gone all macho in trying to thump Mo out of the ground in the same way Haddin had at Cardiff. Rogers and Smith were playing with far more nous against him, staying deep in the crease and playing the ball late, often behind square. It was effective.

Smith moved into the 90s in the next over with a six off Rooty and there was a certain inevitability about them both reaching their hundreds. Smith got there first with a swivel pull shot taken from outside off stump, which summed up the lack of pace in the pitch. Rogers got there soon after with a punched drive down the ground off the same bowler. Neither man could hide his delight at reaching three figures. Why should they? They had both batted beautifully and given only one clear chance between them when Belly hadn't managed to hold on to that Smith edge at slip.

It was Rogers' fifth Test century and his fourth against England. After making a single Test appearance against India in 2008, Rogers had returned to face us in 2013 at the age of almost 36, but he'd carved out a decent Test career in a short space of time and certainly earned our respect. He is a nuggety type of cricketer who knows his own game well. He is not expansive, but has enough scoring shots and we'd found him to be a tough competitor to face.

Australia passed 300 for the loss of just one wicket in the 81st over before we finally got our hands on a precious new ball. We hadn't managed to get the old one to do much, and the effect was much the same with this one. However hard we tried, we found it almost impossible to get the ball to deviate off the straight. The Aussie pair continued to cash in.

With two balls of the day to go, I drew Rogers into an edge. I was sure I had my man, but just as the ball looked to be flying to Belly it died in the air and dropped about a foot short. It summed up our day and summed up the pitch. I was livid. The ball just wasn't carrying through.

The Aussies finished on 337 for one from 90 painful overs of graft from us, with Rogers and Smith having put on 259 unbeaten runs. They'd batted beautifully, but I must admit I was pretty unamused that evening. I was bitterly frustrated at not getting Rogers at the end. I didn't know what else I could do. Edges should carry to the slips on Test pitches, otherwise it becomes an unfair contest. Life is hard enough as a bowler.

Jimmy was put up to speak to the press and showed his experience by managing to play a straight bat through gritted teeth when asked for his thoughts on the pitch. 'You can't judge a pitch until both sides have batted on it,' he said. 'We need to bowl better.'

He was right but inside he was also frustrated. We didn't want to come across as whingers and the point about us still having to bat on it was absolutely valid. But as every team who bats second when the opposition has chalked up a massive first-innings score knows, the added pressure exerted by those runs on the board – or 'scoreboard pressure' as it's known – is vast. One day into the Test match and we were behind the eight ball. Big time.

I didn't know what else I could do. Edges should carry to the slips on Test pitches, otherwise it becomes an unfair contest. Life is hard enough as a bowler.

It was pretty clear to us our management weren't especially happy about the wicket. They assured us they'd wanted traditional English wickets that would provide an even contest between bat and ball, but what we'd hoped for and what we got were two very different things.

I was sore after a long day in the field bowling on a rock-hard deck. I had a massage before leaving the ground for our hotel and slept like a log that night. We were staying at the Langham Hotel, where I'd had problems sleeping the year before after someone had suggested the place might be haunted. There were all sorts of stories about a German doctor who had killed his wife there.

One night, during the Sri Lanka Test, it was so hot in the room I just couldn't sleep. All of a sudden, the taps in the bathroom came on for no reason. I turned the lights on and the taps turned themselves off. Then when I turned the lights off again the taps came on. It was very weird and it really freaked me out. Once I woke up in the middle of the night convinced there was a presence in the room. It was the weirdest feeling. I turned on the light and looked online and could see Matt Prior was online, too. He was wide awake as well. Neither of us could sleep because we were so spooked out. Matt was in a twin room so I ended up sharing with him.

Having stayed there a few times since, I've not encountered the same problems and I was so shattered this time that I slept straight through. The next morning I woke still feeling pretty stiff and with the nagging concern we still had nine Aussie wickets to take before we'd get a chance to bat.

The mood at breakfast wasn't exactly joyous. However, there was one moment that morning which made me laugh. My usual travelling companion Jimmy was not in the cheeriest of moods, even by his standards, and he sat in the passenger seat looking pretty glum as we made our way to the ground.

I drew up at some traffic lights and we came to a halt. I looked up from the wheel and who else's face was staring back at me on a huge advert plastered on to the back of a double decker bus? It was none other than Jimmy himself. He was wearing a cheesy grin with the words 'I feel fantastic' underneath his face in an advert for vitamin company Wellman.

I looked across at him scowling in the passenger seat.

'Do I heck feel fantastic,' he growled. With Australia 337 for one, I don't think any of us did.

Cooky and Trev remained positive as we warmed up and it was true that a flurry of wickets in the morning could still change the complexion of the game, but we needed a breakthrough fast.

Jimmy took the first over and with his very first ball of the morning hit Rogers flush on the helmet with a viciously directed short delivery. There was added reason for concern, because of Rogers' concussion history, and the Australia team doctors spent a fair while assessing him before allowing him to continue. He had a cut behind his ear but hit two fours in the over so appeared to be OK.

I knew that however hard I ran in I was not going to be able to extract a huge amount from the pitch, but kept reminding myself how quickly things can change in Test cricket. A square drive from Smith off Jimmy took the Aussies to 350 for one.

I steeled myself for another over and felt in decent rhythm again. Rogers hit yet another four before I finally made the breakthrough when I snuck one past his defences to see him depart for 173. At 37 years old, he must have known he'd never play a Test at Lord's again and he rightly milked the deserved standing ovation as he left the field.

My dismissal of Michael Clarke in the second innings at Cardiff had been the tenth time I'd got him out in Tests and I was determined to make it 11 now. I got a couple to nip just enough off the pitch to beat his outside edge, but despite bowling a really good spell at him, I couldn't get the second breakthrough we craved.

Woody replaced Jimmy and had some immediate success when Clarke hooked a short ball straight to Gary Ballance at square leg. It was a soft dismissal by Clarke's standards but we weren't complaining. At 383 for three we'd forced a collapse by the first day's standards.

Adam Voges, my old Nottinghamshire team-mate, came in.

'All right, Vogesy?' I asked. Nothing.

With Smith still looking untroubled at the other end, Voges got into his stride with some well-timed drives as the Aussies reached lunch on 424 for three. Relatively speaking, we'd had a productive session.

I had Voges caught behind by Jos straight after lunch, bringing Mitch Marsh to the crease. He played a couple of nice shots before I bowled him with a cutter which, slightly ominously for us, stayed low. It was another wicket, though, and I was pleased with the way I was bowling on such an unresponsive pitch.

Debutant Nevill came in and provided excellent support for Smith as he approached his double hundred. He got there with an effortless whip off his pads for four off Mo and removed his helmet and punched his bat as the crowd rose to him. He'd batted magnificently, giving just one chance in 336 balls. We all applauded him.

With Australia pushing for declaration runs, Smith was finally out for 215 attempting a reverse sweep and being trapped in front by Rooty with the score on 533. Rooty got a second when Nevill hit a catch to Mo to depart for 45 and the Aussies finally called time on their innings when Jimmy caught Mitchell Johnson off my bowling.

Australia's final total of 566 for eight declared from 149 overs made for daunting reading as we walked wearily off the field and looked up at the scoreboard. Yes, the pitch was still flat and playing well. Yes, we batted deep and were 1-0 up in the series. But I defy any batsman to say walking out knowing you're 566 runs behind does not cause a degree of apprehension. We knew we had to bat out of our skins or we could find ourselves in serious trouble.

Australia's final total of 566 for eight declared from 149 overs made for daunting reading as we walked wearily off the field and looked up at the scoreboard.

Having never opened the batting at any serious level of cricket, I can't imagine what it's like to spend more than a day and a half in the field before having ten minutes to get yourself padded up, focused and back out on the field to face the opposition's quickest bowlers. The nervous energy you expend at the tail end of their innings as you begin to think about your own innings, must be immense. Being captain adds to that burden and I've always been hugely impressed by the way guys like Cook and Strauss have managed it down the years. It must take an incredible amount of mental resilience and concentration.

For Lythy, this level of cricket was all new. The difference in intensity between county and Test level is very significant and unfortunately he lasted just two balls as he fenced at a Mitchell Starc delivery he didn't need to play at and edged behind. I felt for him as he walked off dejectedly.

The wicket was just the fillip the Aussies needed, and you could sense their energy levels increase as Gary walked to the crease. Despite scoring a vitally important 61 at Cardiff, there had still been a lot of talk in the press about his position at No.3 in the side.

The manner of a couple of Gary's dismissals in the Tests against New Zealand, where he'd stayed deep in his crease and been bowled, had caused some to claim he didn't have the technique for Test cricket. I totally disagreed. Sometimes you can see straight away when you watch a player in the nets for the first time if they have a flaw that could be exploited. You get a sense fairly early on if someone's going to cut it at international level. I had no doubt Gary had what it took. I still do. In fact, of all England's top-order batsmen of recent times, I find him the hardest to bowl at in the nets. Because he stays so deep, I find he completely messes up my length and I strive to overcompensate and often overpitch. He's a very awkward batsman to bowl at and has far more shots than people might think, even though he played very tightly in his first summer in the side in 2014. He also showed then he has excellent concentration and can bat for long periods. But nevertheless he was under pressure. So it was great to see him clip his first ball confidently off his legs for four.

'Great shot, Gaz!' I shouted from the balcony. I really wanted him to succeed.

Hazlewood and Starc both bowled very good opening spells, and Cooky and Gary had to battle hard just to survive. Johnson came into the attack and Gary welcomed him by hitting his first ball straight past him down the ground. But then, disaster. Just as Gary looked to settle, Johnson bowled him a full one around off stump and cleaned him up. Out for 23, England were 28 for two.

It got worse. In Hazlewood's next over he bowled Belly with an absolute pearler to leave us 29 for three and in serious trouble. We were 537 runs behind and badly on the slide. We desperately needed another Root miracle act. For once, we didn't get one. Johnson, bowling very quickly, got him to play away from his body and he feathered a catch behind to the gleeful Nevill. Gone for 1, this was serious.

Stokesy almost played on first ball but dug in with Cooky and showed plenty of fight. No surprise there. He smashed Nathan Lyon straight down the ground for six and was ready to take the battle to Australia. The pair reached the close on 85 for four, with Stokesy on 38 from 50 balls and Cooky on 21 from 85. As the players walked off, Cooky sought out Steve Smith to congratulate him again on his double hundred. It was a nice touch.

'Tough day,' Jimmy said.

You could say that again.

We desperately needed a big partnership the next morning. In fact, we needed a massive partnership. For a time, it looked as if we might get one as Stokes and Cook batted through the morning to take the score past 150 in the 48th over. Stokesy moved on to 77 while Cooky ground it out as only he can to reach fifty from 142 balls. Slowly, we began to believe we could turn it around again. You could sense the calming effect the partnership was having on the crowd.

Phil Brown

Getty Images

Above: I wasn't surprised to face a lot of short stuff when I came in to bat at the end of day one in Cardiff, but I was still there for the start of the second day.

Left: The picture looks far worse than the reality here during our warm-up game of football – trust me it wasn't a red-card tackle on Jos Buttler.

Getty Images

Getty Images

I get Shane Watson LBW in the first innings, despite him calling for a review, and the wicket helped reinforce our control of the situation.

Above: The bails go flying after I finally strike on the second morning of the match at Lord's, and Chris Rogers is out for 173.

Right: But it had been a frustrating time for a bowler, with the pitch lacking pace and carry – no wonder I gave it a kick.

Like father like son – Joe Root watches on!

My area in the Trent Bridge pavilion – Forest shirts proudly on display.

Jimmy Anderson pretty much needs a room to himself.

We might not have talked much during the series, but I did swap shirts with Mitchell Johnson at the end of it.

I like to do some visualisation exercises before a match, but it isn't always easy, as this scene at Edgbaston shows.

I was in awe of Jimmy's skills as he dismissed Mitchell Marsh third ball at Edgbaston. His six for 47 helped bowl them out for 136 to put us in charge.

Eyes on the ball. My 87-run partnership with Moeen Ali helped reinforce our position, as we ended up with a 145-run lead after the first innings.

A disconsolate Mitchell Johnson heads off the pitch as I join Steve Finn to celebrate his superb comeback performance.

Filming an advert for Waitrose in which I was giving away tickets for the Trent Bridge match – it turned out to be a pretty decent Test.

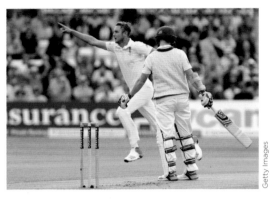

Ottis Gibson and I join in a minute's applause in memory of Clive Rice, and suddenly all the nerves I had about leading the attack in the absence of Jimmy Anderson washed away.

First over and my 300th Test victim, Chris Rogers, is out, caught by Alastair Cook – it was the perfect delivery.

I can't hide my astonishment after Ben Stokes has taken the best catch I've ever seen live. Adam Voges is on his way, and Australia are 21 for five after just 4.1 overs.

The Ashes are back in English hands once again after our crushing victory at Trent Bridge gave us an unassailable 3-1 lead.

Celebrating with Bealey at the end of the match.

Savouring the moment.

Phil Brown

Above: Woody takes the horse for a ride on the outfield at The Oval. We'd lost the Test, but we'd won the Ashes against the odds.

Right: The message behind says it all, as Jimmy and I celebrate a wonderful Ashes triumph.

Below: Alastair Cook deserved this moment – an Ashes-winning captain once again.

Phil Brown

Phil Brown

Stokes looked destined for another hundred when Mitch Marsh, who'd bowled at a brisk pace, forced him to play on when one kept low and he didn't get fully forward. With Stokes out for 87, we were 175 for five and the Aussies were right back on top.

Jos made just 13 before edging Lyon to Nevill. I was a bit surprised to see Jos walk. Each to their own when it comes to walking – and everyone knows where I stand on it – but it looked as if the umpire wasn't going to give it, and replays proved inconclusive even with Hotspot and Snicko. You're never going to have a go at someone for walking, but Jos may have thought twice when he looked at the replays.

Having batted for the best part of six hours and faced 230 balls, Cooky looked destined for a thoroughly deserved hundred when Marsh induced his second drag-on to claim another vital wicket. Cooky dragged himself off the field, four runs short of his hundred, knowing we were in dire straits. He'd played a captain's knock, without a doubt, but at 266 for seven, the follow-on target was still 100 runs away.

I passed him on my way out to the crease. No words were exchanged, but I nodded in acknowledgement of his gutsy innings. I joined Mo in the middle and it didn't need to be said we were in a tight spot.

'Let's just play and see what happens,' I said.

'Fine by me,' he replied. We reached tea on 285 for seven.

Mo didn't last long afterwards, falling LBW to Hazlewood for 39, and Woody came and went quickly as well. I was last out, caught off Mitchell Johnson for 21 as we were all out for 312. Australia led by 254 and had every right to enforce the follow-on, but Clarke decided to let their bowlers put their feet up for a while as their batsmen added more runs.

A few people were surprised by Clarke's decision, but I completely got it. I'm not sure many people really understand the stresses and strains caused by pounding in on rock-hard surfaces. Clarke had given his bowlers a chance to rest. They'd appreciate that, for sure.

Deep down, we knew we were already so far behind the eight ball we were almost off the table. We'd need to bowl Australia out for no more than 100 to stand a realistic chance of chasing down the runs and winning the Test match. We were in survival mode. By the close of day three, Australia were 108 for none with a lead of 362. Only the weather, or a miracle, could save us.

We were utterly dejected in the dressing room. We knew the chances of us saving the Test were now incredibly remote. That evening, we invited former England captain Michael Atherton to pop in. Famed for his obdurate batting style, Athers reminded us of an innings he'd played in Johannesburg in 1995 when he batted for almost 11 hours to score 185 not out and secure a draw against all the odds. It was exactly what we needed to hear. Survival was still possible, and Athers' chat gave us a much-needed boost.

Early the next morning, the strangest thing happened. With Australia's openers cruising along at 114 for none, Rogers suddenly looked seriously unsteady in the middle of the pitch. His partner, Warner, was clearly concerned and moved towards him to put his hand on his shoulder as Rogers knelt down on his haunches then sat on the floor.

Following his blow to the head in the first innings, and his recent history of concussion, there was serious concern for his health. He looked really bemused and had a faraway look in his eyes. It was very disconcerting, not least for Rogers, who for the second time in the match required prolonged attention from the Australian medical team.

After a delay of several minutes, he eventually rose to his feet, but this time the doctors were taking no chances and he left the field on 49. He would later reveal he thought the Grand Stand was moving up and down while he was in the middle and had suddenly become very confused. It was odd and unsettling for everyone. As he left the field, we all wished him well. He would play no further part in the match.

Warner made a controlled 83 while Smith added 58 as Australia ground our noses into the Lord's dust before declaring on 254 for two, a lead of 508. It was stating the obvious that we just had to bat out time. The chances of us chasing down 509 were, in reality, almost zero.

Lythy escaped the ignominy of a pair before nicking his 16th ball from Starc behind to leave us 12 for one. Cooky then edged a cut behind off Johnson to make us 23 for two. The dressing room was very quiet. Gary Ballance made just 14 before edging Marsh behind and Belly could muster only 11 before being caught at short leg off Nathan Lyon.

The Aussies fancied wrapping up the Test that night when Stokesy was run out for 0 when he failed to ground his bat over the line and replays showed his foot was in the air when Johnson's throw hit the stumps. It was a really disappointing way to get out and Stokesy could not hide his anger as he walked off the pitch. We steered well clear of him when he reached the dressing room.

Jos and Mo followed in quick succession as we slumped to 64 for seven. What a time for me to come to the crease. I whacked a few along with Rooty, but the game was gone. Joe and I were out within the space of four balls, and when Jimmy was bowled by Hazlewood for 0 at 5.15pm on Sunday afternoon, it was 1-1 in the series.

After the elation of Cardiff, we'd been taught a lesson at Lord's. We knew they'd come back hard and they'd proved us right. We'd lost by the massive margin of 405 runs. The battle for the Ashes was well and truly on.

ENGLAND V AUSTRALIA (2ND TEST)

At Lord's, London

16, 17, 18, 19 July 2015

AUSTRALIA WON BY 405 RUNS

Toss: Australia
Umpires: H.D.P.K.Dharmasena (Sri Lanka) and M.Erasmus (South Africa)
Referee: R.S.Madugalle (Sri Lanka)

AUSTRALIA

C.J.L.Rogers	b Broad	173	retired hurt		49
D.A.Warner	c Anderson b Ali	38	c Cook b Ali		83
S.P.D.Smith	lbw b Root	215	b Ali		58
* M.J.Clarke	c Ballance b Wood	7	not out		32
A.C.Voges	c Buttler b Broad	25			
M.R.Marsh	b Broad	12	(5) not out		27
† P.M.Nevill	c Ali b Root	45			
M.G.Johnson	c Anderson b Broad	15			
M.A.Starc	not out	12			
J.R.Hazlewood					
N.M.Lyon					
Extras	(B 8, LB 14, W 1, NB 1)	24	(LB 5)		5
Total	(8 wkts dec; 149 overs)	566	(2 wkts dec; 49 overs)		254

ENGLAND

A.Lyth	c Nevill b Starc	0	c Nevill b Starc		7
* A.N.Cook	b Marsh	96	c Nevill b Johnson		11
G.S.Ballance	b Johnson	23	c Nevill b Marsh		14
I.R.Bell	b Hazlewood	1	c sub (S.E.Marsh) b Lyon		11
J.E.Root	c Neville b Johnson	1	b Hazlewood		17
B.A.Stokes	b Marsh	87	run out		0
† J.C.Buttler	c Nevill b Lyon	13	c Neville b Johnson		11
M.M.Ali	lbw b Hazlewood	39	c sub (S.E.Marsh) b Johnson		0
S.C.J.Broad	c sub (S.E.Marsh) b Johnson	21	c Voges b Lyon		25
M.A.Wood	b Hazlewood	4	not out		2
J.M.Anderson	not out	6	b Hazlewood		0
Extras	(B 12, LB 8, NB 1)	21	(B 4, LB 1)		5
Total	(90.1 overs)	312	(37 overs)		103

ENGLAND	O	M	R	W		O	M	R	W
Anderson	26	4	99	0		7	0	38	0
Broad	27	5	83	4		8	2	42	0
Wood	28	7	92	1	(4)	10	3	39	0
Ali	36	4	138	1	(3)	16	0	78	2
Stokes	19	2	77	0		3	0	20	0
Root	12	0	55	2		5	0	32	0
Lyth	1	1	0	0					
AUSTRALIA	O	M	R	W		O	M	R	W
Starc	22	1	86	1		7	3	16	1
Hazlewood	22	2	68	3		8	2	20	2
Johnson	20.1	8	53	3		10	3	27	3
Lyon	16	1	53	1	(5)	9	3	27	2
Marsh	8	3	23	2	(4)	3	2	8	1
Smith	2	0	9	0					

FALL OF WICKETS

WKT	A 1ST	E 1ST	A 2ND	E 2ND
1st	78	0	165	12
2nd	362	28	210	23
3rd	383	29	–	42
4th	426	30	–	48
5th	442	175	–	52
6th	533	210	–	64
7th	536	266	–	64
8th	566	294	–	101
9th	–	306	–	101
10th	–	312	–	103

CLOSE OF PLAY

Day 1	Australia (1) 337-1 (90; C.J.L.Rogers 158*, S.P.D.Smith 129*)
Day 2	England (1) 85-4 (29; A.N.Cook 21*, B.A.Stokes 38*)
Day 3	Australia (2) 108-0 (26; C.J.L.Rogers 44*, D.A.Warner 60*)

9

EDGBASTON

CLASS IS PERMANENT

20-31 JULY

It became very clear to us as we picked ourselves up and dusted ourselves down in the days following the Lord's defeat that we needed to focus more on our own approach and not worry so much about the Aussies. Out of respect for Michael Clarke's men, we'd spent a lot of time in the lead-up to Lord's examining how Australia would react to the Cardiff defeat and not enough time analysing our own performance and where we could improve.

Part of the reason we'd performed so well in the first Test was down to the fact we'd gone into it determined to play the ball and not the man. With Mitchell Johnson, we were not going to hark back to his Herculean displays in 2013-14, but would watch each ball on its merits. If it was there to whack, we were going to whack it. It had worked a treat in Cardiff and we needed to go back to that mindset.

Our success over the summer had been based on approaching each game without fear. That meant almost ignoring what the opposition were going to do, because you have the belief that if you get your own individual skills right as a team, you have the players to outdo your opponents. Looking around our dressing room in the aftermath of the Lord's defeat, I still 100 per cent believed that to be the case.

In the same way our win at Cardiff had probably got people overexcited and carried away, so too our defeat at Lord's saw people go far too far the other way. It was 1-1 after two Tests in an Ashes series, but you'd have thought the urn was already on a 747 back to Australia. In our dressing room, we knew we could hit back hard.

We were bitterly disappointed with the way we performed at Lord's. When we'd batted, we allowed the scoreboard pressure of Australia's massive first-innings total to get the better of us and, for once, Joe Root hadn't been able to dig us out of a hole after a wobble at the top. Our second-innings performance with bat and ball had been nothing short of unacceptable, but in reality it was always going to be a massive undertaking to save the Test match as we were so far behind.

There was a lot of conjecture over our top order with Ian Bell, Adam Lyth and Gary Ballance all coming under close scrutiny. It's as sure as night follows day that as an international batsman your place will come under the spotlight from time to time. If you stay around the England team long enough, it is simply impossible to sustain your form indefinitely. Everyone will have a slump at some point and people will start saying you should be dropped.

Part of the issue for both Belly and Gary was that people were linking their World Cup and recent one-day performances with their Test form. Belly had averaged more than 50 during the World Cup, but had suffered by comparison with some of the astonishing strike rates other teams' openers had achieved, while Gary had struggled at No.3 after the late decision to ask him to bat in that pivotal position. Both men had scored important runs in Cardiff, but it was indicative of the high expectations of the media and wider public that their places were coming under pressure.

A couple of Gary's recent dismissals hadn't looked too pretty, as he was bowled deep in his crease, but I was convinced both he and Belly had big parts to play in the future of the England Test team. With almost 7,500 runs in 112 Test appearances, Belly's credentials were beyond dispute, while Gary had shown himself to have an excellent temperament in scoring four hundreds in his first 15 Tests at an average of almost 50. I remember reading one article calling for them both to be dropped and thinking 'we must have some serious strength in depth to consider dropping two blokes with those records'.

Lythy had scored a vital 37 in the second innings at Cardiff and it was only two Tests since he'd scored his maiden Test hundred. In the 1980s or 90s that probably wouldn't have been enough, but things have calmed down a lot on the selection front since the advent of central contracts and people now understand the importance of keeping a settled team where possible. Some people were highlighting the similarity of some of Lythy's dismissals, caught behind or in the slips playing at balls outside off stump, but how many batsaen don't have a weakness to the ball moving away from them on or around off stump? Calls for him to go were premature in my mind. I had no doubt Lythy would be given another crack.

Trevor Bayliss played a fairly straight bat when quizzed about the possibility of changes for the third Test. 'When you play badly, positions are going to be discussed,' he said in the aftermath of Lord's.

'All I'll say is that two Tests ago these players were considered the best and that doesn't necessarily change after four innings. It's a concern we keep losing top-order wickets and the players know that.'

Jonny Bairstow's county form had been magnificent for Yorkshire. He had already scored five centuries during the season and was averaging more than 100 in the championship. He was making a compelling case. My Nottinghamshire team-mate Jimmy Taylor was also considered, but he wasn't in great form at that point.

In the end, the selectors went for the in-form Bairstow in place of the unfortunate Ballance. I was pleased for Jonny, but had no doubt we'd see Gary again soon in an England shirt. His omission would see Belly move up from No.4 to No.3 in the order, with Jonny slotting in at five.

The other area of concern was Mark Wood's ankle. He had struggled in Australia's second innings at Lord's and the medics were worried that if he played at Edgbaston he could risk being ruled out of the rest of the series. The doctors and coaches had to decide if it was worth playing him at Edgbaston, knowing it could be his last contribution to the series, or leave him out with a view to potentially bringing him back later on. Steve Finn had been bowling superbly in the nets and in one-day cricket in recent months, and looked very much back to the bowler who had burst onto the international scene as a raw 21-year-old five years earlier.

Finny's trials and tribulations have been well documented, after his confidence disintegrated on tour in Australia the previous winter and soon after the then one-day coach Ashley Giles described him as 'unselectable'. His run-up had been messed around and shortened radically while, amazingly, the ICC even introduced a new law making it a 'no ball' if a bowler knocked the bails off at the non-striker's end in his delivery stride. It had been a minor problem throughout Finny's career. He's a lovely lad and a deep thinker and maybe it gnawed away at him a little. The attempts to remodel his run-up were in direct response to that issue and a slight tendency to fall over after delivering the ball. He never settled. When you are not confident in your technique and the pressure comes on, it's inevitable cracks will appear. And they had.

So it was brilliant to see him back smiling and really running in hard to the crease. He had always had a fantastic knack of taking wickets, with one of the best strike rates of any England bowler, but had sometimes lacked control in his younger days. After going back to basics with his action at Middlesex and rebuilding his confidence, he didn't appear to have lost that priceless wicket-taking ability. He is always going to go for a few runs as he strives for wickets, but he's also added more control to his bowling. Ottis Gibson also deserves a lot of credit for the work he'd done to help get him back to his best. He was quite an asset to have waiting in the wings. Mark Footitt and Liam Plunkett were also excellent back-up options but Finny was the standout candidate.

There was a ten-day gap between Tests which gave me time to rest my tired body after getting through a fair amount of work at Lord's, including 27 overs in Australia's first innings. The conjecture over the pitches continued with speculation about how the Edgbaston track would play. We were given further assurances by our management that they had asked for pitches that provided a good contest between bat and ball. It would have sounded like sour grapes if we'd whinged after Lord's. Ultimately, Australia outplayed us across the board and thoroughly deserved to win. But there was undeniably frustration among both players and management about the Lord's pitch. It put far too much onus on winning the toss.

It was important to remind ourselves when we reconvened in Birmingham that the series was all square and, despite some of the doom-mongering in the media, we were alive and kicking. Of all the grounds in England where we would want to play following a heavy defeat, Edgbaston would be right up there. The support we receive is always phenomenal. It's a completely different atmosphere to Lord's and sometimes it can feel almost like a football crowd. The boys absolutely love playing there.

Of all the grounds in England where we would want to play following a heavy defeat, Edgbaston would be right up there. The support we receive is always phenomenal.

The mood remained upbeat within the squad and we certainly weren't letting the Lord's loss weigh us down. I was the victim of one of Root's typically childish pranks in the warm-up the day before the Test began, when he snuck up behind me and managed to pull my tracksuit bottoms down in full view of the rest of the ground. Hilarious. The rest of the boys found it highly amusing and I chased the mischievous little so-and-so around the outfield for a while, threatening all sorts of things. Unfortunately, he was too quick for me and I had to remind him revenge was a dish best served cold.

I wouldn't have minded so much if the whole thing hadn't been caught on someone's camera phone and uploaded on the ECB app with Benny Hill-type music added as backing. Before I knew it, the video had gone viral and created a record number of hits. I don't know who was more delighted – Rooty or the ECB marketing department!

As the Test drew closer, it looked less and less likely that Woody would be risked. It was another fine judgement call for our medics to have to make, but in the end it was decided it was not worth taking the chance in the longer term. With such a high-calibre replacement available in Finn, why take the risk? It was a sensible call. Woody was disappointed, but he understood the bigger picture.

The Aussies also had fitness concerns following Rogers' alarming second-innings turn when he'd retired hurt and played no further part in the Test match. The opener had stayed in London to seek specialist treatment after the Aussies moved north between Tests for a tour game against Derbyshire. His batting partner David Warner had obviously been pretty concerned at the time and gave a frightening insight into what had been said between the two when he gave an interview to the press in Derby ahead of their tour game.

'He actually said to me: "The Grand Stand is moving," and I said: "No it's not." I was worried, I had no idea what was going on, and so was he,' Warner said. 'He said: "I don't know what's happening here," so I said: "Just sit down." I came down the wicket and I had to look twice because I didn't really know what was going on.'

It was pretty scary stuff and a bit unsettling for everyone. With Rogers' concussion history, and the recent tragedy involving Phil Hughes, the Australian medical team were obviously taking the issue very seriously. Rogers had eventually joined his team-mates in Derby after his condition was diagnosed as an 'inner ear' problem and by the time we convened at Edgbaston it appeared he was going to be passed fit to play.

People were asking whether we'd be willing to bowl bouncers at him considering what had happened and, while it may not have been palatable to hear, the answer was unequivocally 'yes'. Once a player is passed fit, they are passed fit. Our job is to take wickets and win Test matches for our country and we do that in the most effective way possible. If that means bowling bouncers, then so be it. I defy any other professional cricketer to say any different. It's harsh, but so is professional sport. Rogers would have expected nothing less.

The day before the Test, I was saddened to hear that the former Nottinghamshire and South Africa captain Clive Rice had died at home in Cape Town aged just 66. Clive was a folk hero at Notts and my dad had known him well as a player. I knew his loss would be hard felt at Trent Bridge and beyond. I took a moment to think of Clive's family and, after speaking to a few people at Nottinghamshire, decided it would be appropriate for me to wear a black armband at Edgbaston in Clive's memory.

There was some conjecture over whether Brad Haddin would return to the Australia team after missing the second Test for personal reasons. Peter Nevill had done a good job behind the stumps and with the bat, but I fully expected Haddin to return with his wealth of Ashes experience and proven track record against us. All due respect to Nevill, who was clearly an exceptionally good cricketer, but I knew who I'd rather face. When Clarke named his team on the morning of the Test, I must admit I was surprised not to see Haddin included.

Haddin was clearly a bloke who thrived in the heat of Ashes battles and as a side we'd come to respect his abilities as a cricketer. His record against us was outstanding. Even in Australia when we got whitewashed, there were several occasions we had them in trouble before he came in and whacked a big score to take the momentum away. He was one of those players who always tried to take the game away from an opposition attack. I've no doubt his omission would have caused a few raised eyebrows among Aussie supporters, too.

With Finny included in our final XI, there was another amusing moment after we'd warmed up before play on the first morning. Finny was last to return to the dressing room and he walked in with a slightly baffled look on his face.

'What's up Finny?' I asked.

'A weird thing just happened,' he replied.

It turned out he'd just been given the silent treatment too as he went on to describe how he'd approached Adam Voges, who he'd played the entire first half of the season alongside for Middlesex, and gone to say 'hello'. Before he knew it, Vogesy had seen him coming and just turned and walked off.

'Get used to it, Finny,' I said, half seriously.

I'm not going to criticise Australia for employing those tactics, but did I agree with them? Not really. At the end of the day, we're just blokes playing sport. I'm not saying you have to be their best friend and tell them how you're planning to get them out, but basic courtesies like saying 'good morning' aren't going to make the difference between winning and losing. But, like their refusal to share a beer with us, it was their prerogative.

We'd been interested to see a fairly even covering of grass on the pitch when we arrived at the ground on the first morning. We'd noticed it in the lead-up to the game, but you never know how much the groundstaff will take off on the morning of a match. However, I was encouraged by the greenness in the wicket. There was little bit of rain around as well, which was going to make for a very tough decision at the toss. As it turned out, Clarke won it and decided Australia would bat. I understood why, especially after the way their batsmen had dominated us at Lord's and this wicket certainly didn't look a bad one to bat on. Indeed, Cooky confirmed after Clarke had explained his reasoning for batting that he would have made the same call. In 2005, Ricky Ponting had famously made the mistake of putting England into bat at Edgbaston and seen them chalk up 400 in a day. I'm sure that would have been playing on both captains' minds.

Jimmy and I looked at each other and, without saying anything, I think we both realised this was a good toss to lose. I certainly didn't walk out that morning with the same reservations I'd had about the Lord's pitch.

Cooky reiterated the message to go out and express ourselves. We had got in among the Australian batting line-up at Cardiff and there was no reason we couldn't do so again.

'This is about us, boys,' Cooky said. 'We make sure we execute our basics and the rest will follow. We have all the talent in the world in this dressing room. Let's go out there and make it happen.'

The atmosphere as we took to the field was absolutely jumping. The hairs on the back of my neck stood on end as I entered the arena.

The rain had abated but it was still overcast and I fancied our chances of doing some damage, even with the form Smith and Rogers had shown at Lord's. Despite my frustrations with the pitch there, I'd picked up four wickets from 27 overs of toil in their first innings and I remained very happy with the way I was bowling, even if the big haul hadn't come yet this summer. I felt as if it was only a matter of time.

Jimmy marked his run and got ready to take the first over. The crowd noise was electric. We were ready to do battle again. Jimmy sped in with the crowd growing louder and his first delivery to Rogers was an absolute beauty, just short of a length and nipping away off the pitch to beat the outside edge. Hello.

The very next ball, Rogers shovelled the ball into the leg side and, following a slight hesitation, called Warner through for a risky single. I sensed a chance and swept round from mid-on before picking up, taking aim and releasing all in one action. My throw was spot on, smashing into the stumps as Warner dived full length for the crease. The boys went up in unison as we thought we'd got our man. We were wrong. The appeal was referred and television replays showed Warner had made his ground by the narrowest of margins. Five years ago, we'd got off to the perfect start to the second Test in Adelaide when Jonathan Trott ran out Simon Katich in the first over of the match without facing a ball. It had set us on the road to victory. Sadly, this time there was to be no repeat.

But the direct hit had got the crowd even more hyped. We were two balls into the day and already, Edgbaston was on its feet.

'This is what home advantage is all about,' I thought to myself as Jimmy prepared to bowl his third delivery.

This time Warner defended solidly before driving the fourth ball to mid-off for no run. The fifth ball swung and squirted away off a thick outside edge for two, before Warner cut the last ball of a highly eventful first over to Stokesy at point. Not that the crowd needed any encouragement, but they were on their feet to applaud.

'Imagine what they'd be like if we'd actually taken a wicket,' I thought.

My first over didn't go quite to plan, with Rogers hitting the fourth ball off his pads through the leg side for four. There was some encouraging carry, although there didn't seem to be any great pace in the pitch, but there still seemed enough in it for us to be hopeful.

In Jimmy's next over, the hope turned into tangible celebrations as he got another delivery just back of a length to jag off the pitch and hit the Australian opener in line. Jimmy was certain he'd got his man and the umpire agreed, raising his finger after some consideration. Warner consulted Rogers before deciding against reviewing and he was right not to do so as television replays showed the ball had pitched in line and was going on to hit the stumps. We were on the move.

Smith survived an LBW shout first ball before getting off the mark and Jimmy's next two deliveries to Rogers were snorters again. There was definitely something in this.

I felt in reasonable rhythm without quite hitting my straps, but Jimmy and I were both getting lateral movement off the pitch and making life extremely difficult for the Australian batsmen. The crowd sensed we had an opportunity to apply pressure and continued to roar their support.

Cooky took the decision to bring me off after just three overs. He was eager to get Finny into the game as quickly as possible and I totally understood that. His last Test had been more than two years previously, against Australia at Trent Bridge in the first Test of 2013, and he was understandably nervous coming into this one. Cooky sensed that, as well as the fact I was a tiny bit down on pace, and took the opportunity to introduce the Middlesex man earlier than he may otherwise have done. It was excellent captaincy and good man management.

His first three deliveries were all around off stump and reasonably full, and Smith, fresh from his double century at Lord's, played them without discomfort. The next delivery saw Smith play and miss a loose shot outside the off stump and the ball flew through to Jos behind the stumps. The crowd were in the game and roared Finny in again.

This time Smith got forward and eased the ball effortlessly through the covers for four. Finn walked back to his mark shaking his head.

'Don't worry, Finny. There's one coming here,' Jos cried from behind the stumps.

How right he was. The very next ball was an absolute beauty which drew Smith forward and caught the outside edge before flying low to Cooky at first slip, where he took a neat low catch. It was a marvellous moment. You could sense Finny's relief. All those months of hard work when, in the darkest times, he thought he may never get a shot at international cricket again had paid off. He'd just got the world's No.1 ranked batsman out on the first morning of an Ashes Test match. He was back in business in a big way and it was fantastic to see. He deserved every high five and pat on the back he got in that moment. It was a defining moment in the Test match.

The Aussies were on the back foot, 18 for two in the eighth over facing two England bowlers with their tails up. The crowd of 25,000 sounded like it was double that number. It was exhilarating just being out on the field.

Jimmy and Clarke exchanged a few words after the Australia captain hit a couple of streaky fours, but it didn't take long for Finny to strike again when he delivered a perfect, quick Yorker which beat Clarke for pace and bowled him. Australia were 34 for three and Finny had two for 6, 14 balls into his comeback after two years in the wilderness. We mobbed our friend and team-mate.

All those months of hard work when, in the darkest times, he thought he may never get a shot at international cricket again had paid off.

Clarke's dismissal brought Voges to the crease and, following their earlier non-exchange, Finny decided the best way to greet him was to bowl a very hostile over at him.

There was a brief rain stoppage, with the Aussies on 38 for three, when Cooky and Trev reiterated the need to carry on bowling tight lines and allow the pitch to do the rest. The new ball was nipping around and looked almost unplayable in comparison to the earlier pitches in the series. In truth, these were exactly the sort of early Test match English conditions which in years gone by would have been considered entirely commonplace. We needed to make sure we took advantage.

Rogers never really settled but hung on in typically dogged fashion, while Voges also knuckled down as Australia reached lunch on 63 for three after an abbreviated session.

There was more rain around during the lunch break, delaying the restart and stopping us maintaining the momentum we'd built up in an excellent first hour.

Jimmy hit his straps immediately after the break. He was in fantastic rhythm and clearly relishing conditions which were tailor-made for a bowler of his skill and control. When there is movement in the air and off the pitch there is simply no better bowler in the world to exploit it. Even if he maintained a stony face, I could tell my old mate was enjoying himself.

With the final ball of his first over of the afternoon session, Jimmy extracted unexpected lift from the pitch and caught the toe of Voges' bat as he made a belated attempt to leave the ball. Jos took the catch gleefully and the Aussies were now in serious trouble, with the inexperienced Mitch Marsh joining Rogers at the crease. Marsh had played some meaty shots at Lord's under completely different circumstances on a rock-hard pitch with his side dominant and chasing declaration runs. Here, the pitch was doing plenty, there was swing around and Australia were up against it after choosing to bat. On top of that, the Edgbaston crowd was reaching fever pitch as the best swing bowler in the world was giving his fans another master class. I looked at Marsh taking guard and didn't envy him.

He lasted just three balls. The first two Jimmy sent down just outside off stump. He blocked the first before leaving the second. His third ball spat a little as Marsh played away from his body and took a healthy edge through to an ecstatic Jos behind the stumps.

The crowd went bananas and so did we. I'd seen Jimmy bowl spells like this time and time again, but I never cease to be in awe of the skills he is able to demonstrate. On his day, he has complete control of where the ball is going and so many subtle variations that are almost impossible to detect. Most recently, he'd taken six for 42 in the West Indies' first innings in the third Test defeat in Bridgetown. Here, in his 107th Test match, he was again delivering for his team when we needed him most.

Australia were 82 for five as another inexperienced player, wicket-keeper Nevill, strode to the crease. He would not have expected this, in only his second Test, after his captain had won the toss and batted at a ground that typically favours batting, for the first few days at least.

As a professional sportsman, there are very few times when you allow yourself to step outside the immediacy of your situation and consider the position you are in. The game moves too fast, is too pressured and too bloody difficult for you to risk losing concentration by losing focus. But for some reason, as I stood at mid-on and Jimmy prepared to bowl, I did precisely that. I stepped back – not literally – but for a moment I was able to consider how unbelievably lucky I was to be in this position right now. I grew up as a passionate England fan. All I ever wanted to do as a kid was play cricket for England after watching my dad reach the pinnacle of his playing career. As a child, I watched Ashes videos on almost continuous loop and I had always dreamt of playing cricket for England. Now, here I was with the best seat in the house. I looked around the ground and thought 'how lucky are you?' I was watching one of England's greatest-ever fast bowlers, if not the greatest – who just happened to be one of my best mates – terrorise the Aussies in front of a full house at Edgbaston. I was right there in the middle, watching at first hand. It felt very surreal. A shiver ran up my spine.

'Wake up, Stuart! Focus!' I thought as Jimmy ran in with another surge of energy from the excited crowd seemingly powering him effortlessly through the crease. His now perfectly tuned action was on repeat mode.

'Oooooohhhh,' went the crowd as Nevill left the ball outside off stump. It was a privilege just to be out here.

Rogers had moved to 40 as he and Nevill combined to block Finny's next over but, with Jimmy now rampant, the Australian wicket-keeper fell in his very next over when he left a booming inswinger, which bowled him all ends up. Wow!

Mitchell Johnson was next to go in Jimmy's following over, when he switched to around the wicket for the left-hander. With his very first ball from the new angle, Jimmy squared Johnson up and he edged a catch high on his bat to fourth slip where Stokesy took a good catch. At 94 for seven, it was carnage. The crowd noise was unlike anything I'd experienced before at this fantastic ground. It felt like the place was going to erupt. At times, we were actually struggling to make ourselves heard above it.

'Have a blow, Finny. Well bowled, mate,' Cooky shouted before giving me the nod that I'd be taking the next over. Rogers reached his fifty with a punch down the ground from my third ball, but we continued to pile the pressure onto the Aussie batsmen.

There was more rain around before tea, which gave us another chance to regroup before going again with another burst before the interval.

Finally I made my first breakthrough, when I trapped Rogers plumb in front on the back foot from around the wicket. I'd worked so hard on this type of dismissal with Ottis in the lead-up to the series. If you imagine I had a piece of string on off stump and had dragged it all the way back to my mark, the aim was to follow that piece of string so I'd hit off stump. It was about aligning my legs, knees, chest, head towards off stump. Although I was bowling around the wicket, it meant the stumps were very much in play. It had paid off again. With only two wickets left, Rogers reviewed. But it was never in doubt and he had to go for 52.

'Nice of you to join the party,' Jimmy said dryly. This time it was my turn to give an England player the silent treatment.

In my next over I joined the party again when Mitchell Starc attempted to leave a rising delivery from just back of a length and Jos took another neat catch from the toe end of an Aussie bat.

One more to go. Lyon walked in. Josh Hazlewood connected with a couple of lusty blows while Lyon was in danger of being on the end of the Anderson hair-dryer treatment when he spanked two fours from the first two balls of Jimmy's 15th over. They proved to be the last two scoring shots of the innings, though, as Lyon played on to the fourth ball, leaving Jimmy with the magnificent figures of 14.4 overs, two maidens, six for 47. After winning the toss and batting, Australia were all out for 136. We'd taken seven wickets between lunch and tea and now had control of the match. Jimmy led us off to a huge ovation from an Edgbaston crowd who had played a significant role in our demolition of Clarke's men. It had been a special performance with the ball. Stokesy and Mo hadn't even been called upon.

Cooky was straight into padding up when we got into the changing room, but he still reminded us of how much work we had to do. That performance with the ball could all have been for nothing if we allowed ourselves time to congratulate ourselves on our performance. We had our foot on Australia's throat and we needed to keep it there.

Lythy and Cooky ran out on to the pitch behind Australia's fielders as rain continued to linger in the air. Lythy took three of the first four overs as he battled manfully in tough conditions against Starc and Hazlewood.

'Come on, Voldemort,' I thought. Lythy had become such a popular member of the dressing room in a short space of time, you couldn't help but want him to succeed. But Test cricket is a brutal place with nowhere to hide and Lythy was learning the hard way just what a tough, unforgiving school it can be.

He'd reached 10 when Hazlewood angled one across him and he edged a catch to Voges at slip. Initially, I thought he may have dropped it, but the ball rebounded from his first attempt and he grabbed it on the rebound before the ball hit the floor.

At 19 for one, Belly strode to the crease at No.3. In the eyes of some, this was a huge innings for him. Despite the 22 Test hundreds, 44 fifties, almost 7,500 Test runs and countless other masterful contributions in 112 previous Test matches, there were still some who were questioning his place in the team. Not one of those people was in our dressing room, I assure you. As he walked purposefully out to the wicket, it didn't appear there were any in the crowd either. This was the perfect place for him to rediscover his form – the ground he'd played so much cricket for Warwickshire down the years in front of a crowd that adored him. Belly even had his beloved Aston Villa shirt hanging on his peg for the duration of the Test.

Johnson came into the attack and straight away starting pushing 90mph-plus. The crowd were loving it. There really is nothing better to watch than a genuine quick bowler charging in. Johnson was getting a lot of stick, but you could tell it was stick born out of admiration for a bloke who was capable of taking the sport to a different plateau simply by bowling very fast and very aggressively. Fortunately for us, in Cook and Bell, we had two of England's greatest fighting our corner.

Cooky looked in really good touch, picking off the bad balls and keeping the strike rotating, while Belly also timed a couple of early boundaries. They took us past 50 as Mitch Marsh also came into the attack and Belly really started motoring when he hit Hazlewood for three successive boundaries to go to 28 from 26 balls. I remembered Collingwood's 'f*ck it mode'. Perhaps Belly was there, too. He was certainly looking to play shots wherever he could.

Then, as we were moving into position to really dominate, Australia were handed the most extraordinary stroke of good fortune when Cooky pulled a short delivery from Lyon fully out of the middle of his bat. Just as we were looking to mid-wicket to see the ball screaming to the boundary, I realised the Aussies were celebrating. Hang on. What's happened here? Somehow, as Voges was taking evasive action at short leg, the ball had stuck between his stomach and arms. He had no idea how, but he'd managed to take the catch. Our captain was out in the most unfortunate circumstances imaginable. At 76 for two, Australia had a sliver of hope again.

Rooty walked to the crease. Clarke brought Johnson back on. Game on. Soon, he was pushing 93mph. The crowd were on their toes and so were our batsmen. With Rooty on 7 from ten balls, Johnson sent down a thunderous bouncer. Rooty got inside the line and hooked with fast hands. He got plenty on it and the ball sailed over wicket-keeper Nevill for six behind the sightscreen.

Belly took a couple of streaky fours off Hazlewood and the boys kept coming at Australia. It was engrossing stuff. Three fours in one over from Starc took Bell to 47 from 45 balls as we closed in on Australia's first-innings total.

Rooty took two fours off the first four balls of Hazlewood's next over before Belly went past fifty from 51 balls in the next over with a classy drive off Starc. Moments later, he chanced his arm against Lyon and was deceived in the flight, hitting a leading edge to Warner at mid-wicket. He was kicking himself for giving it away, but Belly's innings had given us vital impetus just when we needed it. The crowd gave their local hero a rousing reception as he walked off.

The rain came down again in the following over, as Jonny and Rooty saw us through to the close on 133 for three. It was disappointing to lose Belly so late on but, all in all, it had been a fantastic day for us as Jimmy had put us firmly in the driving seat with a magnificent spell of bowling. The day before his 33rd birthday, Jimmy had proved once again just what a pivotal part of our attack he is. Three runs behind Australia's first innings with seven wickets left at the close of day one? We'll take that!

The next morning, Jonny and Rooty were desperate to get us off to a positive start. Ricky Ponting, who'd been well received as an even-handed and insightful commentator for the series on Sky, had made the point that today was a massive day for Michael Clarke as

Australian captain. He called for him to 'stand up' as a leader and, with some bafflement over Haddin's omission in the Australian media as well as the recent dropping of Shane Watson, we knew the Aussies were under pressure. It was up to us not to allow that pressure to ease.

Jonny made a positive start to the day, punching a four through the covers in Hazlewood's first over before succumbing to an absolute brute from Johnson with only his second delivery of the day. A wickedly directed bouncer flicked Jonny's glove as he took evasive action and the ball flew behind to Nevill. The Aussies had the early breakthrough they'd craved.

Stokesy strode to the crease. His first ball was a length ball he worked into the leg side, but the second was another absolutely unplayable delivery which followed him and caught his glove again on the way through to Nevill as he tried to get out of the way. Suddenly, out of nowhere, we were five down for 142. Inside five balls, Johnson had given Australia hope with two of the most devilish deliveries you could imagine. Great bowlers do that. Looking back, it was one of the great Ashes overs.

Jos survived another quick bouncer before Rooty went straight back on the attack in Hazlewood's next over with two trademark punches off the back foot through point. The crowd loved it as he responded to Johnson's double strike in the best way possible. He brought up his fifty from just 49 balls to a rapturous response as he and Jos attempted to blunt the Johnson rapier by counter-attacking.

Even though I was going to have to go out and face him at some point, it was impossible not to be impressed by Johnson's spell. There are few things more special than watching a truly quick bowler in his pomp. I wouldn't describe it as fun to face, but unquestionably it is fun to watch. By taking those two early wickets in the manner that he had, Johnson had shown yet again what a fantastic competitor he is. It was a privilege to witness. No matter how much stick he got from the crowd, he kept running in and bowling sensationally fast and aggressively. He had long since earned our respect in the dressing room and deep down even the most die-hard England fans will admit he's a bowler they fear.

Even though I was going to have to go out and face him at some point, it was impossible not to be impressed by Johnson's spell.

In the meantime, it was up to us to rebuild an innings that was in danger of coming apart after Bairstow and Stokes's swift departures that morning.

Root made 63 before Starc – who'd bowled erratically all morning – got him to jab down on a full ball outside off stump to have our in-form rescuer-in-chief caught at first slip. His dismissal brought Mo to the crease and when Jos was LBW to Lyon for 9 we were 190 for seven, a lead of just 54, and it was my turn to bat.

The next over, Clarke brought Johnson back on. 'Here we go,' I thought.

I got off the mark with a driven two through the covers as Mo and I agreed to just relax and try to enjoy ourselves. We both knew it was a potentially critical partnership. If we'd both been out cheaply, we could have been all out for 200, but if we could put together a partnership we could still secure a decisive first-innings lead. Stick to the principles. Attack. Don't fear the consequences. I kept reminding myself to watch the ball, hit the ball. Watch the ball, hit the ball.

We saw off a couple of Johnson overs before Mo caressed two boundaries off Lyon to take us past 200. We began to enjoy it. Johnson went around the wicket to me in an attempt to rough me up, but I managed to duck, dodge and weave as the Aussie quick began to tire. He'd given his all that morning and could not have been asked for any more. After another four-over burst, Clarke had no choice but to replace him with Starc.

Mo was not at his fluent best, but we hung in there and gradually the runs began to come. A booming drive for four framed by an extravagant follow-through took him to 23 and we reached the safety of lunch on 221 for seven with our lead approaching 100. We agreed to really have a go after the break in a bid to take the game away from the Aussies. A quick-fire 30 could make all the difference in the context of a low-scoring game.

Clarke knew the score and immediately brought Johnson back on after lunch, but we'd moved from survival mode to fun as the runs really began to flow. The crowd, after a nervy morning, were enjoying themselves too as we swished away at everything Australia threw at us. There were a few streaky runs, with Mo playing it a little more textbook than me, but I was doing what I do best with the bat again: getting under the skin of my opponents. We could tell the Aussies were rattled.

One memorable over saw Mo smash three fours off Johnson in five balls, including a magnificent straight drive over mid-off that made a clear statement to the Australians. We had faced Johnson down and seen him off.

Mo brought up his fifty from 66 balls with a single off Lyon. The importance of his innings could not be underestimated and I embraced him in the middle.

'Brilliant stuff, mate. Keep going,' I implored.

In the end our partnership reached 87 before I was out for 31 when I mistimed an attempted pull off Hazlewood to mid-on. As I walked off, I knew our partnership had shifted the momentum of the game right back in our favour. The Aussies knew they'd potentially let their chance slip through their fingers. Yet again, the crowd's response was phenomenal.

We were eventually all out for 281 – a lead of 145 – as Mo and Jimmy followed soon after me, but the vibe in the dressing room was so different from a few hours earlier when Johnson had been threatening another demolition job early in the morning. We had stayed true to our principles and attacked our way out of trouble. Now all we had to do was repeat our first-innings bowling heroics.

When Australia came to bat, it was evident straight away that Warner was pumped up. He was talking to himself even more than normal and clearly trying to gee himself up. I could see what he was trying to do, so I tried to ignore him. He wanted a battle.

He came out all guns blazing, playing shots left, right and centre and running a pretty much non-stop commentary on his innings at the same time. He was hyped, smashing two fours off my first three balls and congratulating himself on doing so. Bit odd that.

I responded by taking the vital wicket of Rogers in my second over as my ploy of bowling around the wicket worked a treat and had him trapped in front.

Rogers' departure did not affect Warner at all. He kept coming hard at us. Finny replaced me after four overs and was promptly despatched for two fours in his solitary over before Cooky turned to Mo in a bid to temper the Aussie run rate. Warner raced to 48 from 47 balls, while Smith was playing a handy support role at the other end. We were starting to get a little twitchy as Australia reached 62 for one at the start of the 13th over.

We needed something special. Finny delivered it.

Switching ends, Finny steamed in at Smith and bowled a quick bouncer that the batsman could not get on top of and miscued a hook up in the air which Jos took cleanly after calling for it. It was the breakthrough we needed.

Australia reached tea on 73 for two, with Warner unbeaten on 56. While he was there in this type of mood, Australia remained enormously dangerous. We spoke at tea about shutting down his scoring options, attacking the other end and trying to frustrate him out. We were up for the scrap.

It took Finny just three balls of his first over after tea to have Clarke brilliantly caught by Lythy at fourth slip when he got squared up to a short ball. Lythy emitted a series of involuntary 'woohoos' as he danced with delight at taking such an important catch.

Finny had the bit between his teeth and, with the crowd behind him, he had Voges caught by Belly at slip off the very next ball.

Pandemonium. Now we were properly into them and we leapt all over Finny as he beamed with delight at reducing the Aussies to 76 for four. The game was well and truly back on our terms again.

The atmosphere was absolutely electric as Finny charged in for what he hoped would be his hat-trick ball to Mitch Marsh. He had five slips in place. Sadly, the ball was just a fraction wide of off stump and Marsh was able to leave it alone as the crowd let out a disappointed 'ooohhhh'. But it had been some over. Finny was on fire.

It's very rare that you feel a bowler can take a wicket with every delivery, but this was definitely one of those times. Finny was absolutely on top of his game and it was thrilling to see.

Warner hit two more boundaries, but two overs later Finn made another breakthrough when Marsh played around a straight one and was bowled all ends up. It's very rare that you feel a bowler can take a wicket with every delivery, but this was definitely one of those times. Finny was absolutely on top of his game and it was thrilling to see. We were watching an amazing Ashes story unfold before our eyes.

Warner was 75 not out from 55 balls as Australia reached 100 for five, but with one end opened up, we felt like we had a grip on the game. We were looking to finish things off that evening when, soon after, Warner attempted a slightly odd flicked pull off Jimmy which he succeeded only in spooning in the air for Lythy to take another catch. Cue more pandemonium as the commentating danger man was going.

'Welcome to the party,' I said to Jimmy with a grin. Nothing.

The crowd sensed blood with Nevill and Mitchell Johnson at the crease, but the pair frustrated us with some disciplined batting which eventually forced Cooky to replace Finny in our attack.

Then, disaster.

Jimmy had been in the middle of another excellent spell when I noticed him holding his side gingerly as he began to run in to bowl. He delivered the ball from around the wicket, but was clearly not happy. I was at mid-on.

'You OK, Jimmy? What's up?'

He grimaced.

'Mate, be careful here. Don't do anything silly.'

He turned to run in and again looked in pain as he delivered the ball. This time, on his return to the top of his run, I was more forthright.

'Jimmy, for f*ck's sake, don't risk it,' I said. 'You could end up doing yourself some damage here. Stop bowling and get some treatment.'

He turned to run in again but this time, perhaps with my words ringing in his ear, he pulled up before reaching the popping crease and agreed to go off for treatment. He left the ground to loud applause, but you could sense the crowd knew something potentially serious was up. Fast bowlers and side injuries are not a good combination and with Jimmy's outstanding fitness record of recent years and an Ashes Test match on the line, we knew he would not leave the field lightly.

With Jimmy out of action, Nevill and Johnson frustrated us for almost 17 overs before Cooky brought Finn back into the attack and another short ball did for Johnson to hand the Middlesex man a thoroughly deserved five-wicket haul and reduce Australia to 153 for seven. They led by just eight.

Nevill and Starc saw them through to the close at two minutes past seven, following an extended evening session to make up for lost time on day one, with Australia on 168 for seven.

We knew the Test match was ours for the taking. That evening a delighted Finny spoke to the media. It must have been a wonderful feeling for him to sit there after a performance like that. He'd worked so hard to turn his career around. It was a story of hope for anyone who goes through tough times playing sport.

Jimmy's injury hadn't looked good and his face told a story when we got back to the changing rooms. He'd have a scan the next day, but it was clear we'd have to do without him for the rest of the Test, if not the series.

The next morning we vowed to finish the Aussies off for Jimmy. In typical Ashes fashion, things didn't quite work out as we'd hoped as Nevill and Starc began playing some shots to back up their hard work on the previous night.

Both players had some luck, but we were starting to become decidedly frustrated when Finny finally got the breakthrough in the

11th over of the morning when Nevill inside edged a lifting delivery to Jos behind the stumps. It left Australia 218 for eight.

But it wasn't the end of our frustration. Hazlewood joined Starc, who by now was playing with real fluency, and the pair continued where Nevill and Starc had begun by giving us the runaround. Starc brought up his fifty with a slog sweep for six off Mo, and you could sense the crowd were getting tense as the Australians extended their lead to 100. Until that point Stokes had had a quiet series with the ball, but he chose the perfect moment to claim a key scalp when he had Hazlewood spectacularly caught by Rooty at third slip. The relief was palpable.

Even then, there was more frustration as Lyon and Starc put on another 20 for the last wicket before substitute Josh Poysden, fielding for Jimmy, took a neat catch off Mo's bowling to dismiss Starc for an excellent 58. With only five first-class games to his name, it was a nice moment for Josh.

We needed 121 to win the Test.

The atmosphere was sensational when Cooky and Lythy strode out to bat, as it had been throughout the Test match. We knew if we could just blunt the potent new-ball threat of Hazlewood and Starc before dealing with Johnson's first spell, we would surely win the Test and go 2-1 up in the series with two to play.

They survived a horrible two-over spell before lunch before resuming after the interval. Lythy got things going with a confident drive through the covers off Starc. Cooky had looked to be positive before Starc bowled him with a superb delivery, full and straight with some late shape, which beat our captain all ends up. Eleven for one.

Belly clipped his first delivery superbly for four before hitting another four off the last ball of the over to settle his nerves and get the crowd going again. Lyth hit another boundary off the next over, before Belly went into overdrive in Starc's next over, crashing three boundaries in four balls to race to 20 not out after eight balls. It was stunning stuff.

Clarke dropped Bell off the final ball of the over, low to his right at slip, and Belly took full advantage hitting yet another four in Nathan Lyon's next over. Lyth had reached 12, with England 51 for one, when the opener was LBW to Hazlewood.

The Aussies had yet another tiny glimmer of hope before Root, in typical style, slapped his first ball for four to calm the nerves again. With Belly batting serenely up the other end after being given a life by Clarke, the pair of them settled into their task well.

Johnson again received sustained abuse from the crowd but carried on manfully as England's batsmen took the upper hand in pursuit of victory. As the target was gradually whittled down, Johnson was reduced to trying all sorts to try to claim an elusive wicket. At one point, he even delivered the ball from 23 yards in a bid to unsettle the batsmen. It didn't work.

A slog-sweep for six off Lyon by Rooty and a square driven four by Belly in the same over took us past 100 and Australia sensed the game was up as the crowd partied in the stands. It was a wonderful carnival atmosphere.

Fittingly, it was Joe who scored the winning runs when he whipped Marsh through square leg for four to spark massive celebrations in the stands and on our balcony.

It was just before 4.30pm when Rooty hit the winning runs. Finn was deservedly named Man of the Match for his match figures of eight for 117, including six for 79 in Australia's second innings. It was one of sport's great comeback stories.

'When I dreamed about it before the game, I didn't think it would go like that,' he admitted to Sky's Ian Ward after the game.

The captain praised Finn and Anderson's contributions and reminded everyone of that old line about form being temporary and class being permanent when it came to Ian Bell. As I said, no one in our dressing had doubted him. Cooky also complimented the groundsman on preparing a sporting wicket that gave our bowlers a chance to bowl to our strengths. Hear, hear!

By contrast, Australia coach Darren Lehmann apologised to Australia's supporters for his side's performance. He also admitted leaving Haddin out had been the toughest choice of his coaching career, but insisted it had not disrupted the dynamic in the Australian dressing room. It was interesting to hear him speak in those terms. With their captain Michael Clarke also badly out of form, the Aussies were definitely feeling the heat.

That evening we enjoyed a few beers in the changing room, but again agreed not to go overboard as we only had a few days' rest before Trent Bridge, and after Root's infamous encounter with Warner in the Walkabout bar in Birmingham two years earlier, it was decided we would ban the Yorkshireman from all nightclubs within a 50-mile radius! He took the ban in the spirit it was intended.

We knew we would be without our leading bowler Jimmy for the Trent Bridge Test – and possibly The Oval, too – and we also knew we had much to work on from this performance. Yes, we'd won and won convincingly by eight wickets, but we knew we could bat better than we had done over the past three days. Too many of our wickets

ENGLAND V AUSTRALIA (3RD TEST)

At Edgbaston, Birmingham

29, 30, 31 July 2015

ENGLAND WON BY EIGHT WICKETS

Toss: Australia

Umpires: Alim Dar (Pakistan) and C.B.Gaffaney (New Zealand)

Referee: R.S.Madugalle (Sri Lanka)

AUSTRALIA

C.J.L.Rogers	lbw b Broad	52	lbw b Broad	6
D.A.Warner	lbw b Anderson	2	c Lyth b Anderson	77
S.P.D.Smith	c Cook b Finn	7	c Buttler b Finn	8
* M.J.Clarke	b Finn	10	c Lyth b Finn	3
A.C.Voges	c Buttler b Anderson	16	c Bell b Finn	0
M.R.Marsh	c Buttler b Anderson	0	b Finn	6
† P.M.Nevill	b Anderson	2	c Buttler b Finn	59
M.G.Johnson	c Stokes b Anderson	3	c Stokes b Finn	14
M.A.Starc	c Buttler b Broad	11	c sub (J.E.Poysden) b Ali	58
J.R.Hazlewood	not out	14	c Root b Stokes	11
N.M.Lyon	b Anderson	11	not out	12
Extras	(LB 7, NB 1)	8	(B 2, LB 9)	11
Total	**(36.4 overs)**	**136**	**(79.1 overs)**	**265**

ENGLAND

A.Lyth	c Voges b Hazlewood	10	lbw b Hazlewood	12
* A.N.Cook	v Voges b Lyon	34	b Starc	7
I.R.Bell	c Warner b Lyon	53	not out	65
J.E.Root	c Voges b Starc	63	not out	38
J.M.Bairstow	c Nevill b Johnson	5		
B.A.Stokes	c Nevill b Johnson	0		
† J.C.Buttler	lbw b Lyon	9		
M.M.Ali	c Warner b Hazlewood	59		
S.C.J.Broad	c Marsh b Hazlewood	31		
S.T.Finn	not out	0		
J.M.Anderson	c Nevill b Starc	3		
Extras	(B 6, LB 4, W 4)	14	(W 2)	2
Total	**(67.1 overs)**	**281**	**(2 wkts; 32.1 overs)**	**124**

ENGLAND	O	M	R	W		O	M	R	W
Anderson	14.4	2	47	6		8.3	5	15	1
Broad	12	2	44	2		20	4	61	1
Finn	10	1	38	2		21	3	79	6
Ali						16.1	3	64	1
Stokes						11	3	28	1
Root						2.3	0	7	0

AUSTRALIA	O	M	R	W		O	M	R	W
Starc	16.1	1	71	2		6	1	33	1
Hazlewood	15	0	74	3		7	0	21	1
Johnson	16	2	66	2	(4)	7	3	10	0
Marsh	7	2	24	0	(5)	1.1	0	8	0
Lyon	13	2	36	3	(3)	11	1	52	0

FALL OF WICKETS

	A	E	A	E
WKT	1ST	1ST	2ND	2ND
1st	7	19	17	11
2nd	18	76	62	51
3rd	34	132	76	–
4th	77	142	76	–
5th	82	142	92	–
6th	86	182	111	–
7th	94	190	152	–
8th	110	277	217	–
9th	119	278	245	–
10th	136	281	265	–

CLOSE OF PLAY

Day 1	England (1) 133-3 (29; J.E.Root 30*, J.M.Bairstow 1*)
Day 2	Australia (2) 168-7 (55; P.M.Nevill 37*, M.A.Starc 7*)

had been given away cheaply and, learning from the mistakes we'd made after Cardiff, we vowed to spend the next few days looking at how we could improve and not worrying about the Aussies. It was an important psychological shift.

That evening, questions were already being asked about my readiness to lead the attack in Nottingham without Jimmy. We were heading to my home ground. I needed one wicket to make it 300 in Tests. We needed one more win to wrap up the Ashes. It was now or never. Bring it on.

10

TRENT BRIDGE
DID THAT REALLY JUST HAPPEN?

1–6 AUGUST

It was indicative of our determination to wrap up the series at Trent Bridge that when Alastair Cook gathered us around in the dressing room at Edgbaston and suggested we travel to Trent Bridge a day ahead of schedule, we said 'yes' without a moment's hesitation.

I made the short drive from Birmingham to Nottingham with my usual travelling companion, Jimmy Anderson, on Saturday morning after a relatively quiet night following the Birmingham win. We knew the series hadn't been won yet, and with an unprecedented run of seven Test matches which had seen us win, lose, win, lose, win, lose and win again, we knew we had to stay sharp or run the risk of another defeat. Cooky joked to the media after the third Test that he wouldn't mind if the win-lose run continued to the end of the series because we'd end up claiming a 3-2 series victory at The Oval. In reality, we were all desperate to get the job done early in a Test Match in my home city of Nottingham.

It was apparent from a very early stage after he'd left the field at Edgbaston that we would have to do so without the world's best

263

swing bowler. Jimmy was understandably pretty down after damaging his side bowling in the second innings at Edgbaston. Fortunately, scans confirmed there was no tear, giving him an outside chance of playing in the final Test, but it was clear he wouldn't be playing in Nottingham. He was gutted. It was particularly unfortunate for him because Trent Bridge is a ground where historically he's enjoyed phenomenal success. Conditions there are generally conducive to swing bowling. No one knows exactly why, but one theory is that with the venue situated just a three-minute walk from the River Trent, the high water table often leaves moisture closer to the playing surface than at most grounds, which can affect the atmospheric conditions at ground level.

Jimmy's absence meant there was more pressure on me. Some people compared his untimely side strain to the moment in 2005 when Australia's leading bowler, Glenn McGrath, twisted his ankle before the second Test at Edgbaston and missed two Tests. Personally, I thought that was stretching the 2005 analogy a little bit too far, but there was no hiding the fact that losing such a high-class performer would inevitably hinder our chances.

The bottom line was that Jimmy's absence meant the spotlight would very much be on me and people were soon asking questions about my readiness to lead the attack. I felt I was ready. I'd been bowling well all summer without getting that really big haul. But I'd been playing long enough to know that it was a matter of when, not if. I hope that doesn't sound arrogant, but I'd learned over time that the most important measure of my bowling was not necessarily the wickets column, but the rhythm I was in and the way the ball was coming out of my hand. That's an important lesson for any fast bowler to learn. Sometimes you can bowl brilliantly and have no luck, other days you might bowl like a drain but grab a lucky haul of wickets. The key thing is to recognise when you have a technical flaw, but not tinker for tinkering's sake just because you haven't taken wickets for a couple of games.

I'd felt in the groove all summer and believed a big performance was just around the corner. I said as much to the press. I felt confident I could deliver in my friend's absence. I'd stood up when the team had needed big performances before and I was determined to do so again.

With Jimmy out, it looked for all the world as if Mark Wood would return to the side after missing out at Edgbaston with an ankle injury. Although he was 25, he was relatively inexperienced as a first-class cricketer and had only once played three back-to-back first-class games. It was always going to be a huge ask for him to get through an entire five-Test series without a break.

Medics are required to tread a delicate path in any professional sport, with players almost always wanting to play regardless of the potential consequences to their long-term welfare. But there was a feeling at Edgbaston that if he'd played, Woody risked being ruled out for the entire series. In fairness, Steve Finn hadn't done too badly as his replacement! With Jimmy ruled out, it seemed like a fairly straightforward decision to recall Woody. He'd been extremely impressive in the four Tests he'd played so far in the summer before his injury and had fitted really well into the team. There was talk among the media about replacing Jimmy with a like-for-like swing bowler such as Chris Woakes, while the name of uncapped Derbyshire left-arm fast bowler Mark Footitt was also being bandied about. Both of them are excellent bowlers but, for me, Woody was the obvious replacement with his naturally skiddy trajectory, which I had no doubt would be well suited to Trent Bridge.

Once again there was a lot of focus on the pitch. The county wickets at Trent Bridge had been pretty green all summer, with plenty of grass on them, but I didn't think for a second we'd be provided with a track like that, however much we'd have liked one. The commercial realities of modern-day Test cricket place a lot of pressure on groundsmen to prepare pitches which 'go the distance'. They're sometimes called 'corporate' pitches because they're prepared to ensure matches last as many days as possible. I was told after the Edgbaston Test that Peter Nevill's half-century on the second evening, which effectively took the Test into a third day, saved Warwickshire well over a million pounds in ticket refunds.

My view is that every wicket should provide an even contest between bat and ball. No one wants to see one-sided games and the most tedious games tend to be the ones where the bat is completely dominant over the ball. In the first innings at Lord's, thick edges didn't carry to the slip cordon. That was frustrating. As a team, we wanted traditional English-type wickets which gave our bowling attack – reliant on seam and swing rather than out-and-out pace – a chance.

The year before, Nottinghamshire had been fined by the ICC for producing a seriously ordinary wicket. We were playing India at home on a ground we loved and where we had enjoyed a great deal of success over the years, but turned up on the first morning of the Test to find the pitch looked more like a sub-continental wicket than anything we'd ever seen on the sub-continent. It was dry, dusty and completely devoid of life from the very first over.

I remember being incredibly frustrated when the first couple of deliveries I bowled bounced twice on their way through to Matt Prior behind the stumps.

With all the talk about the pitches, and the success we'd had at Edgbaston on a lively wicket which exposed the Aussies' frailties against the moving ball, we were all hopeful the wicket this time around would be far more like a traditional Trent Bridge wicket. I felt for our groundsman, Chris Birks, who was under a lot of scrutiny.

While a lot of people associate Nottingham with seam and swing-friendly conditions, the reality is that many England batsmen have enjoyed a huge amount of success there down the years. Michael Atherton and Graham Gooch both scored an enormous number of runs there and my former team-mate Matt Prior loved batting there, too. I hadn't done too badly down the years either, with nearly 400 runs at an average of more than 40 before this Test. It is a ground that gives full value for your shots and good batsmen – and me – can thrive. That's the way it should be.

A few of us enjoyed a barbecue at Graeme Swann's house on the Saturday night before the Test. He'd recently bought a place just around the corner from me in West Bridgford and it was good to relax a little bit with him, Jimmy and my former Nottinghamshire team-mate, Charlie Shreck. Now Charlie is a seriously good cook and we were all really looking forward to seeing what he would make for us. The only problem was that he was terrified of giving us all food poisoning ahead of such a big game.

'I'll be the only person in Nottingham less popular than the Aussies if you boys go down sick,' he said, only half joking. Thankfully he didn't have to worry as he rustled up a superb spread, which we lapped up with a couple of glasses of wine. It was a lovely way to spend the evening.

We met up again the next day for a Sunday roast at my favourite pub, the Larwood and Voce, which is just by the ground and were ready to roll our sleeves up by Monday ahead of the fourth Test.

We had a fairly light training session at the ground on Monday morning before enjoying what was undoubtedly the highlight of my summer in the afternoon – football training at my beloved Nottingham Forest! I'm sure the honour of training at somewhere as prestigious as Forest's indoor training ground will have been lost on some of the boys, but it certainly wasn't on me. I loved every minute as we continued the hugely competitive but fun games of football, which had proved such a bonding factor among the squad over the course of the summer.

We played a match on Forest's full-sized 3G indoor pitch. Their first-team captain Henri Lansbury and striker Dexter Blackstock stayed behind after their own training to watch and cheer us on. I'm friends with both of them but, as a lifelong Forest fan, I was still keen to impress. Unfortunately, on such a big pitch, I felt as if I spent the entire game chasing chickens while running in glue! I don't think they were too impressed. Jos Buttler took the chance to showcase his undoubted footballing skills and seemed to genuinely be trying to push for a contract, while Ben Stokes scored the goal of the day with an absolute rocket from 20 yards which definitely caught the Forest lads' attention.

We trained really well again on Tuesday as well and that night we had dinner as a fast-bowling group with former England captain and fast bowler Bob Willis. If you'd told me two years ago that I'd be sharing a dinner table with Bob, who has the reputation of being one of England's sternest critics in his role as a Sky Sports pundit, then I'd have laughed you out of town. He'd probably have said the same thing, to be fair. When I heard we were having dinner with him, I took a bit of convincing. But in yet another example of the new-found openness we were keen to maintain – and for which Peter Moores had been the catalyst – we invited Bob to join us for a catch-up a couple of nights before the start of this all-important Test in order to share the benefits of his experience. Some younger fans may forget that Bob took 325 Test wickets, including one of the greatest Ashes spells of eight for 43 as England famously won at Headingley in 1981.

It proved an inspired call. Far from the gruff, droll persona Bob presents when on-screen, he proved to be really good company. His humour is undoubtedly dry, but he was very funny and provided valuable insight for some of our younger bowlers in particular on how to take wickets at Trent Bridge.

He spoke about how all the bowlers who'd had success at Trent Bridge weren't the ones who bowled for the top of off stump, but actually the ones who bowled knee-roll height. He told us to think about where the Investec sponsor's logo is on the stump and aim for that. He was spot on. He also talked about the importance of aerobic fitness work over pure gym and weights work. That definitely made sense to me. Lifting weights is fine, but for me there is no substitute for getting miles in the legs. Sometimes, there is nothing better than just going for a run or bowling ball after ball in the nets. Bob's old-school message definitely registered.

We trained well again on the Wednesday. As a team we were in good shape, but I noticed I was feeling far more anxious than I usually would be the day before a Test match. All the papers were talking about how much we were going to miss Jimmy and how it was time for me to step up. I was the local boy on the verge of 300 wickets and nobody was shy of reminding me how much responsibility was on my shoulders.

I was the local boy on the verge of 300 wickets and nobody was shy of reminding me how much responsibility was on my shoulders.

That night, I read something Nasser Hussain had written for a newspaper column. It read:

'Stuart Broad stands just one wicket away from 300 in Test cricket and will lead the attack for his country on Thursday on his home ground — but for some reason he is not as popular as he should be and remains an under-appreciated cricketer. He has lived in Jimmy Anderson's shadow, but it is time for Broad to emerge in his own right. He is just as important a weapon for England and they deserve to be regarded as a double act like Ian Botham and Bob Willis.'

It struck a chord.

I normally have absolutely no problems sleeping the night before a game, but I had a fitful night that Wednesday before waking up earlier than normal on the morning of a Test match. I looked at my alarm and it was 6am. I already had butterflies in my stomach. That was unusual.

Within reason, nerves are a good thing because they focus you and ensure you're sharp in body and mind. I'm nervous before every international I play for England, but this was much worse than I'd experienced since the very start of my international career. I couldn't remember the last time I'd been so jittery before a game. It felt like I was making my Test debut all over again. I struggled to eat much for breakfast and got down to the ground earlier than normal, feeling tense and anxious.

I couldn't have been more acutely aware of the pressure on my shoulders going into that game and Cooky reminded us in the changing room before the toss of the importance of setting the tone with bat or ball that morning.

There's usually not a huge amount of point inspecting the pitch in the days leading up to a Test match, because the groundstaff will normally shave any grass off early on the morning of the first day, giving a more accurate reflection of how it will play.

Despite a slightly green tinge to the Trent Bridge pitch, and a few light showers in the morning, I was very much of the opinion we should bat first and I told Cooky as much. Whenever I mark out my run-up before play in the morning, I always do a bit of visualisation of running in for the first ball and hitting the wicket-keeper's gloves. With a plan for Chris Rogers in mind, it felt a bit weird that morning because I'd be bowling around the wicket first up.

I had a chat with Nathan Lyon on the outfield before the toss and he asked me what I reckoned. As a spinner, he was always going to be in the 'bat first' camp, because he'd want to bowl in the last innings when pitches are normally at their most worn and conducive to spin.

Moments before the toss as I was marking out my run-up, just after I'd spoken to Lyon, Shane Warne came over and asked what I reckoned. I said to him I'd bat first 99 per cent of the time in Test cricket and today was no different. Warney's reply surprised me a bit. He said he was always a bat-first man but he might just have had a bowl today.

That did make me question myself, because I thought 'Wow, if Shane Warne thinks we should bowl then maybe it is a bowl-first day.' That was the point I started hoping perhaps we would bowl after all.

Thankfully, Cooky paid absolutely no attention to me and, when he won the toss, he invited Michael Clarke and Australia to bat. It turned out to be one of his better decisions.

As expected, Woody returned to the side, but while our team and the pitch didn't necessarily provide too many surprises, their team selection again raised an eyebrow or two. All-rounder Mitchell Marsh was dropped, despite having taken some key wickets in the two Tests he'd played, including those of Cooky and Stokesy at critical moments at Lord's. He also scored some pretty handy runs in that second Test, after scoring back-to-back hundreds in Australia's warm-up games against Kent and Essex and was clearly a man in form, despite a disappointing return for him at Edgbaston.

The Australian selectors opted to drop the talented all-rounder for his brother Shaun and retain Adam Voges in the side. Vogesy is a good mate of mine, even though he had chosen not to speak to me all series, but he had scored just 73 runs in five innings before the Trent Bridge Test and, like most of the Aussie batsmen, had looked shaky against the moving ball. Mitchell Marsh had really troubled our batsmen, but the Aussies left him out and changed the balance of their side. With Shane Watson also out of the team after Cardiff, the Aussies were back to having a four-man bowling attack for the first time I could remember. With Mitchell Starc and Mitchell Johnson very much strike bowlers who could be prone to leaking runs, it was a reminder of the invaluable contribution Watson had made down the years to the balance of the Australian side.

Before we took the field, Cooky gathered us round and reiterated the point that this session would set the tone for the Test match. I'd never bowled the first over of a Test match before and I was acutely aware of the additional pressure on my shoulders as the most senior bowler in Jimmy's absence. I walked out on the pitch an absolute bag of nerves. It was now-or-never time.

Before play began, there was a moving tribute to Nottinghamshire and South Africa legend Clive Rice, who had sadly passed away the day before start of the Edgbaston Test match. My dad knew Clive really well from his time at Nottinghamshire and spoke very highly of him. I understood just how highly he was regarded by players, staff and supporters alike at Trent Bridge.

I had never really had the chance to get to know Clive, but I will never forget him phoning me out of the blue the day after I'd taken six for 50 in the fourth Test at Durham in 2013 to tell me that, given the circumstances, it was the best spell of aggressive fast bowling he'd ever seen. He didn't have to do that and it meant an incredible amount to me coming from a man of such standing within the game.

As the crowd burst out into a minute's applause for the great man, I thought of that call from Clive and the hairs on the back of my neck stood on end. I thought of what Clive's family must have been going through following his passing. I'd experienced the loss of a close and much-loved family member when my step-mum Miche died from motor neurone disease aged just 60 in 2010.

I looked up at the members and some of them were clearly upset. Their former captain and coach still meant a great deal to them. Suddenly, all the nerves that had been threatening to stifle my performance just drained out of me. I went from a nervous wreck to feeling on top of the world in the blink of an eye. I realised this was not life or death, it was a game of cricket. I was ready. What would be would be. With Clive still very much on my mind, I found an inner peace which put everything in perspective.

I've never thought to myself on a cricket field 'you're in the zone', because you're so focused on what you're doing that almost by definition if you started to think like that then you would lose that focus. But something felt very different that morning. It was the most amazing feeling. Things seemed to be happening in slow motion and, all of a sudden, I did not have one single nerve left in my body.

I felt incredibly light on my feet and the ball seemed tiny in my hand. I was in complete control. Five minutes before play began in one of the biggest Test matches of my life, it was a good place to be.

There was a very brief delay to the start after a bit of rain but, while Cooky had chosen to bowl and I was ready to give it 100 per cent as always, I honestly didn't think these were the sort of conditions we'd be able to skittle Australia out in. I'd seen the ball hoop around at Trent Bridge before, but it didn't feel like one of those days. As I said, I wanted to bat! The crowd at Edgbaston had been phenomenal and, if early indications were anything to go by, Trent Bridge was set to be just as supportive.

I have a routine I always go through before I bowl which revolves around threes. First, I scratch my mark three times, then I bowl three balls to mid-on, then I visualise bowling three balls through to the keeper before doing three tuck jumps before getting ready to bowl.

I also always scratch the mark where my foot is going to land. If you rough up that hard surface on the crease, it allows your studs to grip that little bit better in your delivery stride. Normally, on Test match pitches, which are usually very good for batting, it's very rare for any moisture to come up. This time I pulled up a decent amount of moisture.

'Interesting,' I thought to myself. Perhaps Cooky was on to something after all.

I'd been so used to Jimmy bowling the first over of a match I'd almost forgotten what it felt like. I got to the end of my mark and could hear the crowd cheering as they always do on the first morning at Trent Bridge. There's an audible lift in crowd noise before the first ball and I felt absolutely ready for the battle. I scraped my boots in the sawdust at the top of my run, just to cover all bases, took a deep breath, and began my run-up.

I was desperate not to get hit through the covers first up. All I was thinking of was 'whack it in to back of a length as hard as you can'. If Rogers wanted to pull me out of the ground first ball then fair play, but I wasn't going to be driven.

The ball landed pretty much exactly where I'd wanted it, just short of a length and fractionally outside off stump. Rogers went back and punched it into the covers, but there was no run. There was a hint of movement away, but I wasn't too bothered about that. I just wanted to get into the game. I was off and running.

My heart was pounding, but I felt calm and in control. I ran in again. Again the crowd roared.

The next ball was slightly fuller and angled into Rogers' legs. He moved across his stumps and played at it, he missed and the ball deflected off his pads and down to the fine-leg boundary for four leg byes. I was frustrated I'd let them get off the mark, though I remained utterly focused.

It was the perfect delivery. If Rogers had missed it, it would have bowled him. I couldn't believe it.

I reached the top of my mark. The crowd were still willing me on. I turned and ran in. I felt like I was floating over the ground as I approached the crease before gathering into my delivery stride and sending the ball on its way.

If I was to draw the perfect delivery to bowl to the left-handed Rogers from around the wicket, this was it. The ball was full, but not full enough to drive, and the Australian batsman was caught in two minds as the angle from around the wicket saw the ball arrow towards middle and off stump before nipping away off the pitch.

Rogers was squared up and the ball caught the outside edge and flew to Cooky at first slip where he took a good, low catch to his left. It was the perfect delivery. If Rogers had missed it, it would have bowled him. I couldn't believe it. It had taken me just three balls to get rid of a bloke who'd been a thorn in our side in recent Ashes series and who'd never before been out for a duck in Test cricket. This was quite a time to hand him a first. I looked up to Ottis on the balcony. Our hard work and planning had paid off again.

On top of that, I'd taken my 300th Test wicket to leave the Aussies 4 for one after three balls. There was a huge sense of relief. I hadn't fluffed my lines. When I watched it back later, I could see some of the members in the pavilion behind me celebrating before Cooky took the catch. The crowd were as pumped as we were.

It's hard to believe I had a tinge of sadness at that moment, but after celebrating with my team-mates on the field, I immediately looked around for Jimmy. I'd played in only five Tests before this one that Jimmy hadn't played in and I was gutted he wasn't out there to share this special moment with me.

I looked up to him on the dressing-room balcony and could see he was smiling. A few months earlier, I'd been there when he took his 400th wicket and it was a shame he couldn't be out there with me at this special time. We'd been through so much together and I think he'd agree that a lot of the wickets he's taken have been in part due to the pressure I've been able to create at the other end. That's certainly been the case for me with Jimmy. Bowling in partnership is so much about building pressure and knowing that the opposition batsmen can't relax at the other end. Jimmy and I have dovetailed brilliantly down the years and I owe him a huge proportion of my wickets.

But what mattered now was keeping the pressure on the Aussies. In Jimmy's absence, I was the leader of this attack and I was determined we should ram home our early advantage.

With everything that was going on, I'd hardly noticed Steve Smith walk out to the crease, and as the warm applause from my home crowd for my landmark wicket died down, I refocused on the business of trying to bag another wicket. And not just any wicket, but the wicket of the No.1 ranked batsman in the world. His double hundred at Lord's was still fresh in all our minds.

The first ball to him gave me huge encouragement, even though he got off the mark straight away from it. The ball was full and outside off stump and Smith came hard at it, squirting it through wide mid-on with a closed face. The Aussie fans cheered the runs and so did I, because it was obvious to me that he was ticking. Most No.3s would have shouldered arms and allowed the ball to pass through to the keeper just to get an early sighter. But I applauded the shot and returned to my mark.

The next ball he climbed into another full delivery outside off stump and absolutely smashed it through cover point for four. Again the Aussie fans in the crowd leapt out of their seats and Smith was fist-pumping David Warner at the other end. It may sound weird, but I was absolutely delighted. No bowler likes being hit for four, but cricket is so much about psychology and clear thought processes and it was obvious to me that Smith's beans were going. I had him where I wanted him.

The next ball was just short of a length and bounced on Smith, squaring him up. It caught Smith's edge and flew to Joe Root at third slip where he took a comfortable catch. I didn't even see the catch. As soon as Smith nicked it, I was off charging around like a maniac high-fiving and celebrating. Australia were 10 for two after my first over. What a strange scoreboard. In my wildest dreams I didn't think I'd take two key wickets in my first six balls. Once again, the crowd was ecstatic as a shell-shocked Shaun Marsh walked out to bat.

As if that wasn't a good enough start, Woody then proceeded to take what was probably the biggest wicket of the lot when he got rid of Warner two balls into his first over.

The ball was nipping around a little bit, not excessively, but the conditions were definitely favourable to our bowlers. Woody bowled one just short of a length which nipped back, caught Warner's inside edge and flew behind to Jos, who took a regulation catch.

Ten for three after eight balls. What on earth was going on? We were looking at each other with wide eyes. We couldn't believe what was happening. Were we dreaming this?

Don't forget how big this Test match was. There was so much riding on it and we were delivering in spades. It was hard not to get carried away.

Cooky kept a calm head and reminded us: 'Keep asking questions boys, don't force it.' It was good advice.

Jos, on the other hand, was a bit more like a fan masquerading as an England player. He had the biggest grin on his face you've ever seen and was completely incredulous at what was happening.

'I can't believe this,' he'd say. 'What on earth is going on out here?' He kept repeating it as the wickets kept falling.

Normally in those positions, you keep focused and talk clearly about your plans for each batsman. A lot of the talk was quite sensible, reminding each other to hit the top of the knee roll, but Jos was like a fan watching it on Sky.

Australia had Michael Clarke and Shaun Marsh both in the middle and yet to score after just eight balls of the Test match. In our wildest dreams, we couldn't have hoped to be in a better position.

Clarke swished at his second ball, inside edging a drive agonisingly close to his off stump and away for four. Woody crumpled in a heap on the floor. It was unbelievably close. The Australian captain survived the rest of the over, but the crowd sensed blood and so did we.

This time, Marsh was on strike and the noise when I reached the top of my run-up was unbelievable. I still felt in control, but the adrenaline was pumping. I'd never felt more alive on a cricket field.

It was never my plan to bowl around the wicket to Shaun Marsh, even though he was another left-hander. I'd planned to go over the wicket to him, bowl a full length and look to run it across him.

Cooky came over for a bit of a chat and, with the dismissal of Rogers very much in my mind, I said to him: 'If I can bowl that same delivery again then it doesn't matter who is facing, because it was pretty much the perfect delivery.' Cooky agreed to back me. We went on instinct and I stayed around the wicket.

The plan worked. After Marsh survived for three deliveries, I got one to nip away again off a full length and Belly took a sharp catch at third slip. It was a decent ball, but not as good as the one I'd bowled to Rogers. If Marsh had left it alone it would have missed the stumps.

Having not played Test cricket for a couple of months, I guess he wanted to get bat on ball and he nicked it as a result. Sixteen balls into one of the most important Test matches of our lives and we had Australia 15 for four. We were in dreamland. It was becoming fun.

Next up was the out-of-form Voges who, along with Clarke, played out Woody's next over relatively untroubled. But then came a moment that will live long in the memory for anybody fortunate enough to have witnessed it.

With Voges on strike, and the scoreboard an already ridiculous 21 for four, I prepared to run in again. There haven't been many occasions in my career when I have felt I could take a wicket with every ball, but this was most definitely one of them. After Finny and Jimmy at Edgbaston, this felt like my time. I had absolute control over where I was going to land the ball and every part of my body felt in sync. My run-up felt smooth and the ball was coming out of my fingers perfectly.

I approached the crease and delivered the ball full and just outside off stump. It nipped away slightly off the pitch and Voges, also eager to feel bat on ball, drove loosely and with his weight not coming forward into the shot.

The ball skewed off the face of his bat and I saw Adam Lyth turn and start to run towards the third-man boundary where the ball looked destined to finish.

In a flash, I saw Stokesy dive at full stretch to his right. I was convinced the ball had evaded him, it was travelling that quickly. Somehow, and I still don't know how, he managed to fling his right hand out low, to his right, and behind him. The ball stuck. It was a ridiculous catch. He later told me the only reason it stuck was because of the dodgy surgery he'd had a few years earlier which left him with a crooked index finger on his right hand which he refers to as 'the claw'. The ball had stuck in the claw!

I couldn't believe what had just happened. It was without a doubt the best catch I've ever seen live and I instinctively held my hands to my face and mouthed 'Oh my God'. I was in shock at the quality of the catch and the situation we found ourselves in.

Everyone was stunned. Lythy was 'woohooing' like there was no tomorrow!

I couldn't believe what had just happened. It was without a doubt the best catch I've ever seen live.

People soon started to compare Stokes's catch to Andrew Strauss's legendary one-handed take to dismiss Adam Gilchrist off Andrew Flintoff at the same ground in 2005. They were both unbelievable catches, but I know which one is my favourite.

The way Stokesy managed to fling his hand backwards with the ball already past him was astonishing. He had about 0.2 seconds to react. I'm not sure if people realise just how good an athlete Stokesy is, but we see things in training that make us double take almost every day. He is a superb fielder – one of the best I've seen. He is also an incredibly strong bloke and one of the fiercest competitors I've ever known.

I've already mentioned the time when Trevor Bayliss saw Stokesy play golf for the first time in Spain. Whereas I consider a round of golf a chance to escape from the pressure cooker of cricket and take it all in my stride, it's fair to say Stokesy brings the same level of intensity to the golf course that he brings to a cricket field. He also brings the same power game. He consistently hits a seven iron more than 220 yards, which puts him in the same bracket as some of the world's top professional golfers in terms of length. But, unfortunately for him, his accuracy doesn't quite match his distance and the fury he can generate over a missed putt or sliced drive really is something to behold. Poor old Trevor couldn't quite believe what he was witnessing as Stokesy swore his way around the Desert Springs, as the rest of us giggled out of sight, desperate not to enrage him further.

Stokesy's dad was a professional rugby league player and, despite doing the absolute bare minimum required in the gym, Ben is able to generate incredible power, while his hand-eye co-ordination is only matched by Jos in our squad. He can do all sorts of clever back flips and is a natural entertainer.

He was clearly incredibly pumped when he took his catch and charged off with his hand raised towards Jonny Bairstow, who was fielding at short leg. As poor old Jonny came towards him to celebrate, Stokesy did his finest impression of Jonah Lomu and just completely steamrollered him. Jonny didn't stand a chance.

Rooty was jumping up and down like an excited schoolboy, while Jos kept saying: 'What is going on here?' Mo was charging around, too. I don't think I've ever seen so much emotion on the field celebrating one wicket. None of us could believe it. Twenty-one for five off 4.1 overs. Really? The crowd seemed equally stunned, delirious even. It was the most incredible experience of my cricketing career.

Peter Nevill was next man to the crease and the atmosphere was electric as he took guard. I suspect he hadn't expected to be standing at the crease less than half an hour into the day's play and effectively facing a brand-new ball. He survived the rest of the over, while Clarke hit a four and a single off Woody's next over as the Durham quick showed his ankle was in decent fettle by repeatedly touching 90mph.

I've enjoyed some decent tussles with Clarke down the years. By the end of the series I'd got him out 13 times, which is more than anyone I've bowled to. I respected him enormously as a batsman and I always enjoyed going into battle with him. It had become the norm in the last couple of series for Cooky to bring me on to bowl when he came in to bat. I'd got him out in Cardiff driving loosely, but I wouldn't go as far as to say I'd got into his head, even though some of my team-mates were saying that.

This time, I was already on, and I was cooking on gas. A bit like Smith earlier, I got the sense he wasn't in the right frame of mind. Who could blame him? He was witnessing his team's Ashes hopes crumble before him.

I'd dismissed him during the first Test of the 2013-14 series in Brisbane when I'd made a big song and dance of putting a short leg in before bowling him a vicious bouncer that saw him balloon the ball up to the close fielder. This time, I wanted to get into his head space again and made the same play of positioning the short leg, making him think I was going to bounce him once more. I was pretty sure that Brisbane dismissal had stayed with him.

There was no way I was ever going to bounce him here, but I set him up in the same way by bringing a short leg in. I did the old-school trick of signalling to fine leg to make him think I might bounce him. Trevor often says 'just get the batsman thinking', and this was one of those instances. I wanted Clarke to wonder 'why is he there?' and mess with his normal thought processes. In the end, I bowled it full and a bit wider than I'd intended and Clarke threw his hands at the ball and slashed a sharp catch to Cooky at slip, which he took brilliantly above his head. It was the worst ball I'd bowled in the spell but arguably my most important wicket.

Australia were 29 for six and I had gone from having figures of one for 6 to five for 6. It was almost schoolboy stuff. I don't think any England bowler had ever taken five wickets inside an hour on the first morning of a Test match. It was the point I began to think: 'This is a bit special now.'

We weren't done yet. Mitchell Johnson came in and started to leave the ball. Although it didn't feel like it at the time, it later transpired that only three of our wicket-taking deliveries would actually have hit the stumps. I think Johnson had twigged this and he actually left the ball really well. If other Australian top-order batsmen had shown the same level of application, who knows what the outcome would have been?

Woody had gone two overs without a wicket so Cooky decided to switch things up at the Radcliffe Road End by bringing Finn into the attack. Despite our commanding position, I think he was quite nervous coming on. It was a bit of a no-win for him. If he bowled poorly and got hit around or failed to pick up any wickets, he'd have felt like he'd let the side down.

As it turned out, he bowled an absolute jaffer two balls into his second over to clean up Nevill. It was arguably the best delivery of the innings and left Australia 33 for seven off 9.2 overs. It felt like everything we tried was turning to gold and, without Brad Haddin in their side, who could have just chanced his arm and rattled up a score quickly, and no recognised batsmen to come, I felt we had a complete grip of the Australian innings.

Although the next wicket took only 20 balls to come around, it felt like an absolute age as Johnson, with Mitchell Starc up the other end, clubbed Finny for a couple of boundaries.

I got Starc with a decent delivery which Rooty pouched at slip but, despite having them 46 for eight, it had felt like an age between wickets, so accustomed had we become to taking wickets with virtually every other ball. You could see my reaction was one of relief rather than elation. Those three overs felt like they'd taken an hour. Apparently, Ottis was getting really frustrated up on the boundary asking Jimmy why I was still bowling around the wicket and berating us for not finishing the job. We were all feeling that way.

That was my seventh over, and I reckon if I hadn't taken a wicket that over Cooky might have taken me off. Luckily, normal service was resumed when I got Johnson two balls later with a very similar delivery to the one that had done for Starc. The ball flew quicker than Starc's edge, but Rooty again did the honours in the slips with a really good catch.

We got together in the huddle and Cooky said: 'That felt like it was seventy miles an hour!' I thought he was taking the mick, so I said: 'Thanks a lot, mate.' But it was to do with how well people were zoned in and switched on; everyone just felt that they had so much time.

I had seven for 11 and they were nine down for 47.

Nathan Lyon, who earlier that morning had agreed with me that it was a bat-first day, walked to the crease. He looked at me and smiled.

'Broady, I think we might have been wrong you know, mate. Maybe it was a bowl-first day after all,' he said, shaking his head.

'I don't know,' I replied, not wanting to admit I'd clearly read it wrong. 'It was a bat-first track; it just needed your batters to turn up!'

Lyon put on 13 for the last wicket with Josh Hazlewood and I was starting to get quite annoyed by the partnership when I began my tenth over. When Lyon sliced me over gully for four, I don't think I have ever been more annoyed at conceding a boundary. I'm not kidding. I was desperate to finish with eight for 11, but in the end I had to settle for eight for 15 as I had Lyon caught by Stokesy off the next ball.

We'd bowled them out for 60 in a little more than an hour and a half, but my initial feeling was relief. Cricket is such a weird sport. There's always something else to do. My immediate thought as we began to walk off was: 'Let's get through to lunch with the bat.'

As I left the pitch, the Nottinghamshire crowd stood as one to applaud. Even a few Aussies stood to acknowledge our efforts. I looked for my old mate Jimmy up on the balcony.

I took a moment to look around the stands and savour the most amazing feeling I'd ever had on a cricket field. We still had a job to do, but in that instant, I knew we had one hand on the Ashes.

As I walked up the pavilion steps of a ground I'd played county cricket on for seven years and had very much come to consider my home, the members applauded me and the team all the way in to the dressing room. We could hear the cheering continue long after we'd got inside. It was an incredibly emotional moment and it was all I could do to fight back the tears. I thought about Clive again and his family. Had he been with me for this? It was so surreal.

The only time I can ever recall feeling like that was when I took a hat-trick against India at the same ground in 2011, but in many ways this was even more fantastic because of the magnitude of the game.

I plonked myself down in my usual spot in the changing room and turned to Belly.

'Did that really just happen?' I asked him, as I started to take all the bits of tape I habitually strap around my ankles and toes when I'm in the field.

'You'd better believe it,' he replied with a grin.

But some things in cricket never change. We still had a job to do with the bat, because if we'd proceeded to be bowled out for 100, all our hard work would have been undone.

Cooky – who had a tricky little 15-minute spell to negotiate with Lythy before lunch – spoke to us and was very clear he didn't want us to lose focus. It was a reminder that professional sport can move on in five minutes.

'Great morning boys, but it's done now,' he said matter-of-factly. 'We have a job to do with the bat here if we are going to win this Test match. I don't want us talking about what has just happened this morning until after this Test match finishes. Are we clear?'

That was that then. Once the captain says that, you can't walk around the changing room grinning like a Cheshire cat giving it the big 'I am'. The harsh realities of professional sport leave absolutely no room for romance. That moment was a perfect illustration. There's always another job to do.

I was dying to talk about it, but knew I had to keep quiet and pretend it was just another day in the office. Ottis sat down next to me at one point and gave me a look with this big West Indian grin that said it all.

But it felt utterly surreal. Eight for 15? Sixty all out? Three hundred Test wickets? Was this really happening?

Thankfully, the boys did exactly what Cooky had asked of them by finishing the day on 274 for four, to lead by 214 as Rooty finished unbeaten on 124. He and Jonny put on 173 for the fourth wicket after another wobble at the top had left us 96 for three. There was no denying we were in complete control of the Test match after one of the most dominant day's performances you could possibly imagine.

That evening, I did the rounds of media after the close. I think even some of the seasoned press pack couldn't quite believe what had just happened. BBC cricket correspondent Jonathan Agnew, a close family friend, looked incredulous.

'My word, Stuart, that was really quite something,' Aggers said to me with a broad grin. Sky's Ian Ward was another one who seemed shocked by the day's events. I don't think any of us could really believe what had just happened.

Of course, I said the right things about the job not being done and the Aussies being fighters, but I knew it would take a miracle for us not to win from here. People ask me if it's a pain not being able to be more free-speaking in those press conferences and it is all a bit of a game, but you're playing the game for your team, not the media. If I'd said then 'it's in the bag, the Aussies need a miracle', which is what I thought, then it would have heaped loads of unnecessary pressure on my team-mates. So I bit my tongue and played my straightest bat of the summer. Inside my heart was soaring.

The ICC Anti-Corruption Unit rules stipulate we have to lock our phones away in a secure box during play, so when I took my phone out and checked it, there were literally hundreds of messages on it.

I took a call from my old mate Michael Lumb after I'd showered and made my way across the outfield to the car park by the Radcliffe

Road. Rather than the usual 40 or 50 diehards, this time there must have been three or four hundred fans all asking me to sign '8-15' on their tickets and programmes.

I was eager to get home, because Bealey had been away on holiday and I hadn't seen her for a week. She was so excited to see me and had cooked my favourite, chicken fajitas. Normally I'd smash six or seven of them down after a day's play, but I could not even manage one. I felt sick. My head was spinning. I was completely shattered from the day.

The doorbell went, it was Dad with a bottle of wine, and I face-timed my sister Gemma down in New Zealand while he was there. That was a pretty special moment and Dad said some lovely things about his three-month premature little boy who'd just starred in the Ashes.

I thought about Nasser's words the night before and smiled.

When I finally went upstairs to bed, I still couldn't comprehend what had just happened. I was elated, but also confused. Did that really just happen?

11

REDEMPTION

RECLAIMING THE ASHES

7–23 AUGUST

The rest of the Trent Bridge Test had passed by in something of a blur. It was surreal. We had Australia on the ropes within an hour of the start of one of the highest-pressure Test matches of our lives and I'd achieved bowling figures you can only dream about as a schoolboy. It didn't feel real.

Late on the first day, just before the close, our analyst Nathan Leamon had poked his face around the dressing-room door and made a kind of statement by saying 'England's most dominant Ashes day ever?'

Cricketers are a superstitious bunch and Nathan – a top bloke who is very popular among the team – was given short shrift by those of us in the dressing room. 'Shut up!' we cried almost as one. Even Belly snapped at him to get back in his box. You know you've crossed the line when Ian Bell is annoyed at you.

In Melbourne in 2010, England had bowled Australia out for 98 before finishing the day 157 for none. We went on to win that Test by an innings and 157 runs. I was injured for that game and I never thought I'd see another day when I would be involved in a similar, if not even more, dominant day's performance over Australia. At Trent Bridge, we were 214 runs ahead on day one with six wickets still intact. It was a position of complete and utter control.

While we would never admit it, we knew that having bowled Australia out for 60 before lunch on day one, if the weather held, it was going to take something monumental for us not to win the Test.

By close on day one we knew we had one hand on the Ashes. Joe Root's magnificent hundred, his second of the series, provided the bedrock of our innings alongside Jonny Bairstow's excellent 74. Moeen Ali and I enjoyed another fun-filled ninth-wicket partnership of 58 to extend our first-innings lead to a massive 331 before Alastair Cook declared shortly before lunch with the score on 391 for nine. In years gone by, he may have just taken the conservative option of batting until we were all out. Why not? There were more than three and a half days left after all. But he wanted to get into the Aussies again. We had more than enough runs already and Cooky knew it.

'Keep focused and get the job done,' he said to us before we went out. 'Finish them off. We have not won this until the last wicket is taken. Don't get ahead of yourselves, boys.'

Despite every single logical thought telling me that we would win the Test comfortably, cricket is such a strange game that when Australia reached 113 without loss, there was a small voice in my head asking: 'They couldn't, could they?' History told us they couldn't, but records are there to be broken and you never know for certain. As Cooky said, the match was not over until the last wicket was taken.

Frustratingly, the ball had stopped deviating off the pitch to anything like the extent it had done in the first innings. Cooky dropped a fairly straightforward chance off David Warner in my fifth over and Belly also shelled a tough one off Ben Stokes, but otherwise we hadn't really threatened a breakthrough.

But, just as had happened so many times in the series already, when we needed someone to step up with a match-winning performance, somebody did. This time, it was Stokesy's turn to shine.

> When we needed someone to step up with a match-winning performance, somebody did. This time, it was Stokesy's turn to shine.

His dismissal of Josh Hazlewood in Australia's second innings at Edgbaston had been only the second wicket Ben had taken in the series. In fairness, with the other bowlers taking wickets, he'd been required to bowl only around 40 overs in the first three Tests. Now, with me, Mark Wood and Steve Finn all struggling to extract much life out of the Trent Bridge pitch, the value of having a fourth seamer in the side became evident.

Almost as soon as he came on to bowl, Stokesy got the ball swinging. And when I say swinging, I mean hooping around corners.

Jimmy had obviously been gutted not to get a chance to bowl on a ground where he'd enjoyed so much success, but it was clear our all-rounder had found the formula for swing.

Stokes bowled for five overs without any luck before Woody thought he had Chris Rogers caught by Root, only for the Aussie to be given a reprieve when a no-ball was called.

The next over, Stokesy finally made the breakthrough when Rooty pulled off his umpteenth stunning catch of the series to leave Australia 113 for one. Rogers was the wicket we needed and the relief around the ground was palpable.

In his very next over, Ben struck again when Warner went for a strange half-hearted paddle pull and top-edged it to me at mid-on. Australia were still 200 runs from making us bat again with eight wickets left.

Six balls later and Shaun Marsh was out for 2, narrowly avoiding a pair when Stokesy got him to nibble at one outside off stump and caught the edge. Two balls after Marsh departed, I picked up my ninth wicket of the match – and moved past Fred Trueman into fourth place in England's list of all-time leading wicket-takers with 308 in the process – when Steve Smith edged to Stokes.

Adam Voges and Michael Clarke hung around before Woody got rid of the Australia captain for 13 when Belly juggled a catch at slip to leave them 174 for five, still trailing by 150 runs. As I ran in to celebrate with my team-mates, I passed Clarke. I caught his eye. It looked completely blank. He wasn't angry, he wasn't upset. He just looked gone.

'Something strange has just happened there, lads,' I said as we gathered in a huddle. 'Clarke didn't even look pissed off as he walked off. He just looked empty. I'm telling you, something's happened.'

The next day, the Australia captain announced his retirement from international cricket.

From then on it was just a matter of time before we wrapped things up. Stokesy, who by now was doing a very passable impression of Jimmy at his best, dismissed Peter Nevill and Mitchell Johnson to claim his second five-wicket haul in Tests and leave Australia 236 for seven shortly before the umpires called time for the day. It was frustrating not to finish the series off that night but, just as at Edgbaston, it meant another Saturday crowd would get to watch some Ashes cricket.

That evening, in another illustration of how our relationship with the media had changed since Peter Moores took over, I invited journalist Ollie Holt over to my house. I'm not a violent man, but not so long ago, if I'd seen Ollie in the street I'd have swung for him. In 2011, he'd written a piece comparing me not walking at Trent Bridge with Lance Armstrong taking performance-enhancing drugs during the Tour de France. Normally, I let that kind of stuff wash over me, but it touched a nerve and seriously pissed me off. It was a ridiculous comparison and I was angry at being compared to a drugs cheat. I'd told Ollie as much.

Now, here he was as the chief sports writer at the *Mail on Sunday*, a paper I've enjoyed writing a column for over the past couple of years, in my house with my family the night after a performance which will probably define my career. I'll never get better figures than eight for 15, that's for sure.

With Nottingham Forest on TV in the background, Ollie and I enjoyed a great chat, recounting the bizarre events of the day before. It was nice having him over. It's easy to form an opinion on someone before you meet properly.

The irony of the situation wasn't lost on Ollie, who has since accepted he went too far with the Armstrong comparison. I enjoyed his company that evening as we worked on a column I never thought I'd be in a position to write.

Arriving at the ground the next morning was an incredible experience. With only three wickets left to take, we weren't actually sure how many people would turn up. Would everyone show knowing it could all be over in a flash? We needn't have worried. The support we received throughout the summer was absolutely astonishing. Yet again, England's cricket fans had shown why they're the best in the world by packing out every day of every Test and giving us rousing support in the process. Here, as we closed in on victory on the third morning of the fourth Test, my home ground was packed to the rafters again.

As we were leaving the dressing room to begin our warm-up, news reached us that Clarke had announced he would be retiring from international cricket after The Oval Test. It was surprising, especially as this Test match was still going on, but it also explained his blank look after he was out the day before. He'd already made his decision.

The noise while we were warming up alone was fantastic. There was a carnival atmosphere in the ground. It felt as if people had come to celebrate with us and it was hard keeping our emotions in check before going out on the field.

'Finish the job, boys. Finish the job!' was Cooky's simple message.

With nine wickets in the match to that point, people have asked me since if I was frustrated not to get on to bowl that morning. I 100 per cent was not. Why would I be frustrated to have nine wickets? I was still floating on cloud nine for goodness sake. I couldn't have been happier that we were in such a strong position.

No Australian sportsman would ever give up on a game while it was still alive, that's what makes them such a proud sporting nation. But with the odds piled so heavily against them, Michael Clarke's men would not have been human if they hadn't felt resigned to their fate that morning.

As we walked out, 'Jerusalem' blared out over the tannoy as it had done on the morning of every day of the series. This was different, though.

'I've never heard the crowd sing it louder than it's being played over the tannoy system!' shouted Woody to me over the crowd's amazing rendition of the famous old hymn.

'Keep focused, boys. Keep focused!' came the cry.

In the end, it took us 10.2 overs to complete our victory. They were ten of the noisiest and most enjoyable overs I've ever been on a cricket field for. Woody had four balls to complete from his over the night before, and the noise as he ran in to bowl to Voges was deafening. I know Cooky had told us to keep focused, and he was absolutely right to do so, but it was hard. Knowing victory was ours, I couldn't help but cast my mind back over the series and what had gone before it.

I thought of my grandparents, Ken and Nancy, who'd played such a large part in me falling in love with cricket as a young lad. I thought back to the long drives we had in Granddad's car listening to *Test Match Special* and wondered if another little boy or girl was listening right now as England wrapped up the Ashes and dreaming that one day they might do that, too.

I thought of my mum, who'd cried at my 21st birthday at the thought of another premature baby born on the same day as me who hadn't survived. Mum has been there all the time for me and I owe so much of my cricketing success to her.

I thought of Clive Rice and his family and all the friends, team-mates, loved ones and coaches who'd helped me get to where I was at this point; standing on the outfield of my favourite ground in the world on the brink of winning my fourth Ashes series with a team of lads who'd been written off a few weeks earlier.

I thought about lying in that Sydney hotel room after we'd been humiliated in the World Cup and being embarrassed to leave my room for fear of the abuse I'd get out on the street. I thought about Mooresy and everything he'd done to help build this team. I thought about the pain of losing five consecutive Tests to Australia in Australia barely 18 months ago.

I thought about sharing a glass of red with Dad just two nights before.

Then, I was back.

Focus, Broad. Focus.

The crowd roared again as Stokesy charged in to bowl to Mitchell Starc. He drew the left-hander forward and the ball angled back in to him and caught a thick edge which flew to Belly at second slip, where he took an excellent catch at shoulder height.

Get in! We jumped all over Stokesy, who now had Test best figures of six for 35 from 18 magnificent overs of high-class swing bowling.

'Awesome mate, just awesome!' Only two to go now.

Josh Hazlewood joined Voges, who survived Woody's next over, and Stokesy's next over passed without any undue alarm for Australia.

Then, with the crowd in full voice, Woody prepared for his 16th over. Voges took a single off the second ball and the third was a superbly directed Yorker, which Hazlewood did well to dig out. The fourth ball was left alone before Hazlewood played and missed at the fifth.

He turned and ran in for his final delivery of the over and this time it was a bull's eye as Hazlewood's middle stump went cartwheeling out of the ground. The inswinging Yorker would have been too good for better batsmen than Hazlewood. The Aussie No.10 had no chance. The crowd erupted again as we danced around in the middle like a bunch of excited school kids.

One more wicket and the Ashes were ours.

Lyon was caught in two minds before deciding to pull the bat out of the way. But he was too late and the ball hit the underside of his bat before cannoning into the stumps.

Voges played out two dot balls from Stokes before scoring a single off the third ball to bring up his first fifty of the series, leaving Nathan Lyon to survive three balls. He left two before playing and missing at the last.

The final Aussie pair played out another two overs before Woody's sixth of the day. Voges took a single off the first ball, leaving No.11 Lyon to face the rest of the over. He left the first ball before leg-glancing the next one for four as Woody strived for another Yorker.

The crowd were on their feet as Woody ran in and delivered a ball he'll remember forever. It was full and around off stump, and Lyon was caught in two minds before deciding to pull the bat out of the way. But he was too late and the ball hit the underside of his bat before cannoning into the stumps.

Pandemonium.

As the crowd erupted, we were all running around all over the place, jumping up and down and hugging each other. We'd done it. We'd won back the Ashes. We gathered in a huddle and Cooky shouted a few words above the noise of the crowd.

'Remember this moment, boys. You've earned this!' he shouted as we hugged ecstatically. He was clearly emotional. He'd come so close to quitting as captain after the whitewash Down Under and suffered so much stick since, this was an incredible moment for him.

I later watched the highlights and Nasser's commentary captured the moment superbly when he said: 'Five hundred and ninety-nine days after losing the Ashes, Alastair Cook has his redemption.' It was his fourth Ashes win in all and his second as captain. That's quite a CV!

I shook hands with Lyon and Voges, who were still out in the middle and obviously gutted to have lost, before waving to the crowd and acknowledging the incredible support we'd received throughout the summer. It was a very special moment.

Cooky handed stumps to Root, Wood and Stokes, which was a lovely gesture for three of our young stars who'd performed so brightly

ENGLAND V AUSTRALIA (4TH TEST)

At Trent Bridge, Nottingham

6, 7, 8 August 2015

ENGLAND WON BY AN INNINGS AND 78 RUNS

Toss: England
Umpires: Alim Dar (Pakistan) and S.Ravi (India)
Referee: R.S.Madugalle (Sri Lanka)

AUSTRALIA

C.J.L.Rogers	c Cook b Broad	0	c Root b Stokes	52
D.A.Warner	c Buttler b Wood	0	c Broad b Stokes	64
S.P.D.Smith	c Root b Broad	6	c Stokes b Broad	5
S.E.Marsh	c Bell b Broad	0	c Root b Stokes	2
* M.J.Clarke	c Cook b Broad	10	c Bell b Wood	13
A.C.Voges	c Stokes b Broad	1	not out	51
† P.M.Nevill	b Finn	2	lbw b Stokes	17
M.G.Johnson	c Root b Broad	13	c Cook b Stokes	5
M.A.Starc	c Root b Broad	1	c Bell b Stokes	0
J.R.Hazlewood	not out	4	b Wood	0
N.M.Lyon	c Stokes b Broad	9	b Wood	4
Extras	(LB 11, NB 3)	14	(B 20, LB 16, W 1, NB 3)	40
Total	(18.3 overs)	60	(72.4 overs)	253

ENGLAND

A.Lyth	c Nevill b Starc	14
* A.N.Cook	lbw b Starc	43
I.R.Bell	lbw b Starc	1
J.E.Root	c Nevill b Starc	130
J.M.Bairstow	c Rogers b Hazlewood	74
M.A.Wood	b Starc	28
B.A.Stokes	c Nevill b Hazlewood	5
† J.C.Buttler	b Starc	12
M.M.Ali	c Smith b Johnson	38
S.C.J.Broad	not out	24
S.T.Finn	not out	0
Extras	(B 14, LB 2, W 2, NB 4)	22
Total	(9 wkts dec; 85.2 overs)	391

ENGLAND	O	M	R	W	O	M	R	W
Broad	9.3	5	15	8	16	5	36	1
Wood	3	0	13	1	17.4	3	69	3
Finn	6	0	21	1	12	4	42	0
Ali					21	8	36	6
Stokes					6	0	34	0

AUSTRALIA	O	M	R	W	O	M	R	W
Starc	27	2	111	6				
Hazlewood	24	4	97	2				
Johnson	21.2	2	102	1				
Lyon	10	1	47	0				
Warner	3	0	18	0				

FALL OF WICKETS

	A	E	A
WKT	1ST	1ST	2ND
1st	4	32	113
2nd	10	34	130
3rd	10	96	136
4th	15	269	136
5th	21	297	174
6th	29	306	224
7th	33	320	236
8th	46	332	242
9th	47	390	243
10th	60	–	253

CLOSE OF PLAY

Day 1	England (1) 274-4 (65; J.E.Root 124*, M.A.Wood 2*)
Day 2	Australia (2) 241-7 (62.2; A.C.Voges 48*, M.A.Starc 0*)

throughout the series. Someone got hold of the match ball and gave it to me in recognition of my eight for 15.

Slowly we made our way into the changing room, which was a scene of complete and utter chaos. Ian Ward from Sky had snuck in with a cameraman and the pair of them were showered in equal measures of champagne and abuse. It was testament to the relationship Wardy had built up with us over the past few months and years that we were more than happy for him to be in there with us.

Mark Saxby, our physio, had found a latex Albert Einstein mask from somewhere earlier in the week, and Rooty grabbed hold of it and put it on, declaring that it was actually the spitting image of Bob Willis. He then proceeded to carry out a full interview with Wardy, live on Sky, while impersonating Bob's droll tones! Who said professional sportsmen give dull interviews?

Poor old Jimmy was trying so hard not to laugh, because it was causing him agony down his injured side. Wardy managed to keep a straight face as Rooty took the mick out of Bob, but it was great to see the team so relaxed in front of the camera. There had been plenty of banter with the Sky boys – and the written and broadcast media as well – throughout the summer, and Rooty's playful bit of mickey-taking summed up our change in approach.

Luckily, Bob saw the funny side. Although he did say Joe sounded more like Brian Clough than Bob Willis which, on reflection, was a fair point.

I sought out Ottis Gibson and Jimmy to thank them for everything they'd done. Jimmy was obviously sad not to have been on the field for the climax of the series, but I reassured him that, without his six for 47 in the first innings at Edgbaston, we may not have been in the position we were in now. Jimmy congratulated me on my eight for 15 and said how gutted he'd been not to be out there when I'd taken my 300th wicket.

In the meantime, there were the presentation ceremonies to go through and media duties to be carried out.

I was named Man of the Match and, as is customary, asked to go up on stage to speak with Michael Atherton before the two captains had their say.

Normally, when you go up for the presentation ceremony, the ground is half empty with only the diehards and media left to applaud your efforts. It's designed as much for television as it is for the spectators in the ground. This time, hardly a single person had left the ground. I can't ever remember a full house for a presentation ceremony.

As we stood, waiting to be called up, I could tell Cooky was becoming emotional. I put my arm around him. All the pain of those defeats in Australia last time, the personal abuse he'd suffered in the months after that series, losing the one-day captaincy. This one moment made it all worth it.

'Double Ashes-winning captain. Doesn't sound too bad does it, mate?' I said.

Cooky smiled. He was fighting hard to keep back the tears.

I was called up first and was truly humbled by the reception I received from the crowd. I'd joked with Nasser a couple of times about what he'd written before the Test. I certainly felt appreciated now as I made my way up onto the podium with 20,000 people shouting 'Broady, Broady, Broady!'

The utter despair of losing in Australia, both in the Ashes and the World Cup, felt like a lifetime ago.

Athers welcomed me on stage with a beaming grin. He seemed genuinely as thrilled as we were to have won back that precious little urn.

He asked me to say a few words and, conscious there were a few million people watching on television, I was quick to pay tribute to the entire team for their all-round contributions. Strangely, the batting and bowling averages appeared to indicate the Aussies had enjoyed the better of the series. But we had players who had stood up at key moments to deliver match-winning performances. Four of our bowlers had taken six-fers or better.

'It's been an amazing series,' I said. 'A lot of hard work has gone into these last four weeks. Our last four innings, different guys have got five-fers and that shows how well we have bowled as a group, and the catching has been spectacular. The balance of the bowling unit has been perfect – the first time we've been able to settle into a five-man attack since Freddie Flintoff was around.'

When it came to the captains to speak, despite the huge number of people who remained in the ground, I can't remember a more respectful silence ever being observed.

For different reasons, both Clarke and Cooky were emotional. For Clarke, who had announced his retirement that morning, it must have been a bitter pill to swallow. Yes, he'd won the Ashes as captain Down Under, but this Australian team had come to England in the genuine belief that were going to win the urn on these shores for the first time in 14 years. Remember Steve Smith's claim that we 'wouldn't get close' to Australia before the series? They had arrived as the team ranked neck and neck with South Africa as the best side in the world and we'd beaten them inside four Tests.

In the days and weeks that followed, Rogers, Brad Haddin and Shane Watson would join Clarke and Ryan Harris in retiring from Test cricket. Steve Smith would take over the captaincy. It felt like an entire generation of Australian cricketers was moving on in the same way we lost Swann, Prior, Pietersen and Trott as a result of the last tour Down Under.

Clarke held it together impressively on stage. 'England showed us how to execute with the ball in this series, we have to be honest and say they have outplayed us in this series,' he said.

'It wasn't from lack of trying, the Australian boys have given it their all, but we've been beaten by the better team. When England have had the momentum they have run with it. Anderson, and Broad and Stokes in this game, showed what you need to do in conditions like this. I'll always hold myself accountable and I have been nowhere near where I want to be, and certainly haven't led from the front. Retirement isn't the hardest decision when you perform as I have performed over the last series. It's the right time to walk away now. I've been very lucky to play over one hundred Tests. I've had the chance to learn from some older players and now have the chance to give back.'

The crowd listened quietly as Clarke spoke before giving him a warm ovation when the Australia captain stepped down. He acknowledged the applause, holding back tears in the process.

Cooky was next up and it was clear from the beginning he was going to struggle to keep his emotions in check. Who could blame him? The bloke had been through the cricketing mincer over the past two years and survived to fight another day. Not only that, but he had done so with his dignity and honour completely intact. Some of the personal abuse he suffered following our whitewash Down Under was shameful. He did not deserve any of it and it brought him to the brink of quitting. But he'd kept his dignity, kept his own counsel and retained the respect of every member of the team. I was so pleased for him. I was choked just listening to a bloke I am proud to call a friend. I look forward to sharing a glass of red with him in 20 years and remembering the moment he lifted the Ashes for the second time.

'When you lose five-nil, there's a turnover of players, but you see what talent there is in the country and we saw the end potential here,' he said. 'Ben Stokes was fantastic here. Joe Root has gone from strength to strength – they have driven this side forward – and the senior players have led so well.

'Broad and Jimmy, the support I receive from them means a lot. It comes down to hard work and a lot has been done over the past months. Peter Moores isn't here, but the development started with him. Today is about the team going through that "journey" and the tough times. That moment when Woody gets the last wicket is what you play for. The players have embraced showing off their talent and I had to try and follow that, too. Trevor has just turned up, so let's not give him too much credit. He has allowed us to go out and play the way we have. Paul Farbrace has been the constant and has led this turnaround. We want to go to The Oval now and put on a good display.'

It was a touch of class to mention Mooresy and the right thing to do. It is hard to overestimate what Mooresy has done to help English cricket, and the England cricket team, and I was delighted to hear Cooky name check him publicly. His little jibe at Trev – who had showed his class by staying in the background in much the same way Andy Flower had when we won the Ashes Down Under in 2011 – drew a wry smile from our coach on the balcony, where he was standing alongside Farbs, Ottis and the rest of the backroom staff who'd contributed so much to our success. It also showed the burgeoning of a strong relationship which, I believe, will serve this country well for years to come.

We spent hours walking around the ground signing autographs, having selfies taken and generally thanking our fans for their incredible support before returning to the sanctity of our dressing room.

It was a little calmer now, although still full of excitement as the champagne kept flowing and the cold beers were cracked open. It is moments like these that you live for as a sportsman.

Cooky spoke brilliantly ... He spoke of remembering this moment, not just for the joy of winning but also for all the time, work, sweat and tears that had taken us to this point.

Cooky spoke brilliantly in there. He's not naturally given to Churchillian oratory and generally prefers to keep things short and concise. But, having just won the Ashes under those circumstances, our captain indulged himself a little.

He spoke of remembering this moment, not just for the joy of winning but also for all the time, work, sweat and tears that had taken us to this point. He asked us to remember the coaches, the parents who'd driven us to practice as kids, the wives, girlfriends and team-mates who'd enabled us to get to where we were today. He also reiterated the importance of moving forward with a young team bursting with potential. This was not the end of the journey, he said, but the beginning.

We sat for hours in the dressing room in our whites. No one wanted to move away. It was our special place. I spoke to Ottis for a long time and thanked the bloke my mum had asked to look after her teenage son on my first away trip for Leicestershire all those years ago. He'd done that and so much more over the years. He knows my game better than anyone and I'm very lucky to have him as a friend and mentor. The work we did behind the scenes at Trent Bridge played a huge role in my success over the series and went a long way towards helping us to win back the Ashes.

Trev, not given to overly lavish praise, even came over and offered a 'well bowled, mate'. It was high praise indeed coming from him. I'd only recorded the best figures for a fast bowler in Ashes history, so I couldn't expect too much, I suppose! His understated nature was part of the reason he and Farbrace work so well together. As assistant coach, Farbs is the real heart of the changing room; he's the one who'll pick you up if you're low. He senses people's moods and knows how to give players confidence. He always says to me: 'Be the man, take control of the game.' Trev, on the other hand, stays in the background. The partnership works really well.

At one point, I took a moment to look around the dressing room and saw young lads like Rooty, Stokes, Jos, Mo, Lythy, Jonny

Bairstow and Woody smiling, laughing and joking. They had all contributed so much to our series win and deserved to enjoy this moment. I was chuffed for Finny, too, after his amazing comeback in Birmingham.

We enjoyed ourselves long into the night. The job had been done, the series was won. We had ten days to let it sink in before The Oval. But whatever happened there, the Ashes were ours.

As it transpired we weren't able to finish the series with a fourth win (which would have been a record for us in England) as Australia won the final dead rubber at The Oval by an innings and 46 runs, after Steve Smith scored a first-innings hundred. We were bowled out for just 149 in our first innings, after which we received our first serious dressing down from Trev. We hadn't seen that side of him before, but he was absolutely right to give us both barrels. In fact, the angrier Trev got, the thicker his Australian accent became. At one point he growled: 'That was just fair dinkum bullshit.'

It was hard not to laugh when Stokesy piped up in his thick Geordie accent: 'What does "fair dinkum" mean?' He was being serious.

Cooky scored a dogged 85 in our second innings, but we never seriously looked like making them bat again after following on.

For us, the most memorable part of the Test were the Ashes-winning celebrations at the end and the moment the Aussies finally called an end to their bizarre silent treatment of us, which they'd maintained throughout the series.

After the Test, they even came into our dressing room and shared that long-overdue beer. We spent ages talking over the battles we'd enjoyed over the series and discussing some of the key moments and pivotal innings.

ENGLAND V AUSTRALIA (5TH TEST)

At The Oval, London

20, 21, 22, 23 August 2015

AUSTRALIA WON BY AN INNINGS AND 46 RUNS

Toss: England
Umpires: Alim Dar (Pakistan) and H.D.P.K.Dharmasena (Sri Lanka)
Referee: J.J.Crowe (New Zealand)

AUSTRALIA

Batsman	Dismissal	Runs	
C.J.L.Rogers	c Cook b Wood	43	
D.A.Warner	c Lyth b Ali	85	
S.P.D.Smith	b Finn	143	
* M.J.Clarke	c Buttler b Stokes	15	
A.C.Voges	lbw b Stokes	76	
M.R.Marsh	c Bell b Finn	3	
† P.M.Nevill	c Buttler b Ali	18	
M.G.Johnson	b Ali	0	
M.A.Starc	lbw b Stokes	58	
P.M.Siddle	c Lyth b Finn	1	
N.M.Lyon	not out	5	
Extras	(B 1, LB 24, W 6, NB 3)	34	
Total	**(125.1 overs)**	**481**	

ENGLAND

Batsman	Dismissal	Runs	Dismissal (2nd)	Runs
A.Lyth	c Starc b Siddle	19	c Clarke b Siddle	10
* A.N.Cook	b Lyon	22	c Voges b Smith	85
I.R.Bell	b Siddle	10	c Clarke b Marsh	13
J.E.Root	c Nevill b Marsh	6	c Starc b Johnson	11
J.M.Bairstow	c Lyon b Johnson	13	c Voges b Lyon	26
B.A.Stokes	c Nevill b Marsh	15	c Clarke b Lyon	0
† J.C.Buttler	b Lyon	1	c Starc b Marsh	42
M.M.Ali	c Nevill b Johnson	30	(9) c Nevill b Siddle	35
S.C.J.Broad	c Voges b Marsh	0	(10) b Siddle	11
M.A.Wood	c Starc b Johnson	24	(8) lbw b Siddle	6
S.T.Finn	not out	0	not out	9
Extras	(B 1, LB 7, NB 1)	9	(B 12, LB 18, W 7, NB 1)	38
Total	**(48.4 overs)**	**149**	**(101.4 overs)**	**286**

ENGLAND	O	M	R	W		O	M	R	W
Broad	20	4	59	0					
Wood	26	9	59	1					
Stokes	29	6	133	3					
Finn	29.1	7	90	3					
Ali	18	1	102	3					
Root	3	0	13	0					

AUSTRALIA	O	M	R	W		O	M	R	W
Starc	8	3	18	0	(2)	16	4	40	0
Johnson	8.4	4	21	3	(1)	16	2	65	1
Lyon	10	2	40	2		28	7	53	2
Siddle	13	5	32	2		24.4	12	35	4
Marsh	9	2	30	3		16	4	56	2
Smith						1	0	7	1

FALL OF WICKETS

	A	E	E
WKT	1ST	1ST	2ND
1st	110	30	19
2nd	161	46	62
3rd	186	60	99
4th	332	64	140
5th	343	83	140
6th	376	84	199
7th	376	92	221
8th	467	92	223
9th	475	149	263
10th	481	149	286

CLOSE OF PLAY

Day 1	Australia (1) 287-3 (79.4; S.P.D.Smith 78*, A.C.Voges 47*)
Day 2	England (1) 107-8 (40; M.M.Ali 8*, M.A.Wood 8*)
Day 3	England (2) 203-6 (79; J.C.Buttler 33*, M.A.Wood 0*)

I grabbed a beer and made a beeline for Vogesy.

I said to him straight up: 'Have I upset you?'

He looked at me and said: 'Sorry mate, let's hug it out.'

Peter Siddle, who'd performed well in the match, having finally been given his chance in the series came over and we sat down together. They explained their decision to give us the silent treatment was just a game plan from their point of view. I'm not sure if it had come from Clarke or Darren Lehmann, but those three hours we spent in the changing room after the series were three of the best hours of the summer and showed just how much the two teams had in common. It also showed a level of mutual respect that is not always present between teams.

It was so enjoyable sitting there sharing a few beers with guys we'd been battling with for the past six weeks. I had a really nice chat with Mitchell Johnson, too. He's a real warrior on the cricket field and I couldn't believe how quiet and unassuming he was now he was out of warrior mode sitting in front of me sharing a beer and not trying to knock my head off.

We swapped shirts and signed each other's. I wrote that it had been a pleasure playing against Mitch and great fun in the process. I meant it.

I had a long chat with Michael Clarke and mentioned the look in his eyes as he walked off following his second innings at Trent Bridge when it just looked as if he was not there. He said it was the moment he realised he could no longer perform at this level. I asked him if he had begun the series knowing he was going to retire at the end of it. He said 'absolutely not'. As it had progressed, he'd come to realise he could no longer excel at that level and he couldn't face being a passenger in the team. It was a real privilege to speak with a player I'd admired so much down the years under those circumstances.

But the lasting memory from The Oval Test, which will stay with me forever, was the moment Cooky lifted the urn aloft. Losing the last Test had not been ideal, but there was no way it was going to dampen our celebrations. If someone had offered us a 3-2 win at the start of the series, we'd have bitten both their hands off. We'd worked so hard to win the series and we couldn't wait to celebrate our triumph in style. We were like excited children when the time came after the match to return to the pitch to lift the urn.

'Shall I go with one or two hands this time?' Cooky turned to me as we walked down the steps from the changing room and back out on to the pitch.

'Eh?' I replied.

'Shall I lift the urn with one or two hands?' he said.

'Oh, right. What did you go with last time?'

'Two,' he replied.

'Go with one this time, then. Definitely one.'

We reached the stage and lined up behind Cooky, ready to celebrate. With his eyes fixed on the prize, the England captain paused, picked up the little urn, took a deep breath and held it aloft.

Against all the odds, England had regained the Ashes.

12

REFLECTIONS

The reaction to us winning the Ashes and me taking eight for 15 has been absolutely amazing. When I returned home from the World Cup, no one approached me in the street. People were a bit embarrassed for us, I think. Ever since that Trent Bridge Test, at least ten people every day come up to me and tell me where they were when I took eight for 15.

When I was younger everyone used to remember where they were when Jonny Wilkinson kicked the dropped goal to win the World Cup or where they were when Manchester United beat Bayern Munich in the Champions League final. To think that people now talk of that eight for 15 in the same way is truly humbling. It's been fantastic to restore some pride in the England shirt after a turbulent couple of years.

I grew up as a passionate England fan. I fell in love with cricket while listening to *Test Match Special* in the back of my granddad's car. *TMS* became was pretty much the soundtrack to my childhood. When I retire from playing, I will go back to being a fan again. So it's been lovely to hear the happiness that spell of bowling brought to people and the enjoyment they got from seeing us beat the Aussies. It's what makes being an England cricketer so special.

I've had bus drivers, window cleaners, rugby players and footballers all tell me where they were on the day. Stephen Fry knows precisely where he was as I ran in to bowl and took all those wickets. I even had a message from a friend whose dad was having some treatment for cancer at a hospital during the Test. He told me the entire waiting room was filled with joyous cheering and laughter as they were told the news of how we had bowled Australia out for 60. To hear stories like that reminds you of the amazing force for good that sport can be.

I still pinch myself at what Alastair Cook and the team achieved. On a personal level, the summer couldn't have gone any better. I mean, eight for 15. Really? There are times when I still can't bring myself to believe it really happened. I mean it when I say I used to dream about a spell like that. Every cricket-loving schoolboy does. To have actually done it is going to take a very long time to sink in.

Since the series finished, I've been inundated with requests and offers which I never dreamt in a million years I'd receive in my lifetime. In September, I was named *GQ* Man of the Year and attended a glamorous star-studded evening at the Royal Opera House. It was hosted by Samuel L. Jackson. Bealey and I got to meet people like Lionel Richie, Oasis and countless other A-list celebrities. It was surreal being surrounded by so many superstars.

I've also been invited to accept an honorary degree from Nottingham University and, by far my favourite offer of all, have had a tram named after me by Nottingham City Council. Honestly, there is now a tram ferrying people in and out of Nottingham called Stuart Broad. How weird is that?

But while there's been time for reflection, the world of professional sport waits for no man or woman. We have some incredibly exciting series coming up including a four-Test series against South Africa in the New Year. As I write this, I'm in a hotel room in Abu Dhabi a few days away from the start of a three-Test series against Pakistan. The international cricket calendar is a relentless wheel which I hope I don't have to get off for a few years yet.

If the 2015 summer proved one thing, it's that the England cricket team is in a really good place. We have moved on from the trauma of losing the Ashes 5-0 in 2013-14 and the nonsense that followed it. Under Alastair Cook's leadership, we have a talented group of young cricketers, with guys like Joe Root, Ben Stokes, Mark Wood, Moeen Ali, Jonny Bairstow and Jos Buttler capable of forging long England careers. Don't forget Gary Ballance, who I'm sure will return in time, while Adam Lyth impressed everyone with his attitude and sheer love of playing for England over the summer. Having Steve Finn back and firing can only be good for English cricket – let's hope his injury setback in the UAE is only a brief one. I just hope they all remember to keep playing without fear.

Under Trevor Bayliss and Paul Farbrace, the team is in good hands, while hopefully the old-stagers Cooky, Jimmy Anderson, myself and Ian Bell can keep creaking on in the Tests as the one-day side goes from strength-to-strength under Eoin Morgan. I still hope to feature in the one-day side again, too.

The ECB seems to have got itself back on an even keel and Andrew Strauss has no doubt had a hand to play in that. It's an exciting time to be an England cricketer and fan. There are many more battles ahead to fight, and I can't wait to fight them.

ENGLAND V AUSTRALIA 2015

SERIES AVERAGES

ENGLAND

BATTING AND FIELDING	M	I	NO	HS	RUNS	AVGE	100	50	CT
J.E.Root	5	9	1	134	460	57.50	2	2	8
A.N.Cook	5	9	–	96	330	36.66	–	2	9
M.M.Ali	5	8	–	77	293	36.62	–	2	2
J.M.Bairstow	3	4	–	74	118	29.50	–	1	–
I.R.Bell	5	9	1	65*	215	26.87	–	3	7
M.A.Wood	4	7	3	32*	103	25.75	–	–	–
B.A.Stokes	5	8	–	87	201	25.12	–	2	6
G.S.Ballance	2	4	–	61	98	24.50	–	1	2
S.C.J.Broad	5	8	1	31	134	19.14	–	–	1
J.C.Buttler	5	8	–	42	122	15.25	–	–	12
A.Lyth	5	9	–	37	115	12.77	–	–	6
J.M.Anderson	3	5	1	6*	11	2.75	–	–	3
S.T.Finn	3	4	4	9*	9	–	–	–	–

BOWLING	O	M	R	W	AVGE	BEST	5WI	10WM
S.C.J.Broad	143.3	34	439	21	20.90	8-15	1	–
S.T.Finn	78.1	15	270	12	22.50	6-79	1	–
J.M.Anderson	87	20	275	10	27.50	6-47	1	–
B.A.Stokes	105	26	368	11	33.45	6-36	1	–
M.A.Wood	118.4	31	391	10	39.10	3-69	–	–
M.M.Ali	123.4	13	546	12	45.50	3-59	–	–

Also bowled: A.Lyth 1-1-0-0; J.E.Root 28.3-1-135-4

AUSTRALIA

BATTING AND FIELDING	M	I	NO	HS	RUNS	AVGE	100	50	CT
C.J.L.Rogers	5	9	1	173	480	60.00	1	3	1
S.P.D.Smith	5	9	–	215	508	56.44	2	1	1
D.A.Warner*	5	9	–	85	418	46.44	–	5	3
A.C.Voges	5	8	1	76	201	28.71	–	2	7
P.M.Nevill	4	6	–	59	143	23.83	–	1	17
M.A.Starc	5	8	1	58	157	22.42	–	2	4
M.G.Johnson	5	8	–	77	141	17.62	–	1	1
M.J.Clarke	5	9	1	38	132	16.50	–	–	4
J.R.Hazlewood	4	6	3	14*	45	15.00	–	–	1
M.R.Marsh	3	5	1	27*	48	12.00	–	–	1
N.M.Lyon	5	7	3	12*	47	11.75	–	–	2

Also batted (one Test each): B.J.Haddin 22, 7 (5 ct); S.E.Marsh 0, 2; P.M.Siddle 1; S.R.Watson 30, 19 (2 ct)

BOWLING	O	M	R	W	AVGE	BEST	5WI	10WM
P.M.Siddle	37.4	17	67	6	11.16	4-35	–	–
M.R.Marsh	44.1	13	149	8	18.62	3-30	–	–
J.R.Hazlewood	112	18	412	16	25.75	3-68	–	–
N.M.Lyon	137.1	25	452	16	28.25	4-75	–	–
M.A.Starc	142.2	23	549	18	30.50	6-111	2	–
M.G.Johnson	140.1	29	524	15	34.93	3-21	–	–

Also bowled: S.P.D.Smith 3-0-16-1; D.A.Warner 5-0-27-0; S.R.Watson 13-0-47-0

TEST MATCH BOWLING RECORDS

ALL-TIME TOP TENS

BEST INNINGS ANALYSIS FOR ENGLAND

	OPPONENT	VENUE	DATE	FIGURES
J.C.Laker	Australia	Manchester	26 Jul 1956	10-53
G.A.Lohmann	South Africa	Johannesburg	2 Mar 1896	9-28
J.C.Laker	Australia	Manchester	26 Jul 1956	9-37
D.E.Malcolm	South Africa	The Oval	18 Aug 1994	9-57
S.F.Barnes	South Africa	Johannesburg	26 Dec 1913	9-103
G.A.Lohmann	South Africa	Port Elizabeth	13 Feb 1896	8-7
J.Briggs	South Africa	Cape Town	25 Mar 1889	8-11
S.C.J.Broad	**Australia**	**Nottingham**	**6 Aug 2015**	**8-15**
S.F.Barnes	South Africa	The Oval	12 Aug 1912	8-29
F.S.Trueman	India	Manchester	17 Jul 1952	8-31

BEST INNINGS ANALYSIS IN THE ASHES

	OPPONENT	VENUE	DATE	FIGURES
J.C.Laker	Australia	Manchester	26 Jul 1956	10-53
J.C.Laker	Australia	Manchester	26 Jul 1956	9-37
A.A.Mailey	England	Melbourne	11 Feb 1921	9-121
S.C.J.Broad	**Australia**	**Nottingham**	**6 Aug 2015**	**8-15**
F.J.Laver	England	Manchester	26 Jul 1909	8-31
G.A.Lohmann	Australia	Sydney	25 Feb 1887	8-35
G.D.McGrath	England	Lord's	19 Jun 1997	8-38
A.E.Trott	England	Adelaide	11 Jan 1895	8-43
H.Verity	Australia	Lord's	22 Jun 1934	8-43
R.G.D.Willis	Australia	Leeds	16 Jul 1981	8-43

BEST INNINGS ANALYSIS IN ENGLAND

	OPPONENT	VENUE	DATE	FIGURES
J.C.Laker	Australia	Manchester	26 Jul 1956	10-53
J.C.Laker	Australia	Manchester	26 Jul 1956	9-37
D.E.Malcolm	South Africa	The Oval	18 Aug 1994	9-57
M.Muralitharan (SL)	England	The Oval	27 Aug 1998	9-65
S.C.J.Broad	**Australia**	**Nottingham**	**6 Aug 2015**	**8-15**
S.F.Barnes	South Africa	The Oval	12 Aug 1912	8-29
F.J.Laver (A)	England	Manchester	26 Jul 1909	8-31
F.S.Trueman	India	Manchester	17 Jul 1952	8-31
I.T.Botham	Pakistan	Lord's	15 Jun 1978	8-34
G.D.McGrath (A)	England	Lord's	19 Jun 1997	8-38

Figures correct to 1 October 2015

TEST MATCH BOWLING RECORDS

ALL-TIME TOP TENS continued

ENGLAND'S LEADING TEST WICKET-TAKERS

WKTS		TESTS	BALLS	RUNS	BEST	AVGE	5WI	10WM
413	J.M.Anderson	107	23826	12134	7-43	29.38	18	2
383	I.T.Botham	102	21815	10878	8-34	28.40	27	4
325	R.G.D.Willis	90	17357	8190	8-43	25.20	16	-
308	**S.C.J.Broad**	**84**	**17498**	**8983**	**8-15**	**29.16**	**14**	**2**
307	F.S.Trueman	67	15178	6625	8-31	21.57	17	3
297	D.L.Underwood	86	21862	7674	8-51	25.83	17	6
255	G.P.Swann	60	15349	7642	6-65	29.96	17	3
252	J.B.Statham	70	16056	6261	7-39	24.84	9	1
248	M.J.Hoggard	67	13909	7564	7-61	30.50	7	1
236	A.V.Bedser	51	15918	5876	7-44	24.89	15	5

LEADING TEST WICKET-TAKERS IN 21ST CENTURY

WKTS		TESTS	BALLS	RUNS	BEST	AVGE	5WI	10WM
573	M.Muralitharan (SL)	85	29157	12040	9-51	21.01	50	20
413	J.M.Anderson (E)	107	23826	12134	7-43	29.38	18	2
402	D.W.Steyn (SA)	80	16716	9040	7-51	22.48	25	5
396	Harbhajan Singh (I)	95	26866	12727	8-84	32.13	25	5
380	M.Ntini (SA)	97	20082	10884	7-37	28.64	18	4
357	S.K.Warne (A)	65	18129	8986	7-94	25.17	21	6
355	A.Kumble (I)	74	22647	11014	8-141	31.02	20	5
311	Z.Khan (I)	92	18785	10247	7-87	32.94	11	1
308	**S.C.J.Broad (E)**	**84**	**17498**	**8983**	**8-15**	**29.16**	**14**	**2**
303	B.Lee (A)	75	16309	9476	5-30	31.27	9	-

Figures correct to 1 October 2015

ACKNOWLEDGEMENTS

There are a number of people I'd like to thank for making this book happen.

First and foremost, I'd like to thank all the England fans who have supported us through thick and thin over the years. I'd also like to thank my England team-mates, coaches and backroom staff associated who worked tirelessly to ensure we turned our fortunes around so spectacularly over the course of 2015. It has been quite a journey.

To my family, and girlfriend Bealey, thank you for supporting me through thick and thin and always being there, with words of advice and encouragement when things haven't gone so well. I wouldn't have achieved anything without you all.

To the team at ISM, and in particular my agent Neil Fairbrother, thanks for making sure I know what I'm doing from one day to the next and that all my off-field affairs are taken care of, enabling me to focus on winning cricket matches for England.

Thanks also to Ian Marshall and all his team at Simon & Schuster for your tireless hard work in putting this book together.

Last but not least, thanks to my friend and ghost writer Sam Peters from the Mail on Sunday, who took hitting a deadline to new levels by delivering this book right in the middle of a Rugby World Cup.

I couldn't have done this without any of you.